THE GOOD GLOW

Charity and the Symbolic Power of Doing Good

Jon Dean

D1612891

P

First published in Great Britain in 2020 by

Policy Press
University of Bristol
1-9 Old Park Hill
Bristol
BS2 8BB
UK
t: +44 (0)117 954 5940
pp-info@bristol.ac.uk
www.policypress.co.uk

British Library Cataloguing in Publication Data
A catalogue record for this book is available from the British Library

ISBN 978-1-4473-4002-7 hardcover
ISBN 978-1-4473-4490-2 paperback
ISBN 978-1-4473-4469-8 ePdf
ISBN 978-1-4473-4491-9 ePub

Cover design by Robin Hawes
Front cover image: 'Du Paradis #2', Ravi Roshan, Unsplash
Printed and bound in Great Britain by CMP, Poole
Policy Press uses environmentally responsible print partners

For Vera Dean, who has done a lot
of good for a lot of people.

Contents

List of figures and tables

Figures

Tables

About the author

Jon Dean lectures in politics and sociology at Sheffield Hallam University in the UK. His research focuses on inequalities within the voluntary sector and youth volunteering, particularly in relation to social class, as well as charity advertising and homelessness. His research has been published in *Nonprofit and Voluntary Sector Quarterly*, *Voluntary Sector Review*, *Sociological Research Online*, and other leading social science journals. He also serves on the steering group of the Voluntary Sector Studies Network, and the publications committee of the Association for Research on Nonprofit Organizations and Voluntary Action. Jon's research interests also include innovations in qualitative methodology, and his first monograph, *Doing Reflexivity: An Introduction*, was published by Policy Press in 2017.

Acknowledgements

We are only as good as the people around us. It is not false modesty to say that I am worse than the people around me, but would be much worse were it not for them.

During the course of the research that has gone into this book, over 60 people volunteered their time to take part in interviews or focus groups. If this goodwill ever dried up and people suddenly decided they didn't want to spend their valuable time explaining how their worlds work, qualitative researchers would have to spend their time talking solely to each other. Readers and audiences everywhere should be delighted that this isn't the case: deep thanks to those people who helped out.

I have been very lucky to have had support with various aspects of this book and the research projects it builds on, from several research assistants. Jack Aizlewood, Hannah Baker, Tom Barker and Georgina Burns-O'Connell are academic and research names to look out for. I hope I did your hard work justice. Much of the research work was kindly supported by the Department of Psychology, Sociology and Politics at Sheffield Hallam University, which, despite the incessant pressures of the modern university, has continued to support research in its myriad forms. Colleagues have always been generous in their feedback, and a guiding set of lights in dark times, especially Carissa Honeywell, Bob Jeffery, Anjana Raghavan, Rob Macmillan, Chris Dayson, Peter Thomas, Julia Hirst, Paul Hickman, Jenni Brooks, Diarmuid Verrier and Andy Price. Final year students on my Charity and Community module have continued to test me (in a good way), have highlighted literature and ideas that have made it into this book, and are the best sounding board one could hope for: attentive, questioning and willing. I wish you all the very best in what you go onto next.

In the wider sociological and voluntary sector research communities, I have been lucky enough to receive the support of terribly decent people. The Voluntary Sector Studies Network, the ARNOVA Critical Perspectives Common Interest Group and the Voluntary Action Research Group all provide stimulating environments and collegiality, and tolerate my nonsense. Thanks especially to Eddy Hogg, Ali Body, Beth Breeze, Angela Ellis Paine, Chris Damm, Ellen Bennett and Tracey Coule. The team at Policy Press and the University of Bristol Press do a fantastic job of encouraging socially attentive scholarship. They are always available to listen to and invest in people. Special thanks to Victoria Pittman, Shannon Kneis and Dawn Rushen.

Finally, without Mum, Dad, Andrew and Nana things wouldn't get done. Without Jenny there would be no point. Everything you do is probably not appreciated enough.

1

Introduction

We have, as the philosopher Immanuel Kant (1996: 212) put it, 'a mania for spying on the morals of others'. This emerges in various ways: from judging the social welfare recipient who dares to own a television, to criticising the millionaire footballer who decides to buy some household products from a pound shop. And we judge people's charity, all the time. Some people give nothing to charity, feel no remorse when walking past someone begging on the street, and see no reason to look out for elderly neighbours. Society judges these people as cruel, heartless and lacking the inner happiness that comes from empathetic action. And at the same time we judge those who do an enormous amount that is charitable, dismissing them as 'mugs' for allowing themselves to be walked over. Or we look at the billion-dollar donations of the mega-rich as merely a way of ingratiating themselves into celebrity and political hierarchies, drawing admiring fawning as a cover for their tax avoidance. Some of these observations may be fair, others not: the point is that they will continue to take place whether we point them out or not, whether accurate or not, the quick moral judgement a long-established part of human nature.

This book is a sociology of charity. Charity is a subject largely untouched by modern sociologists (with some notable exceptions, which will be discussed throughout), often left instead to the policy analysts who seek to understand the logic of *charities*, their management, their delivery of services, their resourcing. Charities, the non-profit bodies themselves, are fascinating organisations, vital for understanding how modern society is organised and how we address our desire to improve it. But in focusing mainly on *charity* and not on charities, I want to re-examine that more ephemeral notion, and bring a new theoretical lens to how charity operates and works in modern society. This includes a desire to focus on the social reaction to acts of charity, and how that reaction plays out in the internal monologue of the charitable individual. In doing a number of research projects around charity for over a decade now, I see the contradiction of both a huge amount of cynicism about charitable acts and individuals – Moore's (2008: 71–2) argument, for instance, that *being charitable* has taken on a particular meaning in contemporary society, one where demonstrating support for a cause is less about the cause and more about the person doing the demonstrating – and at the same time a wealth of giving, volunteering, kindness and love, that is really the day-to-day lifeblood enabling society to keep its head above water. Such a focus does not seek to undo good works, but the nature of sociological critique means this book definitely focuses on the negative side of this equation. I have the luxury of cynicism, but also sociology's driving theoretical force is the notion of revealing society's 'profoundly buried structures' (Bourdieu, 1996: 1), the idea that unthinking orthodoxies must be unpicked. I want to show what it is that makes charity 'good', and how this awareness of charity's goodness drives more charity, in a way that can be rewarding for the demonstrably charitable, but also how this goodness creates huge silences and violences about how charity is both practised and operationalised. The 'good glow' of charity is inherently powerful and sociologically problematic in terms of policy and everyday practice.

To provide an illustrative example, let us focus on how charity plays out in moments from the lives of two iconic Americans: the 45th US President Donald Trump, and Larry David, the creator of *Seinfeld* and the central character in the sitcom *Curb Your Enthusiasm*. One is a bombastic old divisive white man who says whatever he can get away with, and the other ... well, you can finish that joke yourselves. Two stories in their lives tell different experiences of what I shall be calling the *symbolic power of charity*.

In 1996, the charity Association to Benefit Children held a ribbon-cutting event to celebrate a new nursery for children with AIDS. There were a lot of dignitaries in the room: mayors, former mayors, and Steven Fisher, a wealthy donor who had provided the funds to build the nursery. Then Donald Trump showed up:

> "Nobody knew he was coming," said one person. There is this kind of ruckus at the door, and in comes Donald Trump, he just gets up on the podium and sits down. Trump was not a major donor. He was not a donor, period. He'd never given a dollar to the nursery, or the Association to Benefit Children, and now he was sitting in Fisher's seat, the donor's seat, next to Mayor Giuliani. "What should we do?" said one person, "Oh just sing past it." So they warbled into the first song on the programme, "This little light of mine", alongside Trump and a chorus of children, with a photographer snapping photos and Trump looking for all the world like an honoured donor to the cause. Afterwards, two charity workers said he left without

offering an explanation or a donation. The actual donor who had built the nursery, Steven Fisher, was stuck in the audience. The charity spent months trying to repair their relationship with him. (Farenthold, 2016)

Political performances are 'those that seek to communicate to an audience meaning-making related to state institutions, policies and discourses': the space and place in which the performance occurs shapes its impact (Rai, 2015: 1179–80). Here is Donald Trump celebrating and singing 'This little light of mine' with the children, pretending that he was the world's greatest donor, pretending that he was the good man, the best man, of Manhattan. Being *seen* to be charitable, to Donald Trump, is more important than *being* charitable. And because he's on that dais, because all those children and all the audience are looking at him as one of the wonderful donors, we understand that Trump gets to use the symbolic power of charity for his own ends. The symbolic authority of charitable spaces – the automatic assumption of goodness – allows people to take advantage of it. Trump understands that being seen to do good and being offered the space to do good or be good or to demonstrate your goodness can be an integral part of doing good. In fact, the latter may not actually be instrumental to achieving the former.

Farenthold's mass of forensic reporting won him a Pulitzer Prize for National Reporting in 2017 (see The Pulitzer Prizes, 2017, for all the articles and an overview of the findings), and shows in great detail how Trump had, for the most part, failed to follow through on his many public promises to donate money to charity:

> Although Trump had spent years promising to give away his money.... I couldn't find much evidence he'd actually done it. In fact, after trying 450 charities, I'd found only one gift to charity from Trump's own pocket in the years between 2008 and 2015. And it was for less than $10,000. I also found that Trump had used his personal charity, the Donald J. Trump Foundation – which was filled with other people's money – in ways that seemed to break the law. (Farenthold, 2017)

Trump claimed that between 2011 and 2015 he had given over US$102 million to charity, but little to none of this came from his own pocket, made up instead of donated free rounds of golf at his courses, lifts in Trump's plane and gifts from the Donald J. Trump

Foundation, Trump's charity, to which he gave none of his own money between 2009 and 2014 (Kranish and Fisher, 2016: 307–8). According to legal documents released in June 2018 by the New York Attorney General, Trump used US$100,000 of his Foundation's money to settle a legal dispute concerning his Florida-based Mar-a-Lago private club (Isidore and Schuman, 2018), illegal given the established charitable aims of the fund, with the Foundation's overall activity allegedly highly questionable: it is claimed that 'spending at Trump's foundation was so loose that its board of directors hadn't met since 1999, and its official treasurer wasn't even aware that he was on the board' (Farenthold, 2018). In fact, Farenthold (2017) concludes, Trump's personal marketing strategy is to promise big results and rely on the public's assumption that because a promise was made clearly, publicly and 'bigly', that it will be kept: 'For as long as he has been rich and famous, Donald Trump has always wanted people to believe he is generous; he spent years constructing an image as a philanthropist by appearing at charity events and making very public, even nationally televised promises to give his own money away, which he never did' (Farenthold, 2016).

The rather sickening tales of deception *of charities* that Farenthold (2017) documents from Trump – such as a US$250,000 pledge to help Israeli soldiers and veterans, where he didn't pay up and another donor paid his pledge instead – speaks to the 'do anything, say anything to get ahead' attitude you would associate with a New York property developer, but also someone with a certain level of social intelligence to be able to take advantage of the symbolic power that charity has: 'He may be rough around the edges, but would a bad person pledge all that money to charity?' And it doesn't matter that the money never goes to charity, because who in their right mind would promise the underprivileged a substantial amount and then not pay up? No one, obviously. We think of charities as distinct, and charities make claims of distinctiveness to operate in wider fields (Macmillan, 2013). Charities *are* different, their symbolic power, the good glow they bestow around the giver, is a key part of what makes them different, and some people, whether it's Donald Trump or whoever else, are willing and able to try and take advantage of that difference in order to present themselves in a certain way.

In *Curb Your Enthusiasm*, Larry David plays Larry David, the writer of the hit sitcom *Seinfeld*, now semi-retired, occasionally writing and producing, but largely just struggling to fit into everyday society, as he fails to conform to social conventions, retains a desire to point out other people's character flaws, and a general unwillingness to let sleeping dogs lie. In an episode in Season Six, Larry donates to an environmental cause and is presented with a plaque, proudly stating, 'Wing donated by Larry David'. Pretty good, one would think. But the other wing, on the other side of the lobby, has another plaque, this one reading, 'Wing donated by Anonymous'. Larry is unhappy about this: 'Nobody told me that I could be anonymous', he scowls, 'now it just looks like I did mine for the credit.' What makes this worse is that everyone knows that 'Anonymous' is actually actor, and Larry's rival, Ted Danson, who happens to have told everyone important (including the in-attendance US Senator Barbara Boxer) that he was the 'anonymous' donor. Larry fumes: 'I would have taken that option, OK?! You can't have it halfway, you're either anonymous or you're not. "There's Larry David, the guy who has to have his name up on the wall, as opposed to Mr Anonymous, *who's really Ted*!"'

This case is an example of what theatre critic Charles Isherwood (2007) calls the 'philanthropic graffiti' as one moves through the vicariously labelled rooms of the Shakespeare Theatre Company in Washington DC (the Morris and Gwendolyn Cafritz Foundation Grand Staircase, the Paul and Mary Tomkinson Memorial Cloakroom and the Mariah England Ceremonial Toilet [only two of these are made up]). Isherwood feels this shows people only give to make sure they get their plaque – leaving Singer (2010: 66) to ask whether anyone who gives money to a theatre company in one of the world's richest cities could ever be an ideally selfless spirit. What we see here is the anonymous Ted getting the double benefit of charity's symbolic power, basking in the 'warm glow' (Andreoni, 1990) of giving, reinforced by the good glow of people believing you're a good person for donating to a worthy cause, *doubly reinforced* by the fact that they believe this because you didn't want people to know you gave the donation (for further examination of this case, see Caesar, 2008; Gallagher, 2018). Why show off about something when you can show off about it in a way that makes people think you aren't showing off about it?

One of the above experiences involves screaming at the unfairness of the world, of how your good deed is deemed lesser because you were open and honest about it, naive as to the hidden symbolic power of gestures that allow the heightened goodness of anonymity to be used by someone wishing to present themselves in a certain light. The other experience tells of using the symbolic power of charity, the prestige where being seen to be a donor (but not actually donating) enables an individual to present as better than they actually are. It doesn't matter that Trump's place on that dais was phoney – we know this matters little to his success. But the confidence inherent in being able and willing to manipulate the goodness of charity for your own instrumental purposes is the sort of confidence most ordinary people working for charities would feel socially unable to call bullshit on. Fahrenthold's assiduous reporting showed, despite his consistent claims to the contrary, 'no evidence of major charitable contributions from Trump's own pocket' (quoted in Ball, 2017: 29). In both the Los Angeles gallery opening and the New York ribbon cutting, those gathered knew the rules of social engagement around charity. They knew that sitting on a dais means you have done something good for the world, and they knew that wanting to remain anonymous is to demonstrate greater humility than to not. *It doesn't matter that neither of these things were true*, because the symbolism overpowers reality. The rest of this book wants to unpack that symbolism. Giving to charity, being charitable or being part of a charity makes people look good, enabling them to bask in a sociological good glow from others as opposed to the internalised, psychological warm glow you get yourself from doing something nice – but we obscure more than we illuminate if we pretend that isn't true out of politeness.

What is charity?

The word 'charity' comes from the Latin for 'dear', or the Old English word indicating 'Christian love of one's fellows'. A charity is, of course, an organisation set up to provide help and raise money for those in need, with the act of charity indicating the voluntary giving of help, typically in the form of money, but also the gift of time through volunteering, to those in need. Charities come in many shapes and sizes, often grouped together in a 'loose and baggy' sector (Kendall and Knapp, 1995) containing a myriad of organisational forms, purposes and prominence. They may be labelled as charities, or voluntary organisations, or non-profits (terms generally used interchangeably throughout this book, not because they always mean precisely the same thing, but because the differences are not vital for our analysis). But these organisations' bagginess and diversity may mean thinking of a charity 'sector' (or voluntary sector, or third sector, or social sector) makes little sense (Rochester, 2013), as organisations that are vastly different in scale and scope are clumped together, differently in different countries and contexts. (It's worth saying that while this book, as a theoretical exploration of charity is not specifically 'placed' in a geographical location, most of the examples are drawn from the UK, with some in the US and elsewhere, which are clearly not representative of the full gamut of charity policy and practice, but are those best known to myself and to those participating in the qualitative data presented later.)

For example, recent statistics from the England and Wales Charity Commission (2018a), the state-funded charity regulator, show there are 168,000 registered charities, which doesn't include many grassroots or 'below the radar' organisations as a group only needs to register with the Commission if they have an income of over £5,000 a year. Of these 168,000, however, there are still huge differences. Just over 65,000 of them (38.8 per cent) have an annual income of less than £10,000, and only 2,263 (1.3 per cent) have an income of over £5 million – but this latter group account for an astonishing 72.5 per cent of UK charities' income. These UK-based mega-charities are the ones commonly known – Oxfam, National Trust, Cancer Research UK, Royal Society for the Protection of Birds (RSPB) and so on – and come to dominate the picture that the public have in their heads of what a charity is. And just with those four examples, we can see the wide variety in what charities do – deliver international aid and campaign against poverty, preserve historic buildings, undertake medical research into disease, and protect wildlife and the environment.

Charitable status in England and Wales comes from having 'wholly and exclusively charitable' purposes that 'operate for the benefit of the public' (see McGovern, 2017: 3), according to the Charities Act 2006, but given that these 13 charitable purposes include the advancement of education, the advancement of citizenship or community development, the promotion of the efficiency of the armed forces of the Crown, or the efficiency of the police, fire and rescue services or ambulance services, or any other purposes that 'can be recognised' as charitable within the spirit of the law (GOV.UK, 2019), charity ends up in the eye of the beholder, and as we shall see, frequently 'misrecognised'. It is possible for two charities to have opposing aims, as long as each can evidence that it benefits the public or a section of the public in some way (the League Against Cruel Sports campaigns against fishing and horse racing, for instance, but there are many charities that promote these pursuits), and charitable purposes are allowed by law in England and Wales to have negative consequences, as long as any detriment or harm that results from the purpose (to people, property or the environment) does not outweigh the benefit. Perhaps most interestingly for our forthcoming discussions, under current law individuals' personal benefits from charitable activity cannot be any more than incidental: whether everyone celebrating your altruism for a gift you didn't actually give is incidental or more tangible than that is why people are so keen to analyse and judge giving behaviours.

There is an economic argument, rooted in rational choice theory, that charities should not exist and therefore that is why they are so interesting (Krause, 2014: 45): why would people give their money away to other people when they need it themselves? But while human history is often told as a story of kings and queens and battles and conflicts, throughout history people have always helped each other. We have a dependence on others for survival and an instinct to help others in trouble. This dependence on others was witnessed by Kropotkin (1914) among the volunteers of the miners' associations of the Rhondda Valley who rescued those trapped underground. Kropotkin asked why these men came to the aid of each other with the answer, he saw it, in the inherited instincts and education of these communities (Kropotkin, 1914: 275–8), akin to that developed by the animal communities he had observed in the wild, where survival of the fittest may indicate an individualistic attitude, but where it was actually community and teamwork that led to survival. Generations of human psychology and emotional involvement with others who need help or saving, and empathy for others' suffering, means we have always been beneficent and compassionate, but our history of such acts has focused too much on the philanthropic gifts aimed at relieving poverty and not enough on the mutual aid and solidarity (Smith, 1995) that such *charity* can offer. *Charities* emerge as intermediary organisations for the location of acts of giving and empathy for many reasons, with their increased formal social role tied to processes of modernisation and industrialisation (Brown, 1973), with, for instance, the charity schools movement in England showing 'what could be achieved by the pooling of individual effort' (Owen, 1964: 30), but then followed by critiques of 'plenty and lack' in charitable provision in the late-19th and early-20th centuries leading to a more interventionist state. Theoretically, Harrison's (1960) analysis articulates how voluntary organisations serve a purpose, filling the social space where there is a need for bureaucratic methods but also a distrust of centralised authority (Smith, 2000: 10), with a more recent view putting the growth of modern charities and non-governmental organisations in the UK down to the planning initiatives of the modern technocratic state (Hilton et al, 2013). Alongside this, a purist view sees the non-profit sector as a long-time major vehicle for promoting fairness and social justice (Skocpol and Fiorina, 2004; Kim and Charbonneau, 2018), engaging in 'moral work' that upholds and reinforces 'moral values' about 'desirable' human behaviour and the 'good society' (Garrow and Hasenfeld, 2010: 33), but with others seeing the work of charities as an excuse for the state to abdicate its responsibilities.

Fast-forward to the 21st century, and we have a well-established collection of academic journals devoted to understanding charity and charities, giving and volunteering, and in the UK alone, almost a dozen university-based research centres examining the subject. Whether that global research fully understands the full gamut of voluntary action is contested. David Horton Smith (2000) outlines many of the 'flat-earth' paradigms of non-profit research, each of which selects too constrained a lens for analysis and leaves out a significant aspect of voluntary action. These involve well-stated issues, like the 'paid staff' paradigm, where research and social focus is on formal charities with large amounts of paid staff, and views that exclude social movement groups from thinking about voluntary action. But Smith also highlights the 'Angelic' and 'Damned' paradigms, where non-profits can do no wrong, or no good respectively. A tendency to paint charities as perfect organisations, staffed solely by well-meaning and committed individuals, who bring sunshine and light into the lives of the less fortunate, is deeply problematic, both because people's motivations are complicated and temporal, but more because some causes are potentially damaging, or could be dominated by extremists or demagogues. Similarly, those who write off all charitable action as bad, interfering, corrupt, selfish or worthless are unhelpful and swap insight for posturing. While we can dig down into arguments as to whether charities may have lost their 'charitable mission' (Rose-Ackerman, 1990), or more widely that voluntary work may have lost its soul under neoliberalism (Rochester, 2013; Dean, 2015b), in general public consensus seems to be that that in our current form of democratic-capitalist society, charities are generally valuable, if far from perfect.

Smith (2000) also argues that we have been too reified in our definition of altruism. In thinking of it as 'service to others' we have been too virtuous, an impossible objective if we happen to also gain some personal satisfaction from helping someone out. It is not unreasonable, he argues, for altruism to involve some self-serving dispositions alongside the 'other concern' of altruism, because, as social animals, human beings are constantly in a maelstrom of giving and taking. To be a recipient of help is not always a pleasurable experience – it can make one feel inadequate, or pitied, or dehumanised – therefore we should not expect the experience of giving to always be selfless. We need to assess the 'nature and degree of *reciprocity, sharing*, or *exchange*' (Smith, 2000: 18; original emphasis) in any volunteer transaction, not assume it through simple binaries or unrealistic definitions. Food charity researcher Hannah Lambie-Mumford (2017: 5, 138) reminds us that to critically assess a charitable endeavour is not to dismiss the moral imperatives of the cause or the volunteer time or donor resources behind them. They represent generosity and compassion, but they also embody the very structural forces (such as a privatised approach to care) that entail society's need for them in the first place. There has to be a constructive way to critically engage with people's goodness. The rise of food banks, for instance, has 'amounted to a delegation of responsibility from the state to the charitable sector' (Lambie-Mumford, 2017: 14), a responsibility that can only tackle the symptoms of food poverty, not its root causes, causing indignity and stress – and yet ends up being presented as the only way of relieving hunger. We end up thinking the problem is being met (Riches, 1997) when only *a* problem is being met, and it may be causing other problems.

My main point throughout is not to criticise charity, but to critique it, to point out the realities of what we are doing and what is happening when we 'do charity'. 'Doing something for charity' gives undertakings a gloss, a veneer of a higher purpose, and a rationale for activities that may otherwise be socially looked down or frowned upon. Whether it's sitting in a bath of baked beans in a town centre while a Lord Mayor throws fish at you, or eating five kilos of offal in two minutes, as long as it's 'for charity' it is generally held up as fine. Doing 'something' also becomes 'doing yourself' in the occasional charitable endeavour:

> On 6 August 2006 London hosted the UK's first "masturbate-a-thon", a collective event in which hundreds of men and women pleasured themselves for charity, raising money for sexual and reproductive health agencies. They also raised awareness and dispelled the shame and taboos that persist around this most commonplace, natural and safe form of sexual activity. The formula was invented at Good Vibrations – a San Francisco sexual health company – as part of a National Masturbation Month, which they founded and have been hosting since 1995 when the original San Francisco M–A–T took place. (Žižek, 2009: 21)

Now personally I have no problem with this: frankness around sexual health and sexual practices, and dispelling taboos are certainly things that a liberal and tolerant society should push. But the subject matter is illustrative: the very fact that what is effectively a sponsored wank can take place does illustrate something quite special about charity's ability as a concept to allow the unallowable. The tenets of charity ride above the social disgust that may be felt at public humiliation, degradation or masturbation, to provide a symbolic cover: 'Non-profit activity generally is seen as having more "virtue" or being more socially desirable in modern society' (Smith, 2000: 11). In contrasting non-commercial and altruistic non-profit activity with commercial or profit-seeking activity, much of which is egoistic, we can make even the most ostensibly selfish act – masturbating to orgasm – altruistic and community-spirited.

What is symbolic power?

Charity is not always practised inconspicuously:

> [P]eople are nicer when they know their actions are public ... one can induce kindness by promising, perhaps in subtle ways, to make these kind actions known to others. That's why certain charities offer mugs or t-shirts to those who donate; these announce the givers' generosity to the world. (Bloom, 2016: 57)

Partly this is because we are aware charities, and charity itself, are imbued with an immediate authority. 'Doing something for charity' is worthy and immediately praised (even if the individual has always wanted to go skydiving). The organisation or voluntary giving of help in order to help someone or something in need holds a special position in society (although its specialness may be under threat, as we shall see later). Charity is generally respected, revered and imbued with authority – a powerful symbol. But what I want to do in this book is explore how this symbolic power operates, and what happens when this symbolic power is misused and becomes symbolic violence. While usually devoid of formal and statutory power, this book posits that charities do hold sway in their ability to encourage, influence and even (emotionally) manipulate. By focusing on separate case studies – controversies surrounding the remembrance poppy, lobbying and the notion of the 'guilt trip' in fundraising – we will see how charity authority and legitimacy operate, particularly in the UK charity sector.

This authority comes from 'symbolic power'. It is important to set out early, as the phrase will be used throughout the book, what we mean by a focus on the symbolic, in terms of power, capital and violence. Power is seen as the 'capacity for exercising agency' (Elder-Vass, 2010: 87), and the thing that makes 'complex and multiple interactions involving people and resources ... all so necessarily political' (Leftwich, 2004: 109). In Robert Dahl's (1957: 202–3) famous explanation, Person A has power over Person B to the extent that Person A can get Person B to do something that Person B would otherwise not do. But power is not always overtly exercised openly and forcefully; it is also mediated through negotiation, and importantly for us here, *obscured* by institutions and social structures. The sociologist Max Weber reasoned that while states are the body that can legitimately use violence, they generally use non-violent means to maintain order, but these actions must be justified in terms of general social values, with an organised coercive, administrative and symbolic apparatus with sovereign authority (Jessop, 2016: 26–7). Building on Weber's classic definition, therefore, that the state has the 'monopoly of legitimate violence', Bourdieu (2014: 4) posits in his lectures on the varied machinations of the state that, in his view, the state is the entity that possesses 'the monopoly of legitimate physical *and symbolic violence*' (original emphasis). This ties to the strong theme within Bourdieu's sociology that powers and capitals have to be legitimated by dominant actors, and it is the state that ultimately holds the role of legitimator.

Detailed examinations of the role of the symbolic in Bourdieu's work are legion (Bourdieu, 1979, 1989, 1991; for overviews see Swartz, 2013; Dean, 2017), so to briefly summarise: in Bourdieu's (1986) theoretical terms, while the central forms of capital were economic, cultural and social, it is symbolic capital that gives these resources their power. Symbolic capital is many things: it is prestige, where respect is commanded rather than earned because of social status, and those without status are dismissed (Skeggs, 1997; Mckenzie, 2015). This symbolic power is operationalised through a certain obsequiousness paid to the state or existing social order. This is seen in the person applying for a mortgage, and teachers and pupils dogmatically following a timetable (Bourdieu, 2014: 13–16, 171–3), where we all pay homage to 'an individual who is the apparent object of respect, [and] to the social order that makes this person respectable' (Bourdieu, 2014: 35). Symbolic power is reinforced by authority (Pellandini-Simányi, 2014), and therefore there is a symbolic exchange of honour that must be upheld.

Using the metaphor of social life as a 'game', Bourdieu's theory demonstrates how in multiple fields, elite 'players' have not only been heavily involved in the design of the games' rules, but also have the ability to define what a winning hand looks like (Dean, 2017). Symbolic power therefore becomes a target of social life, something to 'win': 'win everything ... belief, credit and discredit, perception and appreciation, knowledge and recognition – name, renown, prestige, honour, glory, authority, everything which constitutes symbolic power as recognized power' (Bourdieu, 1984: 251; see also Pellandini-Simányi, 2014: 655). If a way of thinking is presented and legitimated by the dominant in society as 'just', 'right' and 'the way things should be', the dominated end up accepting this version of how things should be, which is actually a deeply violent control of social symbolism (Sapiro, 2010): certain (middle-class) tastes, values, preferences and behaviours come to be seen as inherently tasteful, knowledgeable and right (Skeggs, 2004a, b; Lawler, 2008). People use 'symbolic strategies' (Bourdieu, 1985, 1989) in order to impose their vision of the divisions of the social world and their position in that world on others around them, visions that are self-interested.

Social structures exist on two planes, as material and symbolic entities, made up of both the distribution of amounts of sometimes-scarce capitals, but also the worth of those capitals that exist as symbolic templates for the practical knowledge and ordinary activity of social agents (Bourdieu and Wacquant, 1992: 7, 9). It is similar to the idea of knowing the price of everything and the value of nothing: a family heirloom may be worthless but priceless; a volunteer stopping by a hospital patient's bed for a chat may be worth a pound on the labour market but may be invaluable to both of the people involved. Objects (like remembrance poppies), gifts (like putting some money in a collecting tin), and labours (such as volunteering in a care home) all have two values, the measurable material that can be traded, and the intangible ephemeral value imbued with a deeper meaning. One would assume that this latter value is not tradable, but this book will show that it often is (frequently, in ways it can be hard to put a finger on), and can be worth much, much more.

That charities possess a symbolic prestige is quite clear. In a recent Ipsos MORI (2014) public trust and confidence in charities survey, it was shown that charities are the third most trusted public institution, behind only doctors and the police. While there is some evidence of increasing public scepticism about ensuring charities spend their funds on charitable activities, with 60 per cent feeling that charities spend too much on administration and salaries, and that they may not act as independently as previously thought, an overwhelming 80 per cent of respondents still agree that charities add something unique to society. What we are attempting to think through here are the potential downsides of this 'something unique'. In the critical youth volunteering literature, for instance, authors increasingly demonstrate how the symbolic power of charity can be used and abused, and how young people are frequently required by structural forces (Dean, 2014) to build their identities and biographies – and CVs – through undertaking a variety of voluntary labours alongside leisure pursuits to present themselves to universities and prospective employers in certain ways (see, for example, Holdsworth and Brewis, 2014; Holdsworth, 2017). These presentations are of 'good', rounded citizens, with a range of experiences, giving them a 'competitive edge' in the context of credentialism (Reay, 2006). Skeggs (2004b: 75) demonstrates how culture is an exchangeable good where participation in activities can enhance the 'overall value' of personhood, be it visiting museums or galleries, which are both seen as morally good but also engender value in later life as tradable experiences for employability and social networking, making an 'intimate link between economic and moral value'. In her blog analysis of (relatively privileged) young British people's gap years before starting university, Helene Snee (2014) shows the enormous range of pressures at this time of life. Despite their privilege, these young people face another pressure, to both have 'the time of their lives', and *to make it look* to their friends and family back home that they are having the time of their lives. Volunteering has the 'moral advantage' of altruism (Snee, 2014: 9), compared with other leisure pursuits, an advantage that is not open to all, as young people from less privileged backgrounds partake in such 'hope labour', which cannot overcome structural inequalities, usually along race, class and gender lines (Taylor-Collins, 2019).

The central idea of this book is not to necessarily say something new about social theory, as hopefully the reader has come for critical charity studies rather than a 'nuanced' (that is, thin; see Healy, 2017) reimagining of Bourdieu, Goffman and so on. Instead, what this book will try to do is to use those theories as devices within the sociological toolkit to explore a widespread and common phenomenon that exists within an underexplored section of the social experience. Equally, the book aims to include a broad range of examples rather than focusing on any one policy, charity or controversy across several chapters. Issues like the collapse of Kids Company, the introduction of the 'gagging bill' or the yearly furore over the Poppy Appeal are issues to which more academic ink should be devoted, and I want to present an eclectic set of cases that illustrate the central theme that charity's symbolic power is another plane that needs theorising and explanation. Applications of symbolic power to charity have been piecemeal, and it's an aim of this text to codify much of that work into a usable tool that others can then work with, in order that we don't continue to sideline this present in potentia part of an everyday phenomenon.

In order to present a thorough examination of how this theoretical framework can be applied in a single field of charitable activity, this introductory chapter now turns to focus on international aid, development and the mega-philanthropy that supports much of it. This research is driven by authors who have focused intently on specific aspects of charitable activity, and who are willing to critique and challenge that which we otherwise could see as beyond reproach – such as Moore's (2008: 68) work on the pink cancer ribbon. Key recent studies useful for our analysis here are Linsey McGoey's and Nicole Aschoff's forensic and explosive examinations of the Bill and Melinda Gates Foundation (the world's largest private foundation with an endowment of over US$50 billion), and Monika Krause's theoretically informed empirical exploration of how development really works.

Taking on the Gates Foundation

There's a prominent internet meme known as Milkshake Duck. So the parable goes, there's a video of a cute duck drinking a milkshake that goes round the world via social media, and everyone falls in love with Milkshake Duck, a charming moment of purity in an otherwise dispiriting world. Then, a day or so later, when someone examines the duck's history, finding a dark and hateful past, the truth is revealed – 'We regret to inform you that the duck is racist.' It's the online version of not meeting your heroes, the fact that the internet's ability to trawl everyone's public and private past immediately means that we should neither take things on face value nor believe in any concept or individual as perfectly good, pure or unchallengeable.

While never referred to as 'milkshake ducking', challengers to the purity of the charitable are key to understanding the basking glow of the symbolic power of charity, but also the shield it can provide. In an interview available on YouTube with C-SPAN (television network) in 1993, and elsewhere in infamous published works, the author and polemicist Christopher Hitchens addresses Mother Theresa – the Saint of Calcutta to her supporters and the 'ghoul' of Calcutta to Hitchens – and her permanent reception of a free pass. Because most people have neither the time nor the inclination to investigate claims about practice and character, especially if they possess the standard Western laziness about issues on the other side of the world, and their character is only framed by media, if you ask the lay person in the West about Mother Theresa, it would go without saying they'd respond that she spent her entire time helping the poor of Calcutta. 'But if you really push them,' argues Hitchens, 'they don't know anything about her at all, they just take it on faith, as saints always are taken.' Various critics, with Hitchens leading the charge, questioned and challenged Mother Theresa's methods, her motivations and her relationships with controversial but wealthy figures.

Today's examples are the tech billionaires, and their increasing desire to 'do good' (Giridharadas, 2018). The fact that large-scale donors are untouchable because of their generosity is highly problematic for developing sustainable and appropriate social policies. With more frequency today, however, these large donations can get pulled apart in the firestorm of public opinion, with some realisation that they may be doing more harm than good, especially in relation to the charges of their anti-democratic tendencies (Barkan, 2013). *No Such Thing as a Free Gift* by Linsey McGoey (2015) focuses on the Gates Foundation and its role in shaping global health policy and education provision in the US. It is highly critical of the Gates and big philanthropy or 'philanthrocapitalism' (Bishop and Green, 2010; for a critique, see McGoey, 2012; Eikenberry and Mirabella, 2018) in general, especially their tendency to avoid accountability through being unquestionable. Bill Gates' emergence as a global celebrity, due both to his wealth – current worth US$107 billion, over 0.5 per cent of the GDP of the US – and his public image – the Gates Foundation commands considerable celebrity accolades from P. Diddy to Jay-Z to Bono – means the Foundation can undertake either ineffective or damaging policy implementation because of the symbolic 'goodness' of his substantial donations to charity. McGoey's book tries to take on the Gates Foundation, not because taking aim at the biggest name is the best way to get noticed, but because charity and especially mega-philanthropy is, by its very essence, hard to critique. We – academics and scholars, tabloid and broadsheet journalists, the general public – would have no trouble criticising the spending priorities or effectiveness of a Whitehall department, or a local council, or a medium-sized charity such as Kids Company. So why, then, McGoey asks, does an organisation with a budget outstripping all of these often get a free pass? Does the very scale of the Gates' generosity mean that reasoned critique just looks like jealous sniping from the sidelines? Looking back a century, McGoey finds parallels with the 'big men' of US industry and philanthropy of the 1900s, Rockefeller, Carnegie and Ford, who, as businessmen, were guilty of price fixing and bribery, were anti-union and anti-welfare, and deployed employee surveillance or were guilty of anti-Semitism respectively (McGoey, 2015: 4, 43, 48–9, 57) – the Carnegie and Rockefeller Foundations also funded eugenics research during the rise of Nazism (Black, 2003) – traits they frequently aimed to soften through their philanthropy. Such softening still goes on today, and ties into a long history of examining the motivations of elites in entering the charitable field to make them appear altruistic, benevolent and morally upstanding (Shapely, 1998). The estimate that over 40 per cent of the Gates Foundation's assets derive from companies whose operations contradict Foundation goals (Thompson, 2014) should be enough of a concern for the questions to be sharper.

Philanthrocapitalism is a form of philanthropy that aims to be more efficient and results-orientated than previous philanthropic efforts, emulating the way business is done in the for-profit world. But its critics call attention to its undemocratic tendencies, with an absence of transparency and accountability. As McGoey (2015: 8) points out, whereas the World Health Organization (WHO) is meant to be accountable to member governments (and, by extension, their voting population) who provide most of its funding, when the Gates Foundation makes up 10 per cent of the WHO budget, any independence is compromised if a private philanthropic concern has 'the power to stipulate exactly where and how the UN institution spends its money', in part because private donations have no guarantee of sustainability.

McGoey (2015: 12–13) recounts a story from Baudelaire, of two men walking down the street, who, on passing a beggar, each put money into his cap. One, noting his friend's greater generosity, offers praise; the other replies that it was a fake coin, because increasing the beggar's contentment temporarily while being seen to do a good deed and to be recognised as charitable by his friend, while still having lost nothing, is to 'pick up gratis the certificate of a charitable man'; in sum, a good deal. But the actions of the would-be giver keep the beggar hungry, a failure to recognise one's own role in poverty and the continued need for charity:

> Charity is the humanitarian mask hiding the face of economic exploitation. In a superego blackmail of gigantic proportions, the developed countries "help" the undeveloped with aid, credits and so on, and thereby avoid the key issue, namely their complicity in and co-responsibility for the miserable situation of the undeveloped. (Žižek, 2009: 17)

We know that rich and immensely rich individuals lobby governments; through large individual donations to political parties they aim to help elect politicians whose policies will be favourable to either them personally or their business interests, and to get a hearing with decision-makers. The fact that election authorities in countries like the US and UK are so scrupulous in documenting these donations, and the press' attention is generally focused on those that break or aim to circumvent the rules, means that the above-board and regular donations are unsurprising and not part of public conversation: we know it takes place, we don't seem to care, and are in no hurry to dramatically alter the rules. And just as we should be worried about big money in political lobbying for personal gain, we should be willing to bring the same critical eye to big money in charity when people like the Gates lobby for various policies to be enacted. There is a clear difference, a symbolic difference, when that lobbying takes place for political attention or when it's being done from a position of effecting changes for the social good, yet that doesn't mean we should ignore it.

The number of charitable foundations in the US has risen steeply in recent years, with nearly half of the 85,000 foundations established in the last 15 years, and 5,000 set up every year (McGoey, 2015: 17), with total capitalisation of more than US$800 billion (Reich, 2018: 9). Yet the overall level of giving in the US has remained at around 2 per cent of GDP since the 1970s. So it does not seem unfair to reason that the move to foundational giving among the US's super-wealthy has worked to boost the profile and spirit of its donors than to actually increase the amount of money given. The growth in foundations has, of course, come at a time of increased wealth inequality, with the market reforms of the 1980s and tax cuts of the 2000s serving to concentrate wealth among the richest. Instead of using general taxes to fund a social welfare system that redistributes wealth more evenly, a reliance on private philanthropy means services are at the behest of the giver, not the democratically elected government. We know that the recipients of charity funds in fields like the arts tend to go to the organisations focused on serving richer, whiter audiences. Reich's (2018) research details the unfairness of the US tax code and how it treats donors differently according to their wealth: poorer donors are unable to claim tax back against their donations, while the wealthiest are able to claim back almost 40 per cent of their gifts. If such gifts benefited the poor this may be justifiable, but as Reich demonstrates, in the *best-case scenario*, at most one-third of all charity goes to help the poor, and millionaires contribute at most one-fifth of their giving to the needs of the poor. It seems almost childishly simple to point out the unfortunate truth that the main beneficiaries of rich people's giving are the rich themselves. In a critique, Rosenthal (2015: 1) argues that philanthrocapitalists promote their charitable work 'as a sign of their moral standing, but many of these donations are merely cover.' As McGoey (2012) observed, blatant self-interest is not a threat to this model of philanthropy, instead becoming a prerequisite. There is a:

> ... common popular belief that philanthropists often have tacit ulterior motive for giving, from earning the tax write-off, to accumulating political favours, to advancing corporate or governmental economic interests in foreign regions. What's different today is that such motives are no longer tacit. They are widely voiced by philanthrocapitalists themselves. The new philanthropists are increasingly proud, triumphant even, about the private economic fortunes to be made through embracing philanthrocapitalism. Not only is it no longer necessary to "disguise" or minimize self-interest, self-interest is championed as the best rationale for helping others. It is seen not as coexisting in tension with altruism, but as a prerequisite for altruism. (McGoey, 2015: 20)

No one, McGoey and myself included, would deny that the Gates do much good, just that there has remained until remarkably recently a 'gaping silence' where there should be spirited discussion around crowding out, opportunity costs, transparency and accountability. There is a public mindset that finds the Gates' philanthropy appealing, but this mindset 'restricts public debate surrounding philanthropy by making even the most judicious criticism appear petty or small-minded' (McGoey, 2015: 27). Many authors (for example, Barkan, 2013; Reich, 2018) have considered ways in which foundations are democratically problematic. Within this, an inability to critique is itself democratically problematic, even if that inability comes from social and cultural pressure and norms rather than any reduction of freedom of speech. The fact that large-scale donors have until recently remained untouchable because of their generosity is highly problematic for developing sustainable and appropriate social policies. When the Gates Foundation makes a decision based on its founders' personal desires, that is, a priority based on personal predilections, it is an unchallengeable priority based on the overwhelming generosity of the person making it. There is crushing weight of goodness that giving away US$28 billion (Tweedie, 2013) can symbolise.

Predilections are problematic in other ways as well. While resources depend on a donor's priorities and media attention, too much media attention can be unhelpful, with, for example, the Indian Ocean tsunami in 2004 being seen by some as a disaster that received a disproportionate amount of resources after an appeal (Krause, 2014: 31). Having a bulging wallet and a big heart doesn't give you the right to intervene, and it doesn't guarantee your intervention will be a success. A similar story that is often held up as indicative of using charity as a tool to prevent poor publicity is that of Facebook founder and CEO Mark Zuckerberg and his wife Priscilla Chan's donation of US$100 million to radically transform schools in Newark, New Jersey, in 2010. Part of the 'venture philanthropy' movement that includes the Gates Foundation and philanthrocapitalism, Zuckerberg worked with then Mayor (now New Jersey Senator) Cory Booker and then Governor Chris Christie to bring in a fundamental shift in how public education was managed locally, including moving towards charter schools, a more privatised and competitive approach to schooling promoted by The Gates Foundation, and heavily criticised by teachers' unions (see Aschoff, 2015: 107–43). However, at the same time as Zuckerberg's gift was announced with great fanfare on *The Oprah Winfrey Show*, *The Social Network*, written by Aaron Sorkin and directed by David Fincher, saw Jesse Eisenberg play Zuckerberg during the early days of Facebook, and the legal battles he found himself in as a result of what the film portrays as law suits caused by Zuckerberg's selfish approach to business, his betrayal of friendships and his arrogant genius. As Dale Russakoff (2015: 32), a journalist who followed this local education story closely reveals, while the donation was planned long before the film's release, and the internal communication team at Facebook recommended against the donation because it would look like cover for bad press, 'there was no question that [the donation] would create a splashy and favorable narrative about the young billionaire at the same time he was being bludgeoned on the big screen.'

To tell the story quickly, the school reforms funded by the Chan-Zuckerbergs were largely a failure, with huge protests from parents and teachers. A key part of the failure was the lack of buy-in from local residents: Russakoff's (largely sympathetic) book *The Prize* documents in detail how residents of Newark had to watch Oprah to learn how their children's schools were going to be transformed, and were then left in the dark until decisions had been made as to how the money was going to be spent: 'For four years, the reformers never really tried to have a conversation with the people of Newark' (Russakoff, 2015: 209). It's difficult to criticise a US$100 million donation, and this was Zuckerberg's first venture into large-scale giving, and he clearly learned lessons from it, with his more recent philanthropic projects aiming to engage with communities before offering models as solutions, but the myriad changes these reforms brought to the Newark schools system, the chaos of implementation and Zuckerberg's inability to get his own way because he was working with machine politicians who had their own personal missions and needed to get all of their backers on side before action could be taken, shows the problems with relying on philanthropy for grand social change. There is often a huge accountability hole and democratic deficit at the centre, and problems in education are both pedagogical and political: there is an arrogance, admitted by reformers who spoke to Russakoff, that because of success in one field, skills can be translated across another wholly different field (see Aschoff, 2015: 131–2); US$100 million buys a lot of no questions: Do you know what you are going to do with the money? Who's in charge? What do the community think about this? All went unanswered, because of another question: Who looks a gift horse in the mouth? Charity's symbolic power can override both a lot of democratic principles and a lot of common sense, and this is especially true if that charity comes in the guise of mega-philanthropy.

Realities of the international development field

Monika Krause's (2014) book *The Good Project* argues that judgements of charity, and specifically international aid organisations, are too often hyper-celebratory and full of praise, or hyper-critical and full of cynicism. Instead there needs to be much more judicious examination of how these organisations *actually do their work*, the choices they make and the constraints they have to work within. There is a logic of practice (Bourdieu, 1990) which stands between those seeking to help and those that need help, and like the rest of the charitable giving relationship, this is often best understood as market logic:

> Donor agencies give money and receive the symbolic benefits of having helped. Relief agencies receive money and the symbolic benefits of having helped. Beneficiaries, even those who do not receive anything, lend themselves as a source of authority for those who help. (Krause, 2014: 60)

Agencies (sellers) have to design aid projects (produce commodities) that donors (buyers) want to give to (consume): 'The project is a commodity, and thus those helped, the beneficiaries, become part of a commodity', thereby projects are often short-term and designed for donors, not beneficiaries, and beneficiaries are, in effect, in competition to be helped (Krause, 2014: 4). There are always more people to be helped than can be helped; therefore projects that are designed and implemented will likely be the ones with greater symbolic potential.

Non-governmental organisations (NGOs) seek legitimacy and 'humanitarian authority', a form of symbolic capital that operates within the field of aid generally, determined by both by the rules of development, but also the positions taken and tactics employed by individual agencies within the field. Within the field of international aid itself, organisations compete for space and capital. They try and differentiate themselves, when the non-expert public may lump them together, not in competition for funding, but for reputation and standing: 'The authority of humanitarian relief draws on the suffering of the people it aims to serve', argues Krause (2014: 113), where the very fact that one has chosen to assist others in a less fortunate position than oneself has an authority to it, distinct from other realms of human endeavour (especially the profit motive).

Aid agencies have to (and do) make calculations about where their work and money can have the most impact, but because of the nature of the field, some of this calculation comes from a reputational strategic position, where the fear of looking like a failure or not achieving enough has to factor in. Again, even at organisational level, there is a balance made between altruistic and instrumental reward and altruistic and instrumental risk. As one aid agency water engineering consultant told Krause (2014: 34), 'There is an incentive to help those who are easy to help.' Long-term problems are uncool and unsexy, 'unattractive' for donors, whereas immediate crises and the promise of short-term results are cool and accessible. Agencies need to show that they can deliver 'good projects', playing it safe and keeping their projects 'small, manageable, and risk-free in order to ensure that they will have the best possible evaluation' (Young et al, 2005: 117), with the additional critique that the structural causes of such problems aren't being solved anyway (Flaherty, 2016).

Krause's work makes us aware of the fact that some beneficiaries are easier to package up and sell than others; symbolic value is extracted from beneficiaries by agencies who get to speak about suffering on their behalf, alongside providing a shield of morality and political authority for donors. This is no one's direct fault per se, but a wholly expected and understandable consequence of how both the system of international development and the charity–beneficiary relationship system have operated and been experienced for years. In such a formulation, beneficiaries get little choice about lending this authority to others, their role limited to acceptance or refusal, dependent on the morality of others, with a giver's compassion verifying their moral standing (Longmore, 2016). Whereas in consumer situations it is the consumer who is afforded most of the rights (of return, for instance), recipients in giving situations are afforded almost no rights, only whether to refuse or not, which is both a Hobson's choice (to starve or not), and also often managed through a charity acting as intermediary, meaning the decision of acceptance is often made before the recipient gets a say. Charity leaderships are rarely accountable to those who require their provision (Lambie-Mumford, 2017: 91), with few avenues for those at the bottom of the giver–manager–beneficiary relationship to exercise agency.

Philanthropic theory tends to focus on the philanthropist or giver, leaving the recipient 'absent' (Ostrander, 1989: 229). There is not enough input from recipients (Ostrander and Schervish, 1990; Breeze and Dean, 2012a) taking an active part in defining their needs, in part because charity is a supply-driven field (Schervish, 1992), concerned with how much donors are willing to respond to appeals rather than how much need there is. When projects apply for funding, funders need some way to assess what is 'good'. Many worthy projects do not often measure up in ways that varied audiences will recognise:

> Recognising this tension helps explain why, for example, some desperate situations abroad become *causes célèbres*, and not others. The movements that gain international appeal are those that figure out how to match what donors want. (Eliasoph, 2013: 109)

There are problems with this funding model: organisations end up chasing funding, diverting them from the populations they were founded to serve and that they are good at serving; and it begets a state of competition where those that are most like the funders, or best at speaking their language (Sampson, 1996), get funded: 'What is being consumed by donors are not pots and pans or tents and food, but the act of giving', writes Krause (2014: 47, 48), 'They pay so that something is done, and they pay for the opportunity to be able to say they supported that something was being done', with examples including the insistence that national flags and corporate logos are displayed in the field, operationalising charity as a demonstration of goodness and of positive contribution. These points may seem both cynical and obvious. But the myriad ways in which the concept of charity works lends itself to these practices, which some would argue are the abuse of the charitable imperative, and turn the good glow into a tool to be used – and abused. The following chapters unpick this across a wider range of examples.

Overview of the book

Chapter 2 starts with Paul Longmore's dogged and personal exploration of that most fluffy of charity spectacles, the charity telethon, as a way to start understanding the issues surrounding charitable giving, whether that be in the form of individual donations, corporate social responsibility programmes or volunteering. Looking at these concepts through a symbolic lens, we ask those undeniably suspicious questions of 'are people only doing this for something in return, and if so, what?' Such explorations in 'the other side' of gifts and charity are contextualised through an overview of Marcel Mauss' (2011) study of gift giving, and how that doing good may always be part of a wider embedded relationship of exchange. The role of someone's charity adding to our impression of them, and how, as such, it results in various strategic decisions, is viewed from the perspective of business, individuals and charity fundraising and fundraisers themselves. While giving is practically always something to be celebrated, this chapter continues the work of this introductory chapter in showcasing how charity is complicated and can be simultaneously positive and problematic.

In Chapter 3, data is presented from a series of focus groups conducted with young people, mostly British university students, exploring their experiences of and attitudes towards charity online, particularly on social media. Taking a framework from Erving Goffman's (1959) theory of how we present ourselves to others day to day, alongside the growing literature on young people's online lives and how charities are trying to engage in such new media to spread their messages and raise funds, this chapter reflects on how charity can be used as a tool to present oneself in a certain way online. Young people discuss facing awkward and complicated online relationships because of the constant worry about what is true and authentic, and what is done to promote oneself as good.

Chapter 4 focuses on charities as organisations, often experts in their field or bestowed with the image of expertise. Going through how and why the UK government has sought to involve the charity sector in the delivery of social policy, the chapter outlines new challenges to charity trust that have emerged, and how the public–voluntary sector relationship has become more complicated as a result. Recent attempts to 'gag' charities in receipt of public income from criticising officials, because charities are holders of automatic symbolic prestige, are discussed, as are several cases in which charities may have misused the automatic assumption of goodness and expertise they have received from the public and policy practitioners. Interviewee data presents a story from sector leaders that the environment for charities has become significantly tougher in recent years, partly because of funding, but also because charities are no longer seen as special by default.

Chapter 5 examines the 2015 collapse of Kids Company, a leading charity for disadvantaged children in London. Applying ideas from the sociology of charisma, and the need for voluntary organisations to find a balance between passion and professionalism, Kids Company is examined as a case where the charity's powerful story and emotional pull, and the effervescence of its founder Camila Batmanghelidjh, led to its closure. Sector leaders are asked to reflect on what the high-profile collapse has meant for the sector more widely, and whether charities' closeness to politicians and the media can lead to high-risk strategies that can turn sour very quickly.

In the final empirical chapter, Chapter 6, we look at the poppy, the fundraising symbol of remembrance for the contribution of the armed services, and more specifically, the yearly controversy that surrounds it. Known as 'poppy fascism', the demand that all public figures must wear the poppy prominently and respectfully during the autumn in the lead-up to Remembrance Sunday, this phenomenon illustrates how the essential goodness of charity symbols can be weaponised and used competitively and judgementally. Examining the yearly poppy outcry through the lens of postcolonial theory, we see how the poppy is forced to bear a lot of cultural and symbolic weight, partly because it is held up as an unalloyed 'good thing'. The problems created by 'poppy fascism' for sector leaders are outlined, and a wider angle is taken to illustrate what this simple charitable fundraising and remembrance tool says about modern Britain today.

Chapter 7 presents an alternative attitude towards the doing of charity, which seeks to encourage us to ignore charity's sociology and its symbolic resonance. The effective altruism movement argues that we shouldn't be giving to causes that tug on the heartstrings but only to those that are most effective in saving lives. The chapter argues that while this movement raises complex moral questions for which we often fail to provide good answers, in arguing for such a normative reorganising of society, the effective altruists' unrealistic assumptions about why people do charity prevents such arguments having wider impact.

Theoretical, policy and practice ideas presented throughout the book are rooted in data drawn from two recent qualitative studies I have conducted on issues within the charity sector, one utilising focus groups with young people about their experiences of charity online, and the other a set of interviews with charity leaders and professionals. A short methodological appendix detailing the data collection processes for these empirical studies is included at the end of the book.

Unpacking the good

In his work on the art world, Bourdieu (1994) demonstrates how cultural products are valued in both economic and aesthetic terms. To study art is not just to focus on the work done (the sculpture sculpted, for instance), but also 'the production of the value of the work or, which amounts to the same thing, of belief in the value of the work' (Elder-Vass, 2018). What is it that gives that art a wider meaning and value? 'Among the makers of the work of art, we must finally include the public, which helps to make its value by appropriating it materially ([through] collectors) or symbolically ([through] audiences [or] readers)' (Bourdieu, 1994: 78). Therefore the multifarious audiences, the consumers of discourses (Elder-Vass, 2018) of value and prestige in the art world, add to and build that self-same prestige that makes the art worth something in the first place. There is a reinforcing process between the material object and the symbolic presence, which incurs a reaction and stimulates value. A similar pattern can be seen in charitable activity. Things that are not actually 'good' often get interpreted as 'good' because of the symbolism surrounding and cultural engagement with the act. There is an assumption that the work done by charities is 'good' because it is done for free, that the billionaire giving money away must be doing good, or why else would they give the money away, or that because someone has been commemorated on a plaque, or in a statue, or in naming rights, they must have done something worthwhile. As forthcoming chapters will show, there has been a decline in this automatic assumption of goodness among charities over the last decade, as charity's symbolic power has been pierced, as have many other institutions, by stronger social forces.

As Kate Brittain of the Association of Chief Executives of Voluntary Organisations (ACEVO) (quoted in Birkwood, 2016) has put it, charities are not villains but nor are they 'heroes by default' anymore, arguing that as the sheen has worn away, the sector has to be far more active in proving its worth. This view echoes the wider social and political decline in belief that society functions properly: 'Over the last eight or nine years, in the UK at least, there has been an endemic scandal in pretty much every major institution: the banks, the media, police, Westminster and so on' (O'Hagan, quoted in Ball, 2017: 271). We have seen a cascade of critical books with eye-catching titles ready to rubbish charity: *Charity Sucks*, *The Great Charity Scandal*, *Toxic Charity* and *When Helping Hurts* are all titles one can find online, published within the last decade. This is not to denigrate these particular books and their arguments, nor (clearly) am I averse to criticising the practice of charities or the concept of charity. But it is fair to say that criticising the charitable imperative has become common, and accepted, and profitable (both socially and financially). In their recent critique from the left, *Against Charity*, Raventós and Wark (2018: 97) posit that, 'Most people are reluctant to speak ill of charity, or can't associate it with scandalous wrongdoing because it is so widely believed to be good per se.' This isn't true in totality anymore: with the media and political crisis in fundraising practice, charity has never felt more criticised (Breeze, 2017: 18–20). But that criticism often precludes critique, reasoned analyses or explanation. Over the rest of this book I want to start this work and assess symbolic power's role in contemporary deployment and abuses of charity.

2

Giving and getting: using charity's symbolic power

From 1966 until 2010, the first Monday of September, Labor Day in the US, was also the day when the comedian Jerry Lewis would host a marathon overnight television show, fundraising for the Muscular Dystrophy Association. This was an annual staple of 'charitainment', similar to Comic Relief in the UK, but without the risqué alternative comedy. Dissected by Paul Longmore (2016) as events full of cheesy paternalism, many saw these telethons as dehumanising of people with disabilities (especially children), framing them as pathetic individuals lacking agency, sexuality or skill, where the beneficiaries of charity were a vehicle for advancing the priorities and agendas of others. But these criticisms from disability rights campaigners were often thrown back at the anti-telethon activists by the charities themselves, with critics bullied for having the temerity to appear ungrateful (Longmore, 2016: 201).

Longmore examines the myriad tensions within such public proclamations of charity. Those telethons with the 'greatest heart appeal' will generate the most donations, not those causes where the money would do the most good, or where the greatest number of people are in need. In a country with privatised medicine and a limited safety net, such uneven focus has exacerbated the inequality within healthcare provision. We see the sheer number of US telethons for other causes, and their success in raising donations, as Americans paying a 'social tax' in lieu of a decent welfare state. Longmore's (2016: 72) work also exposes the commercialisation of charity, dismissing the use of incentives to give as 'expos[ing] a selfish motive behind the boasted altruism'. His glare focuses on every donor who got 'a shot of celebrity' by being name-checked on the TV show, to those who got supermarket money-off coupons for donating, but at its most disparaging toward those large corporations who use the good glow of the symbolic power of charities to shield themselves from corporate misdemeanours, male corporate executives going on television to hand over novelty sized cheques acting as the nation's patriarchs, authenticating their humanity. In one example, Longmore details the travails of the US snowmobile industry, which took off in the early 1970s but saw sales fall dramatically when the number of severe injuries and deaths from the machines started to rise. In order to counter the negative press, snowmobile associations teamed up with Easter Seals organisations (previously the National Society for Crippled Children), offering sponsorship, free camps and rides, and physical rehabilitation schemes: as Longmore (2016: 37) puts it 'Easter Seals offered public relations aid to a business burdened by a negative public image.' He details how other companies, like the nursing home industry and Harley-Davidson, did similar.

By encouraging consumers to buy specific products with a charitable tie-in, Longmore (2016: 40) points out that companies 'get positive PR for merely handing over coins that had come out of customer's pockets' (2016: 40). Big businesses' philanthropy rocketed after the Second World War in turn, and charity became a business, reflecting US corporate culture making use of celebrities and the media to tap into status and power structures, lending business moral credibility and public respect. As one 1989 telethon host in Los Angeles said to the audience about the show's 'Angel Board', which displayed the names of those who gave over US$200:

> If I owned a business in this area, I would call in a $200 or more pledge right now. Get my name up there. Think of the advertising. You wear a white hat in the community because people know that you are helping.... Think of all the publicity that your company will get. (quoted in Longmore, 2016: 49)

Reading Longmore's work, one would find a close connection to the critical discourse that swirls around charities: potential donors are pestered, causes are presented out of proportion, too much is spent on fundraising and administration, there's shameless manipulation, and money is not distributed according to need but often around agencies' abilities to publicise and promote causes. Telethons served to extoll voluntary service and charitable donations as the 'American way', exerting 'enormous influence over what Americans considered compassionate behaviour' (Longmore, 2016: 8, 32–3), including over how public money should be spent in medical research and treatment, which often focused on the issue the charity was lobbying for, thereby profiting from their own lobbying. This included propaganda about the possibility of cures for various ailments: this over-claiming took place because donating for a cure is much sexier. While the charities were doing a great amount of work helping people with disabilities manage their conditions and live fuller lives, this wasn't what a lot of the money was being raised for, but the ends of helping children with disabilities justifies the means of shoddy fundraising practices.

Given recent myriad scandals and ensuing calls for tougher regulation of the voluntary sector in the UK, Longmore's work is evidence of how those at the top of charitable causes can forget why they are there and how charisma and celebrity can mask bad practice. It illustrates how fundraising should and should not be done, and reveals both the mistreatment of the disadvantaged, and also a long view of how positive social change has emerged as a result of the disability rights movement. It is an example which shows how three different groups can operationalise the symbolic power of charity: how fundraisers and those working for charities can 'sell' the option of looking good through emotional appeals, how businesses can shield themselves with the notion that they can't be all bad because of involvement in a worthy cause, and how individuals have multiple and inter-cutting motivations to be charitable, including wanting to present themselves in a certain light. This chapter will take each of these groups – charities and their fundraisers, businesses, and individuals – in turn, in order to think about how the giving of gifts can be turned partially to one's own advantage. This requires an examination of the theories of gifts and giving, which is where we start.

Theories of gifts and giving

The role of gifts in society is a subject long studied by social scientists and philosophers. The central idea one could take from this body of work is that gift giving practically always benefits the giver as well as the recipient, with presents and gifts 'maintain[ing] the everyday order of social intercourse' (Bourdieu, 1990: 99). Marcel Mauss' (2011) classic anthropological study sought to investigate those gifts and favours between people that are, in theory, voluntary but in fact reveal themselves as obligatory when looked at in a wider context. In Māori culture for example, the *taonga* (material gift) carries with it its own *hau* (spirit), which is passed on reciprocally from one individual to the next; however, reciprocity, Mauss (2011: 9) argues, is motivated by the *hau*, which 'pursues him [sic] who holds it'. While gifts may be offered generously and openly, there usually remains a 'social deception' based on economic self-interest. There is a paralleling movement at work in the giving of a gift, that while the recipient will receive the material gift, and the associated obligation to return in favour, or face the penalty of losing 'mana', the giver has honour and prestige conferred on them through giving the original gift. While the material that is given may contain a symbolic importance, the motivating feature of the gift is not necessarily to receive a material gift in return, but rather to increase the authority one may have on other group members, or wider social groups – the intangible benefits of the act of giving provide it with a 'magical property' (or symbolic power), worth more than the gift itself. This brings forth the imagery of the gift as being a type of spectre on the horizon of gift-giving which haunts those who are obliged to receive it, but one that is also part of one's own spiritual existence.

In his discussion on the obligations to give and receive in Polynesian tribes, Mauss (2011: 11) discusses the duties and rights of both parties, the relationship between whom includes the 'spiritual bonds between things which are to some extent part of persons, and persons and groups that behave in some measure as if they were things.' There is an allusion to the paradoxical proximity of the giver and recipient, as involving simultaneous intimacy and distance, which arise from the creditor–debtor duality, which was aimed at promoting friendly feeling in the gift-giving practices of the Andaman Islands. There is a complex relationship between individual autonomous choice and obligation, with individuals taking great care to demonstrate their gift stems from magnanimity, even when it was actuated by the mechanisms of obligation which remain resident within gifts themselves. Gifts contain multiple characteristics – 'at the same time property and possession, a pledge and a loan, an object bought, a deposit, a mandate, a trust' (Mauss, 2011: 22) – but also the social ability to 'bite' and 'sever' (Mauss, 2011: 24), stimulating action and ructions, because return gifts are, in essence, obligatory, expected and of a similar quality or cost to the first gift (although not the same – as Bourdieu [1990: 105] points out, 'the counter-gift must be deferred and different, because the immediate return of an exactly identical object clearly amounts to a refusal'). It is no surprise that Mauss traces a link between today's capitalism, yesterday's barter and the day-before-yesterday's forms of gift exchange, with barter arising from 'the system of gifts given and received on credit, simplified by drawing together the moments of time which had previously been distinct' (Mauss, 2011: 35). This work shows that giving a gift is not just to lose an item; it is to 'accumulate obligations' and 'symbolic credit' (Krause, 2014: 58). Such accumulation should breed caution of gifts' double-edged nature – as recipients feel beholden to the giver, there will always remain silence over how the gift is to be repaid (McGeoy, 2015: 19). As Bourdieu (1997: 231–2) writes, gifts are characterised by their ambiguity, 'experienced (or intended) as a refusal of self-interest and egoistic calculation [yet] no one is really unaware of the logic of exchange' – both giver and receiver know that is a ulterior hidden economy at play, and that the giver will need to recompensed at some undefined point in the future. Larger gifts in this case, such as mega-philanthropy, take advantage of such social relations and can operate as a tool of legitimacy for the rich, another strategy for retaining hegemonic power both economically but also structurally, operating successfully in part because they appear apolitical (McGoey, 2015). Working from such a framing, Bourdieu (1990) sees gift exchange as central to social practice, but a problematic part of it: the purchase and then giving of a gift serves to transform economic capital into symbolic power (Klekar, 2009; Scherz, 2014), perpetuating unequal balances of power. Collectively, we misrecognise the true nature of the act because we are all playing by rules set somewhere else. Gifts entail a form of social domination drawing up a 'veil of enchanted relations' between giver and receiver, to cover the realities of the violence that stems from the dominance and dependence, 'getting and keeping a lasting hold over someone' (Bourdieu, 1990: 126): no one can ever point out the moral obligations created by the 'generous' gift, as a rejection of the social game means you've already lost it, an option only available to the extremely privileged.

To apply this reading of Mauss' ideas to today's perilous social world, and deep concerns over 'getting it wrong' and making a social faux pas, think about those birthday presents, wedding presents or gifts you give when you visit a friend's house for the first time, or go for a dinner party: 'The invitation says, "a contribution towards their future lives together". What did they get us as a wedding present? £40? Shall we stick the same in the envelope? But the hotel's costing us much more than it did them! Yeah, I suppose we'll look stingy otherwise.' Or 'Taking chocolate and wine seems excessive, they didn't bring anything.' Or, 'We buy them a really good present every year, and every year we get something awful in return that's in the charity shop two days later. Can't we just stop?' Or, 'I spend ages thinking of something for them and then just get vouchers in return. Can't we just swap tenners?' Now, it may be that this is appallingly middle class, or that it's just my wife and I who go through this rigmarole on many social occasions (hereby revealing ourselves as the worst people in the world), but a desire not to offend people, combined with a desire to present oneself in a certain way, makes these ordinary interactions damned political negotiations. Gift-giving can engender high levels of anxiety and can create and exacerbate interpersonal conflict (Sherry Jr et al, 1993). Mauss and others' work shows us how wanting to do nice things for friends and relatives does come with an expectation that they will do similarly nice things for us, and that *they expect the same*, destined to be trapped in an exchange calculation. As Bourdieu (1990: 99) puts it:

> Little presents ... must be of modest value and hence easy to give and easy to match ("it's nothing", as we say); but they must be frequent and in a sense continuous, which implies that they must function within the logic of the "surprise" or the "spontaneous gesture" rather than according to the mechanism of ritual.

Such worries are certainly the result of privilege and too much time to think about inconsequentialities, but when teaching Mauss to students, the social pressures here are fully recognised, and the discussion of presenting one's self on social media in the next chapter reveals a Maussian element to the digital world. The impact of generosity and giving for the giver is socially determined – affected by how a gift is given, how it is received and how it is seen both by the recipient and wider society. Smith and Davidson (2014: 7) argue that there is something deeper about generosity that cannot be faked, that people cannot 'reap the personal rewards that generous practices tend to produce by going through the motions of generosity'. If true, that means all the positive externalities of *calculated* gift exchanges (the warm glow of giving, for example) disappear, rendering the activity emotionless swapping. Another cautionary note comes from Bourdieu (1990: 98), as part of his wider sociological desire for us to recognise when, as researchers, we end up objectifying social practices that people are generally living within, that everyday life throws up much more random contusions:

> "Cycles of reciprocity", mechanical interlockings of obligatory practices, exist only for the absolute gaze of the omniscient, omnipresent spectator, who, thanks to his knowledge of the social mechanics, is able to be present at the different stages of the "cycle". In reality, the gift may remain unreciprocated, when one obliges an ungrateful person; it may be rejected as an insult, inasmuch as it asserts or demands the possibility of reciprocity, and therefore of recognition.

We should be humble in recognising the partial or non-universal application of such theorising, while not discounting its usefulness for seeing common experience.

So, while gifts are, in theory, voluntary, 'in reality they are given and reciprocated obligatorily' (Mauss, 2011: 3), with gifts given with the *expectation* that the receiver will need to or feel compelled to make some sort of gesture in return (Moore, 2008: 145). Even close relationships are a constant maelstrom of gifts and exchanges and favours and negotiations, and while beyond the purview of this book, doing things for other people, whatever the field, charitable or not, is rightly always going to help make people look good. There has been some recent analysis showing that Mauss' work may not incorporate enough flexibility for the modern digital economy: people using the Couchsurfing website may well feel a sense of obligation to the host who has put them up for free, but they also have a moral requirement to leave an honest review online because of their responsibility to the rest of the system's users (Mikołajewska-Zając, 2018). Elder-Vass (2016: 33) comments more widely that sociologists have been unwilling to take gift-giving seriously as a phenomenon, both as something to study but also its revolutionary economic power: the more positive thing we learn from Mauss is that the social obligations of giving stabilise social relations, because, in much the same way that tax benefits us all, if everybody owes something to and takes responsibility for everybody else, we function much better. This stability and inter-connectedness is seen in the less individualistic reading of Mauss' work than that presented above offered by Graeber (2004: 9–10) and other anarchist scholars who see Mauss' work as revealing 'the origin of all contracts lies in communism, an unconditional commitment to another's needs', and that societies before or without money have been gift economies 'in which the distinctions we now make between interest and altruism, person and property, freedom and obligation, simply did not exist.' Such a view sees gift practices as important foundations for collective life that prioritise a concern for others, where our needs are collective and fulfilled communally. The renewal of a utopian vision that takes gift economies seriously as a way to live is certainly a more hopeful vision than analysing the properties of gifts as instrumental and inward-looking, which neoliberal culture intensifies, and a book demonstrating how the symbolic power of charity is principally held within individuals probably exacerbates.

Fundraising practices

In 2014, a fundraising campaign for research into Duchenne muscular dystrophy received significant attention. Using the stark strapline, 'I wish my son had cancer', the campaign featured Alex Smith holding his young son Harrison, who had been diagnosed with the disease. This terrible illness destroys muscles: by his teenage years Harrison will struggle to walk, and will probably die in his late teens or early twenties from heart or respiratory failure. When so many people's lives are horrifically affected by cancer, was Smith's tactic of a blunt preference for his son to suffer from a well-known and treatable disease, rather than a mysterious and unknown one, reasonable? The campaign's approach made many people ask a question that fundraisers, commentators and the public return to frequently, namely, how far should charities go in shocking and eliciting emotions among potential donors to generate funds?

UK charities make around 20 billion 'asks' a year (Breeze, 2017) – although analysis indicates this may have declined recently as the sector reflects on its practice (Fluskey, 2019) – but it's not possible to get every one right. Mohan and Breeze (2016) found that the general public are swift to express concerns about charity fundraising tactics, and Breeze (2017: 53) articulates a view that, in many people's eyes, asking for money 'is now perceived as an aggressive act that invites a belligerent response', and she recounts several examples of threats of violence against 'chuggers' (charity 'muggers', the disparaging term for street fundraisers often seeking direct debit sign-ups). Of course, actual acts of violence against fundraisers are incredibly low, in part because the interaction is a sadder, less intense one than the word 'chuggers' suggests: 'chuggers' do not 'mug' people they approach, but they can make use of the symbolic power of charity to offer an instantaneous guilt trip. We would never, MacAskill (2015: 13) argues, invest in a company in the street, 'Yet, every year, hundreds of thousands of people donate to charities they haven't heard of simply because a well-spoken stranger asks them to, or even simply shakes a bucket at them.'

Sherrington (2015) argues that the drive to fundraise can lead to a lack of critical and reflexive practice, with professionals having 'to show they are professional and that they make a difference so they can secure funding, [but they] can't show doubt or failure for fear of being seen as wasting money.' Breeze (2017: 1–2) points out that there is an increasing, and illogical, view that giving is good, but asking is bad: 'Many people see no inconsistency in admiring the work that fundraising pays for while simultaneously disparaging, or simply overlooking those who make sure that the costs of fighting good fights, or doing good deeds, can be met.' It's like loving beautifully cooked food, but resenting having to pay for the ingredients. Where people have an idea as to how to improve the world, if they possess the social and cultural capital to be able to approach others to fund it, and the skill to ask them in the correct way, it is fundraising that bridges the gap (Breeze, 2017). Such a positioning presents fundraisers as trusting people, but who often have to work in similar ways to high-end salespeople: the required skill set is similar, but obviously what is being sold are packaged 'good' products (Krause, 2014), and the opportunity to buy something moral:

> Charity is a *moral enterprise* with a clear social script. It produces heroes and model citizens who give, and deferential meek citizens who accept. It delineates society with a clear boundary between moral and immoral. (Wagner, 2001: 73; original emphasis)

Such social scripts, and unquestioning agreement about what the right thing to do is, can work against charity beneficiaries. Sulik (2010) argues that women with breast cancer are forced to follow 'feeling rules', to experience the disease in a certain way, where women are made to feel guilty if not permanently positive, 'battling' and hopeful. This performance of illness allows charities to fundraise in certain ways: the sympathetic faces of breast cancer survivors have more 'credibility' than prostate cancer survivors, leading to more media attention, public awareness and policy success (Kedrowski and Sarow, 2007; Strach, 2016). Instead, we have to buy into events that, as Longmore addressed above, aren't meant to reference the possible doubts we may have about what's occurring. In a stunning piece of contemporary history, Andrew Jones (2017) unpicks the cultural history and meaning of Band Aid, the twin concerts in London and Philadelphia on 13 July 1985, where a series of the highest profile bands and recording artists in the world performed to raise funds for famine relief in Ethiopia: 'Despite its lofty rhetoric Band Aid was always more concerned with global spectacle and consumer gratification than with challenging the underlying political causes of African famine' (Jones, 2017: 191), a problem exacerbated by its 'success', as the shift toward consumer-led charity became the model to follow and replicate. Jones repudiates Band Aid for failing to embrace its potential as a counter-hegemonic force, instead becoming a mess of meanings, where practically anyone of any persuasion could claim that it stood for what they believed in. Bob Geldof bluntly stated that Band Aid was a 'moral' issue, not a political one: he just wanted as big stars as possible, playing as many of their hits as possible, to raise as much money as possible (Jones, 2017: 198–9). It was about creating a brand as consumable for as many people as possible, and while a huge amount of money was raised, we know that such 'ethical consumption' can only achieve so much in a world of persistent inequalities (Littler, 2011). (The very name Band Aid, while having the obviously double meaning of both a helpful object to those who are suffering and aid given by music bands, does showcase the classic critique of charity from the political left, that this is merely a sticking plaster temporarily covering the wound rather than systematic change removing the danger that causes the wound in the first place.) Some feel that the involvement of celebrities in charitable causes serves to commodify problems, obscure inequalities, and is a generally anti-democratic force that removes accountability (Tester, 2010; Kapoor, 2013): 'Musicians and celebrities who appeared in charity singles were able to simultaneously act as traditional philanthropic citizens, and perform the moral imperative of "self help" through their imagined communities' (Robinson, 2012: 420). At our most critical, we may agree with Dawidoff (quoted in Longmore, 2016: 127), who sees charity spectacles as fuelling the self-absorption and self-interest of those who give but who don't have to live with the condition being fundraised for.

With recent fundraising scandals (Mohan and Breeze, 2016; Breeze, 2017; Jones et al, 2018), the charity sector finds itself more examined than ever before. It appears to have lost its aura, and at a time when public institutions (government, the police, the NHS, journalism) are all rightly questioned and have demands of transparency put upon them, it is perhaps no surprise the charity sector is getting the same attention. This came to a head in the UK in 2015, following controversies around fundraising techniques following the death of poppy seller Olive Cooke (a tragedy a government minister later admitted he purposefully misrepresented in order to establish the Fundraising Preference Service in 2016 [Plummer, 2019]), and the impact of such crises is examined later, in Chapter 4. But we have briefly seen how fundraising, by its nature and by necessity, operationalises charity's symbolic power in offering people the opportunity to buy into moral practices, and receive any ensuing acclaim. We will return to fundraising, and how individuals can be motivated, later in the chapter.

Business and charity

The notion of corporate social responsibility (CSR) is well documented and much criticised. At its core is the simple idea that businesses, alongside motivations to increase profits, build value, and increase market share, and should uphold some ethical values and practices while doing so. 'It's good for the company, and it's good for the community', runs the logic. CSR is, ironically, big business. The website of any large corporation will have a section devoted to outlining what steps the company is taking to 'give back' in some way. CSR policies are myriad, often with a well-paid team of staff running the department, theoretically across all of the organisation's work. Practices can involve moving to more sustainable and environmentally friendly production processes or materials, employee volunteering schemes, educational bursaries and scholarships for deprived populations, the donation of free or subsidised products to charities, donations of money to causes, fundraising days (imagine staff in silly outfits), or, as well documented by Longmore, sponsorship.

Ralph Waldo Emerson famously observed that, 'It is one of the most beautiful compensations of this life that no man can sincerely try and help another without helping himself.' While an exquisitely expressed point about the fundamental, soul-enriching benefits of giving to the giver, its fundamental logic has been reimagined by business and their charity. Such largesse and commitment to CSR gets heavily promoted and encourages consumers who wish to consume ethical products to engage with certain brands and corporations. In the UK, the annual Comic Relief and Sport Relief fundraising events work closely with retailers Sainsbury's and TK Maxx that stock red noses and t-shirts, purchases which add to the fundraising total, and at the same time get shoppers after these products into store, who may happen to buy several other items at the same time. As the reasoning goes, win-win (see Giridharadas, 2018): donations are raised and the company profits and its image improve.

What does this mean in practice? Well, as Longmore (2016: 155) found in his detailed exploration, '[i]n any era, donation typically went to institutions that promised the greatest public approbation', companies would seek out the charitable causes that were going to help them the most, leaving charities tackling less favourable problems floundering. Asheem Singh (2018) cautions that the business world is so desperate to take advantage of the symbolic power of doing good, that it often gives itself a poor reputation by over-playing its hand. The grafting on of CSR onto core profit-making work 'appears to be something of a confidence trick constructed by the public relations people for a quick headline and a spike in sales' (Singh, 2018: 77). Singh himself favours social enterprise, a form of business–charity endeavour that uses business means for social ends, although where profit can still play a (large) part (for an overview, see Ridley-Duff and Bull, 2019). Similarly putting the boot into CSR, charity critic Iqbal Wahhab (2016: 85) dismisses it as merely where 'one of the nicer people in the company gets to build an alternative career as the corporation's conscience.'

At the launch of the RED Emporio Armani clothing line, which sees a portion of the price of each item sold go to charity, Giorgio Armani said that one of the results of such an endeavour would be that 'commerce will no longer have a negative connotation' (quoted in Richey and Ponte, 2011: 5; see also Thorup, 2014: 33). This washing of corporate branding through association with charitable ends has been well documented in the sponsorship of fine art exhibits or leading theatre groups by oil companies. Oil and pharmaceutical companies associate with high art in order to fulfil a role as corporate citizens; this CSR 'artwashing' (Evans, 2015) helps them maintain a socially acceptable public image (Wu, 2002), just as where Rockefeller's use of the proceeds of Standard Oil to strengthen civil society embeds both the family and the company in the fabric of society, with whatever they donate repaid 10-fold in social legitimacy, according to artist and activist Mel Evans. Naomi Klein (2001: 35) has cautioned that companies' funding of big events helps convince the public that 'creativity and congregation would be impossible without their generosity', and frequently a 'convenient way for business magnates to extend their reach over domestic and foreign populaces' (McGoey, 2015: 4). Such practices also extend to 'greenwashing (Pettinger, 2019: 167), where companies have green office policies, such as automatic lights, which save energy and feed into sustainability agendas, but also save money.

Charities and causes will team up with industries that cause health problems, even problems that the charity is seeking to eradicate or alleviate (Longmore, 2016: 55). On *The Daily Show*, the long-running US satirical news programme, in a segment that can still be found on YouTube, comedian Sam Bee shows how the breast cancer foundation Susan G. Komen can partner with brands like Kentucky Fried Chicken and a shale gas fracking company, to raise money for breast cancer awareness, through the 'awareness-raising' conduits of a pink bucket of fried chicken and a pink drill bit. Products that it has been shown to cause cancer sponsoring cancer charities, and the companies involved symbolically benefiting from such an enterprise, is the tacky end of CSR. (If you are so inclined, search online for pictures of pink machine guns sold to raise money for breast cancer charities, if you've ever wondered if it's possible to pass out from exposure to irony.) But as Frank Guistra, a mining financier who, in working with Bill Clinton's charitable Clinton Global Initiative managed to tie up uranium deals with the Kazakhstani government put it, generosity 'can be very profitable' (quoted in McGoey, 2015: 35). Charity has access to symbolic resources that business does not (and that can't be bought). Business has access to material resources that charities desperately need. Such relationships reveal connections rooted in a logic of practice that is frequently (although far from always) less than edifying.

An individual's giving decisions

Intrinsic reasons for giving at the individual level include empathy and sympathy, pity and fear, guilt, and the need for self-esteem (Sargeant et al, 2000). Giving can provide psychological boosts such as improving one's self-esteem (see the review in Bekkers and Wiepking, 2011: 938–41), which can be felt as empathic joy, or the joy of giving, most famously documented by Andreoni (1989) as the 'warm glow'. While volunteering for personal satisfaction is still volunteering (Cnaan et al, 1996) it can be looked on as 'impure altruism' (Andreoni, 1989). Some research has demonstrated a physiological side to the warm glow. Moll and colleagues (2006) used MRI imaging with experiment participants, finding that the brain's reward centre, the part that produces the dopamine-fuelled rush associated with sex, money, food and drugs, is similarly stimulated by donating. (Empathy may also have a physiological basis – watching a loved one experience pain triggers the same brain areas as experiencing pain yourself [Singer et al, 2004].) The warm glow may be a physical not just psychological experience, and provides support to the characterisation of charitable work as habitual (Dean, 2016a). It may be that the warm glow is a useful and necessary part of giving: it is part of what keeps the giver coming back, and if made explicit and revealed, it turns what is often a one-way relationship (Ostrander, 1989; Ostrander and Schervish, 1990; Schervish, 1992; Breeze and Dean, 2012a) into a two-way, more egalitarian, one.

Recent research for the Institute of Fundraising by the polling company YouGov (Gunstone and Ellison, 2017a, b) tells us the story of who gives in the UK, how, why and what they do afterwards. Evidence suggests that people whose giving is driven by large national charities and campaigns are less determined, flakier givers. Donors who mainly give to large national organisations are significantly more likely than donors who tend to mainly support small, local charities to say that they would not have donated without being asked (35 per cent against 25 per cent) (Gunstone and Ellison, 2017b: 6). Younger people are more responsive to calls to donate: a significantly higher proportion of 18- to 29-year-olds say that their last donation to charity would have been smaller had they not been asked (Gunstone and Ellison, 2017b: 5). In terms of the self-benefits of charity, young people (aged 18–29) who give are also more likely to feel better or more positive about themselves and in general as a result of donating than the general population, 35 per cent versus 24 per cent (Gunstone and Ellison, 2017a: 6). As Figure 2.1 shows, however, people's descriptions of their giving motivations vary widely, from the very specific belief in the specific cause donated to, to the much more general belief in the inherent goodness of charities, or indeed having 'no reason' to give. Only 2 per cent of donors in this survey stated that they gave because they 'thought they'd get something in return': we don't know if this is genuine, a lack of honesty as not to contravene social norms, or because the 'something' one gets from giving is so imprecise. 'Something' suggests a material swap as opposed to 'it made me feel good' or related symbolic credit.

We know that there are a number of 'hidden benefits' to giving, including the aforementioned greater propensity to health and happiness, but also enhanced reputation and access to elite networks (Bekkers and Wiepking, 2011), which operates differently across countries and contexts: there is more of a 'prestige motive' for giving and philanthropy in the US than in the UK, for instance (Breeze, 2017: 140). Bourdieu's forms of capital contribute towards the membership of popular groups. For instance, the acquisition of social and symbolic capital is particularly crucial in determining the 'social positions within

Figure 2.1: Motivations for last charitable donation (multiple choice, *N*=1,290)

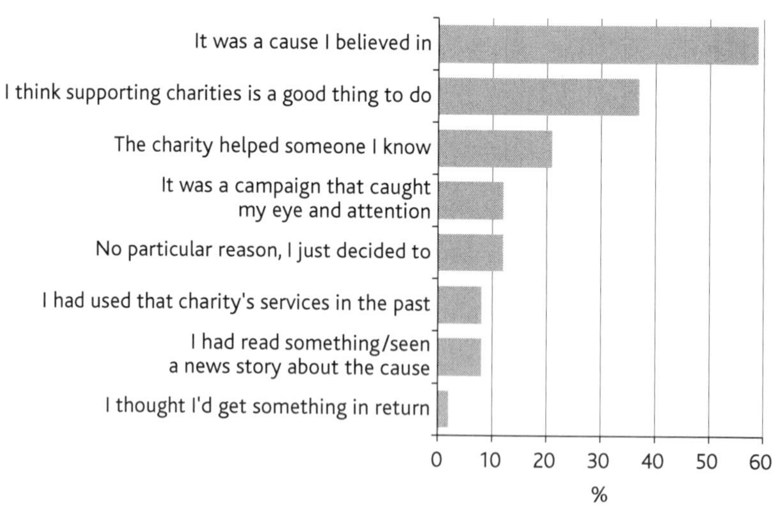

Source: Adapted from Gunstone and Ellison (2017b: 3)

the power structure of the market' (Bullen and Kenway, 2005: 52). Charity's relationship to social networks means that there is a danger that those not connected to the right networks will never be asked to get involved (Rochester et al, 2010), and charity's normative element – this is something that is good to do that you should do – follows from certain specific networks and social cues. Of course, and unfortunately for government policy trying to push volunteering (Dean, 2014), this doesn't work in all contexts: we know that many young people view volunteering as uncool (Smith, 1999; Davies, 2018), and any participation as potentially subject to informal penalties such as damage to one's reputation, being 'slagged and bullied' as a result.

Practices of generosity toward others are positively associated with greater happiness: as revealed in Smith and Davidson's (2014: 15) survey, Americans who give away a substantial part of their income (over 10 per cent) are much more likely to be 'very happy' than those who do not give that much (38 per cent to 28 per cent), and much less likely to be very or somewhat unhappy (10 per cent to 15 per cent). There is a strong correlation between how much time someone volunteers and their happiness, and people who are more neighbourly are also happier (Smith and Davidson, 2014: 17, 21), and these relationships work both ways – volunteering leads to happiness and good health, just as happiness and health lead to volunteering. These 'softer' benefits of volunteering, such as improved subjective wellbeing, are outcomes regularly pushed by volunteering agencies and non-profit organisations as reasons to volunteer. However, recent longitudinal research from a team of European researchers has shown that these effects can be very small in terms of their actual benefit to an individual. De Wit and colleagues (2015) found that volunteering could only be attributed to a 1 per cent rise in health and wellbeing outcomes, and could find no link between volunteering and employment or career outcomes, echoing UK-specific research (Ellis Paine et al, 2013). Much of this result is down to self-selection: those people who choose to volunteer are likely to already be healthier, with wider social networks and stable employment than those who are not. In short, 'we should not expect miracles from participation in third sector activities' (De Wit et al, 2015: 12). The idea that it will solve unemployment, end loneliness and cure health problems is a simplistic and dangerous notion and, allied to the critiques of charity (for example, Raventós and Wark, 2018), provides the state with an easy way to abdicate responsibilities. The personal rewards that volunteering can offer individuals is no antidote to structural inequalities (Dean et al, 2019).

Anonymity

As Peter Singer (2010: 65) writes in *The Life You Can Save*:

> Jesus told us not to sound a trumpet when we give to the poor, "as the hypocrites do in the synagogues and in the streets, so that they may be honored by men." Instead, he advised, we should give so secretly that not even our left hand knows what our right hand is doing. Only then would we be rewarded in heaven, rather than on earth.... Similarly, today when people give large sums with a lot of fanfare, we suspect that their real motive is to gain social status by their philanthropy, and to draw attention to how rich and generous they are.

It has been shown that when appeals are designed where giving will benefit the donor, donors give much more when they are told their donations will be private than public; conversely, if the appeal is designed to benefit others, donors give much more if they believe their donations will be public (White and Peloza, 2009). This clearly shows how giving is socially determined and occurs within the gaze of others, where the presence of public accountability for decisions leads people to manage the impression they leave in a certain way. The same study also showed, however, that if people believe that acting in self-interest is the social norm, they do that. Both results demonstrate how charitable giving is in a milieu of competing interests, norms, customs and contexts, and negotiating this requires a constant appraisal of thinking both about what you want to do and how you want others to perceive you. Peer pressure can cause 'reluctant altruism' when people feel they have to give because others will be informed of their donation (Reyniers and Bhalla, 2013). Giving circles (Eikenberry, 2009; Eikenberry and Breeze, 2015) have grown as altruistic concepts, where people group together to hear appeals from various causes, and decide collectively how to donate. It's a pleasant and democratic concept, where a collation of donations can have more impact, alongside the community-building element, rather than traditional individualised giving decisions. But some laboratory-based research has shown that such group giving can lead to larger donations due to increased public recognition (Karlan and McConnell, 2014), as people look to perform their giving in a more public setting.

The role of anonymity in donations challenges the principle that people want to bask in the socially rewarded glow of giving. Many donors 'want to make sure that their gifts are publicised so that they can attract approval for their generosity' (Elster, 2011: 74; see also Schokkaert, 2006). Yet in one study, Theresa Lloyd (2004) found many respondents who reported donating anonymously, sometimes to avoid controversy or to avoid 'fuss', with some stressing that they feared their donation would be misconstrued. Anonymity serves the purpose of cutting through social norms, which, as we have seen, can cloud the charitable imperative somewhat. But this desire for anonymity can make the work of fundraisers difficult due to the need for charities to get publicity, and the view that having a 'name' behind a donation would encourage others to donate in support. Charity is not a closed system, simply a donor–beneficiary relationship. There are a vast amount of other influences (friends, celebrities, media) all of which contribute to wider social subjectivities that mean largely or exclusively economic interpretations of charitable behaviour which treat exchanges as if they happen in 'snow globe' or laboratory conditions (Khan, 2011) absent the mess of real life are insufficient. This is why a wider, cultural and political sociology of charity, concerned with the realities of giving, can start to unpick some of these wider webs of influence and control.

Does motivation matter?

Guilt is an incredibly powerful emotion, and a tool used by fundraisers within charity sector advertising and messaging (Dean and Wood, 2017) in order to stimulate donations and raise awareness. Auger (2014) showed how 60 per cent of social media Tweets from a set of charities used rhetorical strategies, particularly that of pathos (emotional appeals using humour, guilt, love or shock), to try and engage with donor publics. Leading charities were most likely to play on their supporters' feelings of guilt, as well as use the heritage of their organisation as a tactic. Charity appeals frequently depict hard-hitting cases, with charities rather than consumer brands more likely to use 'guilt appeals'. The role of emotion in fundraising, and whether or to what extent potential donors feel, or should be, guilted into giving, is much discussed (Basil et al, 2006; Bennett, 2015; Lim and Moufahim, 2015; Dean and Wood, 2017), but it has been shown that campaigns can be more successful if they focus on the most extreme side of an issue, or present beneficiaries as dependent and pathetic: for example, fundraising campaigns for disability issues are often most successful when using the dependence of people with disabilities to elicit feelings of sympathy, guilt and pity in potential donors (Sargeant and Woodliffe, 2007: 282; see also Eayrs and Ellis, 1990). The most extreme side of an issue is often the image that the general donor public have in their heads of an issue, making it illogical for a charity to present the issue differently (Dean, 2015a; Breeze and Dean, 2012b). This isn't always the case, however: Allred and Amos's (2018) recent work, making use of images of children with heavily contrasting degrees of cleft palate, shows that while the more severe image evoked greater empathy for the sufferer among potential donors, actually the image of the relatively minor condition evoked greater intentions to donate to the cause. (It must be said, some charity appeals don't quite get the emotional pull right: one widely mocked fundraising appeal for the Royal Opera House said donors could help by donating just £31 to cover the cost of 365 crystals required to decorate one of the Caterpillar's shoes for a production of *Alice's Adventures in Wonderland* [Wood, 2017].)

Within fundraising guilt is often looked at negatively whereas empathy is seen as a much more positive emotion to elicit, yet empathy and guilt are inextricably linked (Basil et al, 2008). The former is mediated by the latter, with personal relevance to a cause alongside assessment of self-efficacy feelings of being able to do something meaningful to help, enhancing one's guilt and likelihood to give. Similarly, individuals with a sense of responsibility towards the cause are more likely to engage with a guilt appeal (Basil et al, 2006). Some evidence suggests people get turned off complying with a request when it appeals solely to fear, guilt or shame (Brennan and Binney, 2010), and potential donors with pre-disposed scepticism towards advertising tactics and potential manipulation are less likely to feel guilty when shown emotive adverts, in one study's case from children's charities (Hibbert et al, 2007). Smith and Davidson (2014: 73) argue that helping out of a sense of fear or guilt are neither healthy nor reflect genuine generosity, merely helping from a sense of self-absorption that prevents the standard social benefits we associate with charity. By thinking through the issue of guilt, and fundraisers potentially playing on the emotions of potential donors, this issue demonstrates how charities have the ability to use their symbolic authority to emotionally manipulate the general public. This isn't necessarily a bad thing: charities have a responsibility to tackle problems, need funding, and the general public should not be insulated from societal woes. But as we have seen, the myriad motivations that cause people to donate can all result in the same thing: x amount of money pledged or y amount of hours volunteered. As Nina Eliasoph (2013: 1) puts it at the start of *The Politics of Volunteering*:

> You have probably done some voluntary work. Maybe you did it because you cared about someone. Maybe it was a requirement for high-school graduation. Maybe you needed a line on your CV, to demonstrate to future employers that you were a good person….

Volunteering because you cared about someone? Well yes, although the United Nations' (United Nations Volunteers, 2011) standard definition says volunteering should be outside the family and close friends, so that's debatable and depends on context. Requirement for a graduation? Again, the UN definition says volunteering cannot be forced, and must be of the individual's own free will, so if there was no alternative, this just seems like unpaid community work. Yet strangely, doing it to build your résumé is considered volunteering: a person's motivation, it is reasoned, shouldn't be taken into account. Yet, when asking the public, surveys suggest they'd have some trouble classifying an activity motivated thus *as* volunteering (Dean and Verrier, 2018). This 'duality' within volunteering sees motivation incorporate both altruism and self-interest, whereby individuals want to be useful members of society and help others, but are also looking to meet new people and develop their own skills and personal growth (Wardell et al, 2000). Employers prefer volunteers to non-volunteers (NYA, 2007; v, 2008), not only because of the practical and soft skills they have developed, but also because they tend to perceive volunteers as more 'honest' and 'genuine' (Anderson and Green, 2012). In an article for the *Stanford Social Innovation Review*, Sean Stannard-Stockton (2008) writes that 'only an incredibly narrow view of life holds that helping others is somehow separate from helping ourselves…. The fact that helping others also helps us does not diminish the act of giving.' Yet, not only is volunteering a characteristic that is likely to add to a person's prestige and respect (Wilson, 2000), but those of a more dominant social position are also more desirable to organisations (Hustinx et al, 2010). Jones (2006) argues that if an individual gives either time or money, there is the potential for the act to be a demonstration of their moral worth, presenting those values that are regarded as 'tasteful' or desired, and that participation in such acts can be a way for individuals to gain such symbolic credit (Bourdieu, 1984), just as Bekkers and Bowman (2009) point out that the presence of volunteering on a CV is a shortcut to being a good person, because obviously only good people volunteer. And in research on food banks, charity managers report that the process of donation embodies relational generosity and care for donors, giving them an opportunity to perform a moral imperative (Lambie-Mumford, 2017: 63). Charity, it seems, frequently has to be about more for the charitable giver than merely moving resources around: Hobbesian philosophy, which argues that we all act in our own self-interest, can be made to work with altruism, rather than, as we would assume, against it. If one feels better from relieving the pain others are in, then it is egoistic to give, but as charitable in the effect as any 'pure' altruism (Singer, 2016a: 59).

Conclusions

The act of giving is almost always something to be celebrated. While there is a sociological tendency to look at such practices cynically, perhaps emerging from our need to look at it critically, for the vast majority of us, generosity, gifts and presents are things that bring warmth and joy, the realisation that other people buy us things is a reminder of the kindness that exists, and the love and respect they have for us. Similarly, giving to charity is a good thing, a behaviour we want to encourage more of, where those of us with what is ostensibly spare money give it to those without. The charity sector exists partially to conduct such behaviours, with fundraisers seen by some as 'moral trainers' (O'Neill, 1994), acting as midwives to virtue and generosity, helping move money from those who have a surplus of it to those who need it. Yet just because such behaviours are generally accepted as good, this doesn't mean that they all are, or that they are simple. As we have seen with our examinations of the gift, gift-giving can be an incredibly complicated process, where even minor interactions are intensely political, in that they concern the distribution of resources between two unequally resourced actors. And this resource is not just material; it is also symbolic. Gifts are an extension of the giver, frequently saying something quite deep about the individual, and something fundamental about what they think of or their relation to the receiver. This might include judgements about both perceived and actual need (in terms of deprivation) or in terms of lack (in terms of taste or lifestyle). The fact that we may give to a person (because we owe them one) or a cause (because they are suffering when you are not) out of guilt is part of such a symbolic relationship, because of what need looks like, and how charities can take advantage of it. As part of fixing our guilt, we may revel in the adulation we receive, killing two birds with one stone, or, as we have seen for certain businesses, deliver our social responsibility in a way aligned with our corporate strategy, generally in a way that builds brands and profits. It is fair to say that businesses probably can't win: if they anonymously run community programmes or a foundation, they have no response to critical questions about what they are doing with their profits. A CSR section on a website, however, is showing off and brand-washing through ethical capitalism. But such behaviours are logical when we know that, to reassert, most people think that most charitable activity is great, and that social rewards are there to be claimed by the charitable or bestowed on them regardless.

Within such discussions, a suitable theory for understanding what's going on comes from Chris Rojek's (2013) notion of 'event power'. Here, the symbolic power of charity, people's need to feel empowered and part of something, pursuing a lofty ambition that makes them feel good (with some of that feeling coming from the everyday adulation of others), means that charity becomes something we buy into. Those memorable moments like Live Aid, the Tsunami fundraising effort or the relief offered after Hurricanes Katrina and Harvey, make us 'conscious of being part of an international community' of givers, where the 'logic of capitalism appear[s] to magically vanish' (Rojek, 2013: vi). People don't want to feel left behind like they're not a part of something, whether that's a new film, new meme or a cronut, and so therefore charitable appeals need to borrow the buzz that often only the marketised advertising strategies of the private sector can offer. Charity's angle, that you're not just part of something, but part of something good, is an extra attraction.

The photograph below (see Figure 2.2) indicates this on a local, everyday level. Taken in the Cancer Research UK charity shop next to my university office, purchasable for a pound to carry the bargain goods you've bought that day away, the slogan leaves us in little doubt that the charity is aware of the good they do, and the value of that good as a tool of self-presentation for their customers. The slogan is logical in how it uses and builds on the processes of retail. While there's certainly an innocent interpretation of the bag, there is a value judgement in the missing next lines: 'You don't shop at Cancer Research UK. You don't save lives. You should feel bad.' In the next chapter, we will see how the use of goodness in self-presentation is a hugely problematic issue for young people trying to navigate the antagonised environment of social media. Such expressions and public demonstrations show how we're all – givers, non-givers, charities, beneficiaries – aware of the symbolic power of charity, and that we're all caught up in the complex and iniquitous machinations of using it, and feel the force of its operation, as acts of fundraising and cause-related marketing bounce people into giving donations to certain causes.

Figure 2.2: Cancer Research UK shopping bag

3

#humblebrags and the good giving self on social media

So it's time for Humblebrag of the Week. They're all over social media, boasts disguised as moans. Here's one:

> "Just gave up my seat for an old Gurkha soldier. He didn't want to accept it – I insisted. #nicefeeling."

This is another classic:

> "A huge thanks to Donna at Pitsea station who saved my pashmina. It was from Thailand when I volunteered teaching English at an orphanage."

Oh sod off! Yeah, I get it, you're great – if you were really that great you wouldn't tell anyone! (The Elis James and John Robins Show on Radio X, 24 October and 25 July 2015)

Social media enables you to update the world on only those bits of your life that you want others to see, and with the options to frame exactly how you want them to see it. Of course it's not perfect: one person's Instagram post documenting how proud they are of a personal achievement is another person's showing off; similarly another person's carefully crafted Facebook status detailing a personal setback can be interpreted as an attention-seeking tale of woe: the Urban Dictionary (2011) defines the 'humblebrag' as, 'When you, usually consciously, try to get away with bragging about yourself by couching it in a phony show of humility.' Due to the delicacy of such phoniness, this form of impression management is far from flawless, but it can be seen as an attempt to remove the risk from ordinary social interactions. The likelihood of committing the social faux pas of saying the wrong thing, doing the wrong thing or of being misjudged are, one could argue, significantly reduced if we get the time to reconsider and rewrite every text reply or status update, or retake every photo. Yet of course a whole new set of failed interactions and interpretations are created, such as not being excited enough about a friend's new Facebook update, and, as the writer Nancy Jo Sales (2016) has documented, such minor infringements of the new digital social etiquette loom large over the lives of Western teenagers, particularly girls.

In the wake of such changes, charities have to consider the growing dominance of the digital in people's lives, contemplating what strategies they should use to engage with donors and support online (CAF, 2017), how to best encourage 'giving habits' in young people that will sustain the non-profit sector (Falco et al, 1998; Dean, 2016a), and whether organisations that are often run by older generations can use social media to attract support from young people (Charity Commission, 2017). These sector narratives intersect with wider social debates about the role of social media in everyday life, particularly around the nature of authenticity, trust and 'fake news' (Ball, 2017) online. Non-profit research into social media needs to be aware of these wider social trends that are shaping how young people live online, and what this means for non-profits and voluntary action.

This chapter examines these issues. Drawing on the research into charities' use of social media (Browne et al, 2013; Guo and Saxton, 2014; Saxton and Wang, 2014; Harden et al, 2015), and wider discussions of how social media is shaping the youth experience (Lange, 2014; Sales, 2016), it centres on asking young people what their perceptions and experiences of charity and voluntary action online are, and what the implications of these practices might be, when contextualised against wider social media and youth discourses. Findings show that despite the supposedly globalised nature of social media connections, friends and family still drive young people's giving online (see Dean, 2020). A lack of disposable income mixed with a grudging duty to give to those close to them means that participants 'stay local' in what they donate to and support. Young participants are also quite negative about online messages that ask them to 'Share to show you care' and 'Retweet to spread awareness', finding them cloying and annoying – and generally an inauthentic attempt to engage an audience with a charity issue. Young participants report awkwardness about asking for donations and feeling that they may be 'guilt tripping' others into giving by requesting donations from friends. They also worry that talking about charity online could be perceived as 'showing off' how good they were, or 'humblebragging' in a faux presentation of goodness, and, in the wake of several scandals in the non-profit sector, were concerned about authenticity in the charitable acts and good deeds of their peers. Contextualised within the sociology of youth on social media (see, for example, Binns, 2014;

Lange, 2014; Sales, 2016), such findings indicate difficulties for non-profits online, as wider social media behaviour shapes the reception of charity. Many of these findings are demonstrated later in the chapter, after first thinking about how we do online life, and charity's role in that experience.

The presentation and authenticity of goodness online

Erving Goffman's (1959) famous symbolic interactionist study, *The Presentation of Self in Everyday Life*, was a qualitative survey of everyday human behaviour, particularly focused on how humans modify their behaviour to present themselves to each other:

> As performers we are merchants of morality … the very obligation and profitability of appearing always in a steady moral light, of being a socialized character, forces one to be the sort of person who is practised in the ways of the stage. (Goffman, 1959: 243)

Focused on the expressive components of social life, Goffman thinks through the impressions we try to make on others and others on us. Detailing how, when in front of other people, individuals 'have many motives for trying to control the impression they receive of the situation' (Goffman, 1959: 26), such as wanting to look good or to fit in, this approach has been applied widely within the social sciences to explore why prospective candidates, fearing stigma (Goffman, 1963), try to cover up their tattoos in job interviews (Timming, 2015; Timming et al, 2017), or why those working in retail put on a more polite front when serving customers than they may do in the staff room (Cutcher and Achtel, 2017). Goffman suggests a dramaturgical model to understand how individuals approach impression management and present their activities before others. A certain amount of stagecraft and stage management are required, with props brought into play as people try to leave a favourable or specific impression on others. Cynical people will try to establish a conviction in their audience about their aims and desires, usually for self-interest, but also for the audience's own benefit (a general who feigns confidence as a way to inspire, or a doctor who prescribes placebos to stimulate recovery). However, Goffman's ideas have rarely been applied to the study of charity (one notable exception would be Swan's [2018] research, which shows how charities can use impression management to maintain legitimacy with their beneficiaries while having to implement unpopular policies).

Given that one of the most obvious critiques of the charitable is that 'they're doing it to make themselves look good', you would expect this to have been fertile ground for those looking to understand the lived realities of charity.

Goffman used an extended dramaturgical analogy to explain the ways in which individuals 'perform' particular 'roles' in their face-to-face interactions with others in order to present a particular impression of themselves to their 'audience':

> At one extreme, one finds that the performer can be fully taken in by his own act; he can be sincerely convinced that the impression of reality which he stages is the real reality. When his audience is also convinced in this way about the show he puts on – and this seems to be the typical case – then for the moment at least, only the sociologist or the socially disgruntled will have any doubts about the "realness" of what is presented. (Goffman, 1959: 28)

Individuals' experiences of themselves come in part from the standpoints of others, shaping our understanding of our self and our action: how our habitus is perceived can be as important as how it actually is (Dean, 2016b), with a tendency for actions to be motivated partly by others' perceptions (Ariely et al, 2009: 544). As previously noted, Sulik (2010) argues that the way society thinks about breast cancer means that women are forced to follow 'feeling rules', where they are required to perform the illness in a certain way, partly in order to assist fundraising.

Such performances, and issues of identity formation and management, are present in Goffman's work and exponents' applications of said theory to the internet. It has been recognised for a long time now that the internet presents opportunities for individuals to experiment with their identities in ways usually unavailable or much riskier in 'real' life (Valkenburg et al, 2005), often as a form of 'edgework' (Hart, 2017). Researchers surveying how school pupils use online chat and instant messaging services in the Netherlands found that 50 per cent reported experimenting with their identity at least some of the time while online (Valkenburg et al, 2005). Younger youth (aged 9–12) were much more likely to experiment with and manipulate their identity than those aged up to 18, with the authors finding:

> Younger adolescents, girls and extraverts significantly pretended more frequently to be an older person than

older adolescents, boys and introverts. Boys and introverts presented themselves more often as a macho persona, whereas girls, younger adolescents and extraverts presented themselves more frequently as a more beautiful person. Finally, boys presented themselves more often than girls as a real-life acquaintance and as an elaborated fantasy person. (Valkenburg et al, 2005: 392)

There were also variations in the *reasons* for engaging in such identity experiments, with younger youth experimenting in order to facilitate social interaction, girls more likely to want to explore their identities than boys, and, perhaps unsurprisingly, introverts more likely to experiment than extroverts (Valkenburg et al, 2005: 395). These departures from offline selves can be found in studies examining users of the online virtual world *Second Life*, but there users will replicate their offline identity to a certain extent – shying away from 'identity tourism' (Nakamura, 2002) – instead engaging in editing facets of self, and highlighting or embellishing certain aspects of their identity (Bullingham and Vasconcelos, 2013). Interviewees also described the difficulties of fully separating their professional and personal selves, meaning differential approaches to the divided self online. Similar findings can be found in Binns' (2014: 82) work on teenage girls' use of social media, where the majority of respondents said that their online self would generally add up to 'the real them', because 'some girls are concerned not just about managing their self-presentation, but also being judged for managing their self-presentation (being "fake" or "two-faced") and even ... burdening others with their emotions.' (Fears over the damage such technologies may be doing to young people's wellbeing have been a frequent refrain over the last decade, but it appears such fears are found to be significantly overstated [Orben et al, 2019].)

Such work raises interesting questions about what constitutes the 'real' or 'true' self, and the extent to which this self is realised or expressed online. The concept of identity tourism suggests the potential that online worlds hold for experimentation with identity, and even outright fakery, as users are able to cloak themselves in anonymity. The psychoanalyst Sherry Turkle (2011: 12) expresses concern about the temptations for us to amend our personalities and identities online: 'We can write the Facebook profile that pleases us. We can edit our messages until they project the self we want to be.' At the other extreme, others might think that it is, in fact, the 'real' self that comes out online, as people feel liberated from the constraints and expectations of real-world discourse. John Suler (2004) has written of the 'online disinhibition effect', in which the features of certain online environments, such as their anonymity and asynchronicity, have the effect of encouraging people to express opinions or say things that they wouldn't say in ordinary life.

While many have sought to apply Goffman's ideas to online behaviours and interactions, it is important to note that his applicability to cyberspace has not gone unquestioned. Hogan (2010: 381) has argued that, while people certainly try to present particular, idealised versions of themselves on social networking sites, the often asynchronous nature of communication on such sites means that the appropriate metaphor is one of a museum of gallery *exhibition* rather than a theatrical performance, where one's artefacts are displayed, curated by the online platform. Alternatively, Banks (2017) has argued that Goffman's account of the self unduly privileges the human, and leads us to draw too sharp a distinction between the virtual and the real, with its frontstage/backstage dualism (Banks, 2017: 432). Instead of thinking of our offline lives as 'the real us' and our online selves as always affected by performance, selves are a network of intersecting identities, different in different contexts.

So Goffman's text has been reimagined as a theoretical guide for the digital age, with a growing literature on how individuals have substantial control over managing their own personal brand online, examining the notion that individuals seek to engage in image or impression management on social networking sites. When studies of charity and social media do take a Goffmanesque, if not Goffman-inspired, approach, they note similar things. Saxton and Wang (2014: 864) argue that '… pressures deriving from one's social network – and the desire to improve one's standing in that network – appear to be driving much of the donation decision on Facebook', also pointing to the prevalence of 'impulse donations' and small donations on social networks, and to the success of particular types of charity on social networks, particularly health charities. Although the authors do not discuss Goffman explicitly, their point about wanting 'to improve one's standing' in one's social network through conspicuous behaviour is backed up elsewhere. Eranti and Lonkila (2015) explore the social significance of the Facebook 'like' button, revealing the complex psychosocial processes and multitude of meanings behind the seemingly simple act of 'liking' something on Facebook. Applying Goffman's concepts of 'face' and 'face-work', the authors argue face-work online entails the monitoring of one's 'liking behaviour' while attempting to maintain a positive impression among all participants in the environment (Eranti and Lonkila, 2015). They explain how many Facebook users maintain a strong sense of who in their network may be observing their liking behaviour, an awareness made up of both the *actual* 'network of previous likers' and the 'imagined network audience' – the individual's perception of which specific people in their network will be observing their 'like' (Eranti and Lonkila, 2015). While a very small study, it revealed a wide range of different reasons for and considerations behind 'liking' an item on Facebook. Different 'types' of like reported include 'friendship like' (the user who posted the item is important to the respondent), 'façade like' (the respondent liked an item in order to try and look good in the eyes of their Facebook friends) and a 'letting steam out like' (to make the respondent feel good).

It is easy to see how such psychosocial processes and considerations are relevant in our discussion of charity, with some people keen to look good in front of their friends and peers on social media through liking a charity's page or sharing a post connected to a campaign. Indeed, the concept of a 'façade like' invokes the idea of 'virtue signalling', originally attributed to James Bartholomew. In an article for the right-wing periodical *The Spectator*, Bartholomew (2015) wrote of the apparent trend for conspicuous statements made by individuals (often on social media) intended to convey their kindness, decency or virtue, citing public condemnations of racism or support for the UK National Health Service (NHS) as examples. Bartholomew feels virtue signalling is, at heart, boastful and self-serving, and increasingly takes the place of genuine, tangible acts of kindness. Critiquing the concept as political propaganda, however, Tanya Gold (2017) eviscerates virtue signalling as a 'slur … part of the Trumpian scream', where empathy, fellowship and love are dismissed as vanity purely in order to present political opponents' viewpoints as coming from somewhere else than sincerity. Bartholomew, the 'inventor' of the term, Gold points out, is anti-public NHS, anti-minimum wage and anti-foreign aid: in his view, she argues, publicly supporting these things is not about political principles and morals, but merely about presenting oneself as better than everyone else. Supporting this argument, *The Telegraph* commentator Michael Deacon (2017) writes that the insult of 'virtue signaller':

> … says more about those flinging it than those they seek to belittle. To me, it suggests fear. Deep down, the people shouting "Virtue-signaller!" are scared. Since they feel no sympathy for those less fortunate than themselves, they

refuse to believe anyone else feels sympathy, either. Those expressing sympathy, therefore, must be lying; they must just be saying it to earn brownie points and look superior. The people who shout "Virtue signaller!" need to believe that. Because the alternative – that they themselves are simply selfish, small-minded, and emotionally shrivelled – is one they can't bear to contemplate.

Yes, no one doubts that there is an enormous amount of insincerity online, alongside both deep-rooted hypocrisy and the natural inconsistencies of some people's views, but the establishing of virtue signalling as a commonly used phrase and concept provides critics of those who share charity messages with a shorthand for accusing them of taking advantage of charity's symbolic power without having to engage with either the cause or the argument.

While the concept of virtue signalling per se does not appear to have been taken up by academic researchers, some recent research has shown that those with narcissistic personality traits such as excessively high self-esteem and relatively low empathy are more likely to engage in conspicuous but low-cost prosocial behaviours. In a large (N=9,062) study of the 2014 ALS 'Ice Bucket Challenge' (where people were encouraged to tip a bucket of ice water over their heads, mimicking the paralysis of the disease, then both donate and nominate others to do the same), researchers found that those who had posted a video of themselves completing the challenge but did not make a donation to the charity scored higher for narcissism than those who made a donation but did not post a video (Konrath et al, 2016: 185). Similarly, Koffman, Orgad and Gill (2015) argue that there has been a rise in 'selfie-humanitarianism', identifying a prominent trend in recent humanitarian campaigns for the focus to be shifted *away* from the prospective recipients of aid (typically in the Global South) *towards* the donors or volunteers (usually in the Global North). They cite the UN Foundation's Girl Up campaign as a prime example of this phenomenon, which 'seeks to spark a grassroots movement among American girls in support of their Southern "sisters"', and operates through online appeals, 'awareness-raising' conferences featuring celebrities, and merchandising (Koffman et al, 2015: 161). Examples of Girl Up's specific campaigns include 'Tweet it Out', in which American girls were encouraged to Tweet about why they stand up for girls around the world, and a campaign in which pharmaceuticals and toiletries company Johnson & Johnson agreed to help fund the schooling of 58 Liberian girls in return for the 'donation' of selfies from American girls (Koffman et al, 2015: 162). As the authors state:

> Rather than a dialogic two-way communication between Northern and Southern girls, the production of media content is self-oriented, contained within the sphere of Northern girls' lives. The images and tweets produced are overwhelmingly centred on Northern girls: it is their images, thoughts and feelings which are made public via social media rather than that of those girls in need of help.... This selfie-gaze outlines a highly narcissistic form of caring for the suffering of others.... (Koffman et al, 2015: 162)

When young people increasingly expect rewards from their volunteering activities (Hustinx and Meijs, 2011: Dean, 2014), this sort of campaign strategy is not surprising. Companies need positive media campaigns, and why not use the everyday habits of teenagers to get it, rather than just merely supporting the education of Liberian schoolgirls without the fanfare? (In 2019, Johnson & Johnson were valued at US$360 billion.)

Our actions are not scripted, but we draw on a repertoire of actions that are well rehearsed and practised, and are 'known to have certain effects on certain audiences' (Moore, 2008: 15). We don't always get it right, however, and being online gives us many opportunities to get it wrong. As Durkheim (1982: 51) wrote, the laughter and social disdain one can elicit for not acting the right way or wearing the right clothes, or, in this case, supporting the right causes or promoting the right charitable paraphernalia, has the same effect as any real social penalty:

> People are ready – even eager – for celebrities and strangers to fall, as though by exposing someone as "bad" they can automatically mark themselves as "good".... Yet the mechanics of social media (such as likes and retweets) can arguably bring out these traits in all of us. Online disinhibition is a phenomenon whereby we say things to others we wouldn't say in real life. Who hasn't had a vulnerable ego when their latest selfie only gets five likes? And strong emotions are frequently the most rewarded online. (Tait, 2017)

In an article for the *New Statesman*, the digital journalist Amelia Tate (2018) focuses on the growth of YouTubers, people who make a living from producing social media content, particularly videos, and how charitable acts and emotion-pulling stunts increasingly play a role in their search for clicks and advertising revenue. These include videos where 'influencers' sell their expensive trainers to provide toiletries for the homeless, or film the reaction of a homeless man as he's given US$100 every 10 minutes. It's both manipulative and a good deed, and given the enormous reach of YouTubers to influence a young generation, there is some indication many are inspired to do charitable works locally as a result. But her discomfort at such videos does lead Tate to the reflexive self-assessment we all need to make:

> It's about now that I should admit that I'm a hypocrite. When a friend raises money online for a charity via a crowdfunding service, you are often given the option while donating to write your name or stay anonymous ... sometimes I don't. Sometimes I want my friend to know that I care about their cause. That I support them. And yes – Lord have mercy on my eternal soul! – that I donated £10 more than Bethany, whom I hate.

Such debates are in people's minds as they navigate the relationship between their offline and online worlds. As one interviewee who worked for a student charity in Sheffield told me:

> Like, I could help somebody across the road on my way home tonight, but I'm not suddenly going to around telling everybody, but lots of people, that'd be the first thing they put on Facebook.... It's that constant kind of "I need to tell people that I'm a really nice person", whereas, to me, really nice people are just really nice people. They don't go around telling everybody that they are all the time, or what is that even about? If you've done something that gave you a sense of satisfaction, then that should be enough. Why is that sense of satisfaction not enough? You need 30 people to comment and go, "Oh, well done. You're amazing", and then they feel satisfied and think, "Mmm...." It's a slippery slope, isn't it? I don't know where it ends. I dread to think. We'll all have TV shows about ourselves, or something....

The doing of charity online can be understood as a 'technology of the self' (Foucault, 1988), whereby subjects are hailed by the promise of technologies that they can actively take up in order to work on themselves as intelligibly better people. But what happens when the performance of the 'good' charitable self goes wrong, and is interpreted as irritating, boastful or misguided? Research has shown that presenting the self on social media is prone to 'context collapse' (Marwick and boyd, 2011), where impressions cannot be fully managed, as the obligation to present a singular identity becomes difficult as diverse groups of people flock to social network sites. What the data below shows is that young people are having to navigate difficult moral terrain when doing charity on social media.

'Look at all the best parts about me!' Charity and impression management online

Most research into charity activities online focuses on large-scale data (see, for example, Guo and Saxton, 2014; Saxton and Wang, 2014; Svensson et al, 2015; Cox et al, 2018), examining what gets shared widely, and the role of social networks in spreading messages. Instead, a qualitative approach allows us to better understand the lived experience of charity online, and how those individuals most likely to use social media are thinking when confronted with non-profit messages on their feeds. A series of participatory focus groups were carried out with mostly UK university students (aged 18–25). Participants discussed their experiences of giving and charity online (such as requests to donate, sponsorship invitations from friends and family, campaigns they liked or shared) and how they perceived such requests, such as whether they found them genuine, or whether they scrolled past them. Participants were also given a tablet computer with a sample Twitter feed on it. This feed contained a variety of material from voluntary organisations and fundraising initiatives, including infographics, pictures, videos and links. Participants were invited to engage with the material as they would their own social media feeds, and asked to reflect on what they liked and did not like. This elicitative process (Harper, 2002) worked as an interactive recreation of their own social media experiences, in order to try and assess reactions through 'live methods' (Back and Puwar, 2012). For a more detailed discussion of the methodology employed in this study, and its limitations, please see the methodological appendix at the end of the book.

Participants frequently expressed the idea found in the literature cited above that people present a certain form of themselves online:

> You only post the absolute best photos of yourself and you really Photoshop them. I think you can do that with your

personality as well. You can only post things that make you look absolutely amazing and you could even lie about it. (Alicia, 21, F)

I mean everybody's profile, on any form of social media, and it's the same on LinkedIn, you construct the ideal profile and you are conscious of that, whether you notice it or not, what you're doing, what you're putting on your wall, and stuff like that. (Liam, 21, M)

Yes, you definitely want to present the best version of yourself there is. People, if they have done something good, probably want to share that and be like, "Look, I'm a great human being...." That could be a nice thing to share but also you might be doing it for personal gain, because people think you're nice. (Lucy, 18, F)

Part of this came from the fact that reality can be less than perfect at times, and offering a micro-snapshot of one bit of a day didn't need to reflect that reality:

We select the best things about us. We're not going to put online, "Oh, I've had an argument with my friend today." (Ani, 21, F)

When you're on Instagram, you always check whether the post is worthy, don't you?... You don't want to put an ugly post on, as it were. (Ally, 18, M)

You can put your best foot forward on social media. On Instagram you only post on the days that you're out and done stuff – you don't post when you're inside watching Netflix all day and crying! (Evy, 23, F)

In this instance social media serves the purpose to 'create a bit of a myth about people', where one's Facebook profile 'just turns into "Look at all the best parts about me!" Yes, I think there are issues with that sometimes' (Erica, 21, F), echoing the research documented earlier in this chapter.

When it came to discussions of charity on social media, authenticity was key. Reflecting on what they think when they scrolled through their own feeds, young people realised how many judgements they make about their close friends and relatives and more distant acquaintances: 'I think a lot of the time you can tell the levels of sincerity that they have towards the cause', said Neil (18, M), 'if they're going out of their way to run a marathon, to raise money, then they can't just be doing that to showboat, really.' This cynicism about small acts of kindness was widespread, and had been stimulated by the web's power to provide a shortcut to morality:

> I think the social pressure does end up with people that pretend to do things though, like they pretend that they've donated, they'll pretend that they'd done this. You know when someone lets everybody know that they've done a random act of kindness, like, "Ooh, I gave money to a tramp today, yay me." Not everyone needs to know about it. You can just do it quietly. (Irma, 21, F)

Whether motivation mattered or not was discussed widely. Recent research has shown that young people are less likely to consider an activity counts as volunteering if it is motivated by instrumental motivations (Dean and Verrier, 2018). However, in this research, the potential selfish motivation of giving in order to brag was generally dismissed as a necessary evil, and even beneficial for charitable causes looking to generate momentum:

> I guess even if someone is bragging about giving to charity, they have given to charity at the end of the day. (Yelena, 21, F)

> If people feel they have to do it, at least they're still doing it, but I don't think it's good that people do feel that way. (Isobel, 21, F)

Stephen (22, M):   It's better to brag about giving to charity than it is to, I don't know, about....

Harriet (22, F): How much alcohol you buy!

Stephen: Yes, exactly, [or] showing off a nice watch. It's better showing off how much you've donated, I guess, but I think people have a natural thought about people who are showing off in general. There's a natural reaction to that, I think.

Harriet: I think that can also encourage competitiveness among other people on social media, which may create some sort of domino effect. Like the "Ice Bucket Challenge" is an example of that, but maybe even more subtle things.

Neil (18, M) ultimately argued that while 'a lot of the time you can say that they're doing it to look good' because 'it does a lot of good for charity', the beneficence of the symbolic power of charity doesn't really matter if good is being done. It may be helpful for the individual donator or volunteer, but it's not a big deal, unless it's performed to a tiresome degree:

> I was going to say that, like when you have people posting about how much they've done, and how much they've raised, and posting pictures of themselves. Like, okay. It makes you feel like they're kind of gloating about it a little bit, it's just like one post is okay. But when you have 10 of them on your wall, within a week, it's just like, it's a bit much, isn't it? Like, there's a difference – I post a lot, but I post to get people to comment, whereas I see a lot of posts saying, "This is what I've done", kind of post. And it's just like, okay, but you've said it already, we get it. So yes, it can feel a lot like that. And even when they're asking for sponsorship, they'll just talk about how amazing it is, that they're doing it, it just makes me want to give you less! [Laughter] (Abrielle, 21, F)

The social pressure to perform goodness in the right way was also discussed at length. This pressure comes from a variety of places – 'you do tend to get a lot of [people] that say, "Are you going to share this or retweet that?" and then I'm like, "I don't know," I suppose the view on charities, if I'm going to be doing something, at least it should have a small amount of belief in it or I want to see it succeed as opposed to something I've never had any interest before in or have any knowledge of' (Leon, 25, M) – and can result in a variety of behaviours, where friends 'pretend to do things' (Irma, 21, F):

> If it's something that was going round, say, your group of friends, and literally it was so popular and everyone was donating to this person, you'd be like, "Well, I'm going to do it now. Everyone else is. I should." Do you know what I mean? I don't know. I don't think it's necessarily to look good, but I feel like people kind of feel like, "Everyone else is, I probably should." (Yelena, 21, F)

This was seen as a totalising thing – 'I think everyone does, even if they deny it, they're lying, everyone does it' (Zak, 20, M) – but there were occasional dissenting voices that rejected – or at least denied – this presentation of self:

Jon: But would you [retweet a cause] if you don't believe in it, to make it look like you would believe in it?

Eddy (23, M):   I wouldn't do that. I'm not about that.

But the general consensus was this was a common thing people did on social media. (Or that *other* people did – participants were generally suspiciously hazy about things in this mould that *they* had done to present themselves differently.) This behaviour was read as normal and expected, with little particular blame for doing it:

> I think every institution and person, no one wants to have, not their bad side but their least public friendly side revealed, you always want your best image. It's like an interview, you don't really want to go in in trackies, when you've just woken up, you always want to present yourself best. So, I think every institution does that. (Joseph, 20, M)

> I'm not saying they're a bad person, but they want to look like a good person, so there's this pressure and, "Look at me. I've done such a good thing today. Please, all applaud me." (Andy, 24, M)

> I think people obviously want to give to charity, but a lot of people won't give £50 to a charity and then not tell someone about it. I think most people would say, "I've done this. How about you do it too?" or something along those lines. I think that's just human, really. (Harriet, 22, F)

Such instincts about activity on social media could bite when it came to one's own charitable activity. The fact that 'everyone does it' (Zak, 20, M), and that everyone is aware that 'everyone' is doing it, did create problems for those young participants who had done some charitable activity recently and had fundraised for it. Two young women who were friends had recently completed a three-week volunteering trip to Tanzania renovating a school, and reported some wariness in their fundraising:

Jon:	When you were fundraising for Tanzania, was there a fear that people would think you were only fundraising because you wanted to go to Tanzania for three weeks?
Andi (21, F):	Yes, I'd say so.
Annika (21, F):	A little bit.
Jon:	How did you deal with that?
Andi:	I felt really awkward keeping posting on Facebook, but we needed to raise the money.
Annika:	Especially when you have to post a lot. You're just feeling bad really! [Laughter] People just probably get really annoyed at you, but you also have to try and raise money, so you've got to do it because you've got to get it out there and that's the fastest and easiest way to do it.

Similarly Luke (20, M), who had recently been part of a group who had completed a 150-mile bicycle ride for a heart disease charity and had had to 'come to peace' with the fact his requests for donations online could be seen as boastful or arrogant, found that:

> [I]t's the only thing I've ever done really, for charity, so I haven't donated anything much since, and I didn't do anything before, so it feels like I'm not just doing it for the sake of doing it. Whereas I do know people, I don't want to say they are doing it for the sake of doing it, but there's certain people who do that stuff all the time, like probably say, post [on social media] loads. I posted a lot around the time … if you post every day, leading up to it, the message will get hammered home. And it might put some people off, but then again it might not.

Telling young people not to care what other people think is a clichéd banal piece of advice, but in these examples, Andi, Annika, and Luke all internalised the message themselves that because they knew they were fundraising for an altruistic reason, and had a need to push their message, stimulating internal negative reactions in a few Facebook friends or Twitter followers was something to shrug and move on from, rather than be stymied or ground down by.

In his encounters with people who've been publicly shamed on social media, journalist Jon Ronson (2016) shows how even minor perceived misdeeds, such as badly phrased jokes, can lead to anonymous social media 'pile-on' shamings, but also devastating consequences, such as the loss of jobs, or even suicide. He concludes that the anonymous crowds of the social media swirl create prejudiced barbarians of us all. While nothing as near as dramatic was discussed in the focus groups, this wider context of social media enabling you to be slighter coarser, slightly harsher and less feeling was part of its wider ability to detach individuals from real life, removing the need to be authentic:

> My opinion on this, I think that although I don't necessarily [do it] intentionally, I think it's the same for a lot of people, I think we present ourselves differently on the internet anyway. I think that might more stem from the fact that there is less emotional – I think the stuff we're posting on Facebook particularly the stuff we say on Messenger, this has put me in trouble with ex-girlfriends and stuff, who were girlfriends at the time. It's just the first thing that comes into your mind, that raw, emotional response is often something that's just so easy to send away. You don't have to go to the effort of even talking. You're not looking at someone's face quite the same. Even if they've got a profile picture of their face, you get used to seeing that picture and suddenly it's just there. You're not talking to someone face on and so I don't think you emit the same level of respect as you otherwise might. I've since started trying to act more as I would in person on the internet but I do think that people act differently online. (Lester, 19, M)

I am not a social media researcher, but it was fascinating to sit down with groups of young people and ask them about the roles their friends and acquaintances play on social media, the rules they followed to manage their online lives, and to find that it was something they all wanted to comment on, had strong opinions about, and could remember specific instances and issues (much better than they could of the specific charity issues we discussed). It's perfectly possible that, in the minutes before the focus group started, they'd been checking Facebook or Snapchat, and seen a status or message they felt was inauthentic or was obvious impression management, or made them 'mini-hate', as Tate (2018) outlines, because of some tiny, potentially imagined slight. The characteristics I asked them about were identifiable: they all knew someone whose behaviour on social media could be described as 'putting up a front' (Yelena, 21, F), or that 'everyone's got that one person on their Facebook' (Eddy, 23, M) who 'everyone knows' is faking it, or 'playing' their contacts, but who no one would challenge or call up on it, because *it's just not worth it*. As one interpretation from Bourdieu might say, we all have to accept the rules and play the game. 'Everyone's normally got one' said Nelson (22, M), pessimistically. This level of distrust wasn't universal, and was often targeted at certain friends and acquaintances: it 'depends on their reputation.... If it is someone you know that can be a bit sly, then I don't think you are going to listen to it as much' (Yasmin, 19, F). These social practices would then emerge in various charity-focused scenarios:

> If it's somebody that you know in actual fact isn't much of a nice person but they're taking part in the cause, you're like, "Well, why have they done that? They don't give a crap." [Laughter] (Natasha, 21, F)

> Everyone knows someone that when they post something on Facebook, like, "Everyone should support this charity", you think, "Oh here we go. This guy again...." Because some people you just know too well, and you know they are not genuine. You know they are just doing it to try and look good, because everyone thinks they are annoying. (Noah, 19, M)

As Noah continued, this level of distrust only focuses on certain people:

> You never see them doing anything charitable. All of a sudden, they are like, "Everyone should donate to this charity", even though you probably know they definitely haven't.

Noah's language here is redolent of the problem young people face in this situation: his dismissal is still caveated with 'probably know'. Of course, finding out the genuineness of the friend or acquaintance's supposed donation is hard, and would risk insult and blowback if one were to enquire, and possible stigma and shame if the person had donated.

Young people could imagine these scenarios quite vividly, able to provide case studies of what such behaviour would be like and how they would react to it *in their minds*:

Sometimes as well, like we were talking about earlier, it's a way of them saying, "Look at me, I'm a really great individual", making themselves look glamorous in front of their charity's sign, and putting it on, not because of the charity. Because if it's just about the charity, get out of the photo. [Laughter] Just take the photo, and put that on. So, I don't know. I think it's sometimes too in your face, if it's on all the social medias, because most people have got Facebook, they don't really enjoy going on it, but they've got it. [Laughter] And if it was on all of them, the same charities, all on every social media, it would just be like, "I've had enough now." And again, we'd be coming to, "Well, just get out of my face", sort of thing. And you just wouldn't, you would never give. (Sid, 19, M)

Yes, but like they'll also say stuff like, "Oh, I'm doing this amazing thing, and I'm giving up chocolate for a month. Please sponsor me." [Laughter] And it's just like, "I'm doing this amazing thing, I'm giving up chocolate, and I'm sacrificing so much, to raise money." Like, those kind of statuses are annoying. (Abrielle, 21, F)

As Sales (2016) documents, young people are having to navigate paths in these worlds for which no one has made any rules, which is both exciting and terrifying. Everyone acknowledges such practices are bad and yet will and must happen. There was a sense that there was 'manipulating your own online identity in the same way' (Liam, 21, M), and that social media is an inherently shallow medium where 'you're only giving this version' (Michael, 21, M). There is a sense of conspicuous consumption or partaking of ethical behaviours and practices that are then presented back at the world:

A lot of people do that on Facebook. They make sure that you know they've run a 5km or they've run a marathon. Maybe not even to give to charity, a lot of people like other people to know that they've done charitable work. (Helen, 20, F)

If someone gives £10 in the forest, and doesn't tell anyone, have they actually given anything?

Conclusions

The data that emerged from this work was wide-ranging and showed a myriad of issues for charity sector researchers and practitioners to be wary about. They must remember that charity doesn't exist in isolation from other social activities. Young people have developed a set of strategies for dealing with life on social media. These are the unwritten, rarely articulated, informal rules of managing any new social network or situation. What was most evident in these discussions was that they had never articulated these before, especially in relation to personal views about charity, giving and questions of morality and selfishness, but yet they were largely consistent and agreed upon. They're not saying in the focus groups what they have done, or what they would do per se, but what they think they would do, and it turns out that their peers have developed very similar internal rules.

Discussing his excellent movie *Eighth Grade*, about an awkward teenage girl who's far more confident and comfortable with herself online, the comedian Bo Burnham said of young people struggling with the new nuances of online that they've been 'forced by a culture they did not create to be conscious of themselves at every moment.' Speaking to young people about charity on social media reveals an unexpected level of self-consciousness, where one may have expected self-absorption or self-aggrandisement. Humblebrags are about such self-aggrandisement, showing off in a humble way that serves to double-down on your showing off. Yet the students I've spoken to *know this*: charity on the internet provides another thing to be conscious of, to be worried about, to go wrong. At a time when young people, especially those from more disadvantaged backgrounds, are pushed into volunteering as 'hope labour' (Taylor-Collins, 2019), where the cult of experience cultivation will hopefully lead to a solid future, it helps us to see charity on social media as a tool where they can document such labour, but also an (unwitting) reinforcer of the ontological insecurities of age and new media. Talking about something good you've done for charity online is perfectly reasonable – but operationalising the symbolic capital you've generated for yourself can raise all manner of complications.

4

Charities, expertise and policy

In his book *In Search of Civil Society*, Nicholas Deakin (2001: 205) states that while voluntary action has long been the state's partner in a broadly dually beneficent relationship, as the 21st century progresses and this relationship changes, we must ask 'on whose terms will this change be made?' In this chapter, we will examine the relationship between charity and policy, and the role that charities' symbolic power plays in helping or hindering their position as influencers, and their role as a set of bodies with considerable expertise in tackling social problems, and as contributors to policy direction and delivery (Hilton et al, 2013). It will briefly examine the changing nature of the UK charity sector's relationship with government over recent years, focusing on why government wanted the sector closely involved in delivering policy, and then how the UK voluntary sector has become less favoured (and increasingly challenged) under the coalition and Conservative governments post 2010, in part due to a perceived decline in charity's status as 'special'.

While the role and contributions of non-profit organisations in the policy process have been outlined as to identify issues, develop solutions and promote those solutions through mobilisation, demonstration and advocacy (Evans et al, 2017), the ability and the right of the UK voluntary sector to do so has been questioned. Drawing on interviewee data, this chapter will look at how the sector gets (or doesn't get) its voice heard, and how in the UK a more critical approach to austerity politics has affected its ability to intervene in political debate. As with many institutions, the charity sector is struggling to come to terms with a new harsher financial landscape while finding itself under immense social scrutiny and political pressure. The data shows how interviewees feel the sector is caught in a web of competing interests, and therefore frequently fails to make best use of its resources. Interviewees offer at times competing normative views of the sector as a political entity, and provide a set of critiques of current practice within the sector, including relationships to power and symbolic positioning. Several recent cases in which charities are demonstrated to not be living up to what is expected of them are discussed, and the chapter concludes by examining how interviewees reflect on the issue that sometimes charity 'goodness' is an excuse for opaqueness or bad behaviour, and the automatic assumption of heroism works against them, or can mask significantly damaging practice.

Charities as special partners

Since Deakin posed his question, numerous authors have sought to reassess the relationship between the public and voluntary sectors in the UK, most recently in the wake of the seemingly defunct 'big society' agenda and the impact of budget cuts, with most current analysis quite concerned for the future. The voluntary sector has struggled to manage in a tougher financial landscape (with the significant growth in UK government funding to the sector seen from 2000 to 2009/10 stagnating and reversing slightly) while finding itself under heightened scrutiny and pressure. For example, there has been the feeling among many Conservative Party figures that the voluntary sector operates as an extension of the political left, framed by the sector's increasing need to raise concerns about inequality, austerity and cuts to key public services. As a result, with a government hugging the voluntary sector less tightly, sector debates seem increasingly *politicised*: from the National Coalition for Independent Action's (NCIA, 2015) focus on the increasingly challenging environment for service-providing voluntary organisations, to the media's focus on transparency in the wages of sector officials, controversies around fundraising techniques following the death of poppy seller Olive Cooke and the establishment of the Fundraising Preference Service, financial mismanagement and the collapse of Kids Company, and the stemming of freedom to lobby and campaign if in receipt of state funding. Such a difficult atmosphere is relatively new. The 1990s and early 2000s were, while not perfect, a relative boom time for the sector as politicians sought to take a 'third way' (Giddens, 1998) approach to delivering public services, between public and private sector-led approaches, that saw a great role for voluntary sector provision, driven, in part, by the (symbolic) effects charities could engender, alongside envisaged partnership and reciprocity between the sector and the state:

> Not all small local VCSEs [voluntary, community, social enterprises] are forces for good but the value of this group of small organisations as a whole cannot be doubted.... Small VCSEs are truly an expression of the force of civil society.... (McGovern, 2017: 2)

The 'difference' of charity and charities – often staffed by volunteers, often locally embedded, potentially flexible and dynamic, driven by need rather than the profit motive or statutory duty – presents the option to use such characteristics to develop an identity as a space of and for 'goodness'. This difference, or comparative advantage (Billis and Glennerster, 1998), or distinction (Bourdieu, 1984; Macmillan, 2013), means that charities have a different offer, and have the authority to decide how to use it. As Pauline McGovern (2017: 5) puts it, the charity sector offers a space for a valorised configuration of social relations where in which the 'ordinary laws of the economy can be suspended, a place of trust and giving.' Oftentimes voluntary organisations are preferred to private ones in the delivery of welfare services because they create moral capital while fulfilling the role (Heckler, 2018). In apparent agreement, the recent UK Government *Civil Society Strategy* (DCMS, 2018: 20) states that:

> ... complex challenges facing society cannot be solved by the government alone, but by bringing together the energy and resources available across society. We will convene partners and deploy capital to harness the expertise of charities and social enterprises and the power of the private sector.

while in the field of responding to natural disasters or events such as terrorism, or the Grenfell tower fire disaster:

> National organisations can bring their capability, expertise and resources to bear, while local organisations understand the needs of, and are trusted by, their local communities. (DCMS, 2018: 33)

The fact that voluntary organisations can lay claim to be 'different' or 'special' is well documented by field theorists such as Rob Macmillan, who try to explain the space in which charities operate and how they can operationalise their 'distinctiveness' or symbolic power at certain opportune moments: 'Distinctiveness appears to become strategically more important in "difficult times", presumably because it may help third sector organisations in the increased competition to sustain and secure otherwise constrained resources' (Macmillan, 2013: 45). Phillimore and McCabe's (2015) work has shown that grassroots organisations are often distinct because volunteers blur the lines between political, personal and civic actions: their 'experiential knowledge' of the problems the organisation was trying to solve aided them in seeming non-hierarchical and non-bureaucratic. As we saw in the response to the Grenfell Tower tragedy, official authorities such as the police, the council and the Home Office struggled to work with local residents because of a lack of trust built up over a period of time, emerging from negligent approaches to safety and violent immigration policies. Small-scale organisations, embedded in communities, are part of a wider view of local charities, which is they 'can be trusted because they are altruistic and community-orientated rather than focussed on making a profit' (McGovern, 2017: 41; see also Hogg and Baines, 2011). Yet, in traditional determination to cut through the over-promotion, Mohan (2016: vi) asks whether we must consider if the voluntary sector has 'a distinctive impact and added value in its own right, or is that the terrain of claims made by disingenuous politicians or by the sector's self-interested publicists?' As Breeze (2017: 109) points out, the professional advice given to charity staff and fundraisers veers between exceptionalism and inclusion, with some claiming 'anyone can do it' if they apply themselves, and others arguing that charity staff are a 'special breed'.

Charities in the UK have always been able to point towards high ratings from the public for levels of trust. In recent years, however, the reality is somewhat murkier. Some studies show that trust in charities has stayed relatively high across the last 10 years, and some show it has fallen significantly. When presented with a list of UK institutions and asked the extent to which they trust them, 64 per cent of the UK population say they trusted charities 'a great deal' or 'quite a lot' (nfp Synergy, 2017). This compares to just over 70 per cent for the NHS and the armed forces, with institutions like the government, newspapers and political parties scoring quite consistently paltry results, at around 20 per cent. There was a mid-decade wobble, which charities appear to have recovered from, where trust declined to 47 per cent in 2015; in parallel, trust in the regulation of charities has doubled to 35 per cent, perhaps indicating that the public saw there was a problem with how charities were operating, and measures have been put in place to do something about it (although how much the public actually knows, or needs to know, about charity regulation is debatable [Hogg, 2017]). Yet research by the Charity Commission (2018b: 5), using a methodology different to nfp synergy, suggests that charity trust took a significant decline between 2014 and 2016, and has not yet recovered. Several leading UK charities have been fined for misusing donor data, by trading details and piecing together donor profiles from different sources, in order to generate new funds (BBC News, 2017a). In Ipsos MORI (2014) research, two-thirds of the public agreed with the statement that 'some of the fundraising methods used by charities make me feel uncomfortable'. Fraud in the UK charity sector is estimated to cost around £1.9 billion per year (PKF Littlejohn, 2016), but declining finances mean regulators cannot focus on everything, and must take a 'risk-led' rather than 'complaint-led' approach to investigating potential malpractice (McDonnell and Rutherford, 2017). While people associate charities with 'trust', 'integrity' and 'good morals and principles', this does not give organisations free reign, as a certain amount of monitoring is required in order to maintain such principles (Hogg, 2017).

As the left-wing parties of the US, UK and Germany sought to respond to the neoliberalism of the 1980s, they sought to develop a 'third way' (Giddens, 1998) approach to the delivery of public services. This meant that services which were previously provided by state actors were either privatised or contracted out to private or community sector partners. In statements like Bill Clinton's 'The era of big government is over', we see the left's loss of faith in government and instead an attempt to borrow the reputation of charitable providers, where charities came to be conceptualised as 'both a cohesive moral force in civil society and also as entrepreneurial competitive providers' (McGovern, 2017: 21). As an example, in 1992, only 2 per cent of home care/help hours in the UK were provided by non-governmental providers, but by 1997, this had risen to 44 per cent (Hogg and Baines, 2011: 343). These shifting state discourses about charities have intensified around their need to be enterprising, more professionally organised (discussed in the next chapter), and ape private companies (McGovern, 2017: 4–5). The deepened relationship between the state and the voluntary sector has been widely critiqued. The third way move to accept neoliberalism, for instance, has, it is argued, led to a situation where 'government and civil society increasingly harmonize their interests with the needs of the market, often tuning out the broader spectrum of public opinion and interest' (Grattan, 2012: 195), a point similarly made by working-class researchers and activists who argue that the charity sector demonstrates a superior attitude, positioning itself as a leader rather than servant of communities (McGarvey, 2017). Spade (2011) sees the lobbying done by non-profits as too often focused on non-structural issues, thereby continuing their ability to pursue 'good work' while looking like radical activists; and the development of close relations between senior politicians, civil servants and the leadership of third sector organisations as 'part of a new, covert political elite of insiders', reminiscent of critiques of Tony Blair's wider 'sofa government' (Murray, 2006). Similar criticisms are raised in the development sector: Fowler (2000) asks where non-governmental development organisations' (NGDOs) legitimacy and moral authority to act in and on society come from. If it comes from the civic constituency that make up their staff, volunteers and beneficiaries, this cuts against a situation where it is borrowed from association with and resources from (popularly mandated) regimes and governments:

> It could be argued that when official funds predominate in their resource base an NGDO has, in effect, traded a legitimacy and moral authority derived from civic rootedness for legitimacy by association with governments, ie legitimacy from the public domain. This is one effect of dependency on tax-based finance. Unfortunately, experience shows it is difficult for public domain legitimacy not to become allied to a contractual relationship and accommodation of values propagated by the state. (Fowler, 2000: 641)

Fowler cautions against collaboration and partnership, addressing fears in the field where NGDOs are 'co-opted' into compromise in terms of adopting a government's paradigm, priorities and practices, and that many organisations still have problems in responding to queries about their accountability. There is a reason organisations like the Royal National Lifeboat Institute and Médecins Sans Frontières choose to receive very little or no money from government (Krause, 2014: 106).

The above section has sought to briefly sketch out the policy positioning of charities, particularly in relation to their holding and operationalisation of symbolic capital, and to amplify some critical voices – longer examinations of the relationship between the voluntary sector and policy-making are available elsewhere (see, for example, Kendall, 2003; Evans et al, 2017; Smith and Grønbjerg, 2018). But hopefully the idea that the charity sector is seen as distinct has been introduced, and this has been something policy practitioners have sought to 'use' for both ideological and practical reasons in various ways down the years, and some of the problems and questions that have emerged as a result. The following section reflects on the relationship between charities and politics and politicians, to see if charities' symbolic resources are no longer enough.

Politicians and charities

Whether it's holding up a big novelty cheque, cutting a ribbon with over-sized scissors, revealing a plaque or doing something silly, politicians have an occasional relationship with charity, where the everyday conversations of policy and practice are forgotten and the pictures of events tell the story of people who 'are human after all' and willing to 'muck in' and 'do their bit'. Power is maintained and legitimated through specific cultural mechanisms, such as education and religion, writes Bev Skeggs (2015: 213) – and charity. Actors at the state level share in the state's sovereignty and symbolic capital, but such resources are contingent on relationships with non-state actors, with the strength of these relationships often determined by trust (Agnew, 2009). In her ethnography of the work lives of Members of the UK Parliament, Emma Crewe (2015) does the hard job of trying to understand the lived realities of doing Westminster politics, and in particular, how local concerns play up against national concerns, and personal political ideologies have to be balanced with party politics and job concerns (both getting re-elected and advancing in Westminster). She finds that MPs and their offices are 'locked into a web of relationships within their (local) area with contacts in the council, businesses and voluntary organizations' (Crewe, 2015: 95), and notes the difficulties politicians have in being inclusive: they represent constituencies which are hugely diverse and contain voters on both sides of practically all issues. Voluntary groups are just one part of this matrix of voices, and so the idea that MPs would act one way because a charity with symbolic legitimacy advised them to is unrealistic. But people are swayed 'not only by the logic of an issue, but how they feel about the people advocating for it' (Crewe, 2015: 186), and one only has to read a selection of the UK charity sector press in recent years to find that the way politicians view the relationship between themselves and charities is one that is both necessarily murky and ideological:

- Former Labour Cabinet Minister Lord David Blunkett advised that charities should 'pretend to collude while you actually oppose [policies] ... be as nice as possible even through gritted teeth, all the time for ministers ... while encouraging and supporting backbenchers, trying to encourage people to understand what's going on and then to raise their voices to change things' (quoted in R. Cooney, 2015).
- The (then Conservative) MP Sarah Wollaston (articulating one of those statements that everybody knows but nobody says out loud) said that the Tories disliked charity campaigning because charity workers were much more likely to be Labour supporters, 'biased' against her party (Birkwood, 2015).

- In a long and weighty investigation for Civil Society Media, Kirsty Weakley (2016) exposes how confidence in the regulation of the charity sector is under threat in part because of the politicisation of the board, with Sir David Norrington, the former commissioner for public appointments, saying that a recent government review into how public bodies appoint their leading figures was an attempt to return to the days of political patronage (Neville, 2016).

Garthwaite's (2016: 59) ethnographic work on food banks details how relationships between the Trussell Trust, the most high-profile UK food bank provider, and the Conservative government, declined as the charity increasingly pointed out the link between cuts to welfare benefits and rising food bank use. Former Department for Work and Pensions (DWP) Minister Iain Duncan Smith accused the trust of 'political scaremongering', supported by a senior DWP source, who stated the Trust was 'misleading and emotionally manipulating' the public for publicity, and that it was the Trust's own increased 'aggressive' marketing that led to more people asking for help with food poverty. (This argument was shown to be a political smokescreen when, in February 2019, the new Work and Pensions Secretary Amber Rudd admitted that the government's benefit reforms were increasing the need for people to use food banks [BBC News, 2019].)

Forty years ago, Bolduc (1980) conducted a wide-ranging ethnographic study of a civic association in Hartford, Connecticut, in order to study its representativeness of the local community and its legitimacy in acting as a mouthpiece of local residents. Bolduc moved his family to the area as he was fascinated by the efforts of this organisation to preserve the racially diverse middle-class area's identity. In his study he explores the relationship between the association and the community, and why it was given such prominence and respect by local residents, and he is worth quoting at length:

> In one sense, the Civic Association carries with it a form of authority which is somewhat analogous to Weber's "charismatic" authority. While devoid of any religious connotations, it is legitimacy granted on the basis of the perceived and actual qualities of the leaders which are considered "unusual". Many Association leaders, for example, have, and are generally believed to possess, an unusual skill in dealing successfully with "City Hall". They know the "ins and outs" of the Zoning Commission and have been particularly masterful at oiling the right wheels

to get them moving. They are far more articulate than the average resident, and have the savoir faire to represent the neighborhood in various aspects of public relations.

Additionally, they are among the most successful members of the neighborhood, as is clearly evidenced by their expensive homes, apparent incomes and prestigious professional occupations. Ironically, the fact that the oligarchs are also the elites seems to carry with it a certain legitimacy. Another factor contributing to the neighborhood's acceptance of the Civic Association is the fact that is recognized, in a relative way, by officials who have unambiguous claims to authority, such as the Mayor, the Police Chief, and the Legislators. Related to this source of legitimacy is the prior existence of the Civic Association before most residents moved into Blue Hills. The Association was started in the mid 1960's when most present residents lived elsewhere. They moved into the neighborhood and found the Blue Hills Civic Association healthy and active. Also, the two major Hartford newspapers as well as local television stations regularly report Association events, and on at least two occasions, essentially endorsed and praised the Association's attempts to "preserve the neighborhood as a viable integrated neighborhood". (Bolduc, 1980: 172)

This example shows how the traditional status of a local voluntary association, and its charismatic leaders, can, as an oligarchy, make the association itself legitimate and a local authority, by utilising its cultural and social capital. Historic examinations of similar situations, such as in Victorian Manchester (Shapely, 1998), reveal the local eulogisation of the benevolent elite who used charity to acquire and reinforce their symbolic capital in order to become local dignitaries of the highest class. Upper-class women have also been shown to operationalise the good glow of charity, as centrality to their communities and service to arts and philanthropic organisations reinforces their class privilege, while philanthropy is used to keep their husbands' wealth untouched by taxation and their families connected to power (Ostrander, 1984). In his career Bourdieu provided descriptions of the legitimation of symbolic power, showing how there are some (generally hegemonic white, middle-class and heteronormative) behaviours, tastes and dispositions which become natural and legitimate over time. It seems like the civic association above made use of its social and cultural resources to cement its legitimacy, without direct democratic right. Symbolic capital is the resource available to an individual or organisation which provides prestige, honour or the right to be listened to, and can be used to hold position or power in a situation without legal reason. Whereas economic capital is clear and obvious (only those with x amount of money have the power to purchase something), the powers of cultural and social capital are more complex and are based on the extent of (mis)recognition of these as valuable, dependent on setting. Symbolic violence is 'the violence which is exercised upon a social agent with his or her complicity' (Bourdieu and Wacquant, 1992: 167), and can be seen in charity as a charity's knowledge that they have a social status that enables them to take advantage of the cultural resonance of their name and organisation type, and the individual's acceptance that they 'should' give in because of the charity's inherent (and socially inherited) goodness. 'Why should I donate to charity A rather than charity B?' 'Well, charity A is a favourite of the Mayor and their Chair is always in the newspaper.' Charity A's authority is increased because good presentations and celebrity endorsements are considered social *signifiers* of quality and prestige, whereas actually it means little in terms of the necessary effectiveness of one's donation. Now smaller charities hold some symbolic power (being small, local, run by volunteers, person-centred and the 'glue that holds communities together are all 'good things' [see Dayson et al, 2018]), but have less opportunity to operationalise these, to bend the will of others.

The relationship between policy practitioners and charities is not always so close, of course; it is often 'adversarial' as a result of diverging views on both problems and potential solutions (Najan, 2003). In fields like refugee and asylum-seeker rights, where an ideological gulf frequently exists between charity and government (McGhee et al, 2016), and where the requirements of funding arrangements have led to the sidelining of overtly critical voices (Vickers, 2014), charities are forced to weave together narratives of conformity (around deservingness, for instance) and contestation (around required policy changes), required to take on some of the macro assumptions 'in order to overcome some of the marginalisation resulting from their adversarial positioning' (Tonkiss, 2018: 131). The following section presents a recent case in which it was felt charities' use of their symbolic resources in adversarial positioning was going too far and had to be clipped.

Gagging

While the UK government continues to be keen to praise the special contribution of charities, such messages do cut against other government-led changes in the public–charity relationship that have sought to reduce the amount that charities in their role as expert bodies can influence the government and their policy decisions. The Lobbying Act 2014, originally purported to stem the influence of corporate lobbyists, became known popularly as the 'gagging bill' for legislating how much money charities which receive public funding can spend on campaigning during elections. It was felt such changes were in part instigated by Oxfam's decision to campaign on the issue of inequality in the UK, and other charity campaigns (ostensibly from the political left) organised against the coalition government. Changes brought in by the Act seek to limit the symbolic authority of charities and voluntary organisations in stemming their ability to voice grievances, at a time when the general public distrust politicians and the wider establishment. The role of charities as influencers and experts on various social issues is questioned for political ends, made worse by the charity sector's lack of political capital as it has no one to bat for it at a senior level (Flannagan, 2017).

In the wake of the collapse of Kids Company, a new clause was announced (recommended by the Institute for Economic Affairs, a think tank and educational charity that does not reveal the sources of its own funding) that was to be inserted into charity grant agreements preventing money from that grant to be used for 'influenc[ing] or attempt[ing] to influence Parliament, government or political parties, or attempting to influence the awarding or renewal of contracts and grants, or attempting to influence legislative or regulatory action' (Cabinet Office, 2016). The National Council for Voluntary Organisations (NCVO) pushed back against such a clause at the time, arguing that the broad use of the word 'influence' as opposed to the more problematic 'lobby' or 'campaign' would prevent charities from being able to tell government what works and what doesn't, and that several organisations had already felt stymied by the anti-advocacy clause (White, 2016). The *Civil Society Strategy* (DCMS, 2018: 70) does detect this contradiction, and merely notes it has 'a job to do' to reconcile how it works with charities. The difficulty of this job was revealed in a recent Department for Digital, Culture, Media and Sport (DCMS, 2017) appeal for bids for organisations to spend the £15 million per year raised through VAT on sanitary products on issues such as violence against women and girls and mental health. The bid documentation wanted successful bids to raise awareness and challenge stigma, while simultaneously banning those bids that promised to campaign and raise awareness (Sharman, 2017).

In other areas charities have felt their ability to influence curtailed. There have been reports on how charities are worried about speaking out against certain policy proposals because the law is so unclear (Asthana, 2017). Smith (2015) tells the story of the Poppy Project, an organisation supporting women saved from traffickers, which closed in 2015 because its submission to run services was outbid by a larger, less specialist charity, and because its Chief Executive Denise Marshall was a leading critic of government policy, a 'species of advocacy and campaigning [which] does not go down well with some Tory MPs, who see it as an example of charities biting the hand that feeds them.' As Smith puts it:

> The risk to charities that dare to criticise government is high. Earlier this year, a report from a panel set up by the Baring Foundation [Independence Panel, 2015] identified "worrying and growing threats" to the independence of the voluntary sector. Its chair, Sir Roger Singleton, said he'd been told about "gagging clauses" in contracts for public services and "active threats by some local authorities" to charities that speak out. Singleton, who ran the children's charity Barnardo's for many years, also revealed a startling conversation with the food bank charity, the Trussell Trust. They "told us how they were threatened with closure when they raised issues with the Government that could have led to fewer people going hungry".

Similarly Ellie Waugh, CEO of small, local homelessness charity Humanity Torbay, claimed her organisation was barred from receiving certain funding by officials because she frequently criticised the government's hugely controversial welfare reforms, a claim that was denied (Littlejohn, 2018). Such a denial seems, however, to fall flat in the face of a *Times* investigation which found that dozens of charities and more than 300 companies with government contracts worth a total of £25 billion had been gagged in various ways, *including* charities that worked with people claiming Universal Credit who had to agree to not 'attract adverse publicity' to government ministers in charge of welfare, and must 'pay the utmost regard' to the minister's 'standing and reputation' (Morgan-Bentley, 2018). The report also found that in 2015 dozens of other charities working with former prisoners were banned from criticising the then Justice Secretary.

As the 'big society' withered, the Conservatives' brief love affair with the charity sector died pretty quickly (Walker, 2015). The legal limits put on charities' campaigning (Morris, 2016) after being told to 'stick to their knitting' (Mason, 2014), the challenges made on chief executive pay (Hillier, 2015), and now a potential sidelining of charities as opposed to social enterprise and socially minded businesses (Bennett et al, 2019), all seem to stem in part from certain charities taking a stand against the political decision of austerity. There was discontent among politicians toward third and faith sector organisations when they spoke out about the negative impacts of cuts and austerity among disadvantaged communities:

> Thus the indications are that the sector acts as an important buffer in meeting welfare needs; but many of the organisations that comprise it do so with a strong sense of their independence, moral purpose and the need to speak truth to power. These characteristics perhaps explain growing strains behind the façade of the Big Society, as voluntary organisations increasingly speak about the impact of austerity on the most vulnerable citizens and communities. In response, government ministers have betrayed frustration with the sector, telling it to keep out of politics and "stick to its knitting", motivations which partly underpin the introduction of the Transparency of Lobbying, Non-party Campaigning and Trade Union Administration Act 2014 (the "Lobbying Act"). For the Conservatives in particular, "social action" in the voluntary, community and faith sector tends to be seen more as independent service to the community rather than campaigning for broader social change. (Rees et al, 2015: 117)

The 'social compact' agreement between government and the third sector formally acknowledged the right of the sector 'to campaign, to comment on Government policy and to challenge that policy irrespective of any funding relationship that might exist' (Home Office, 1998, para 9:1), but also signalled closer working and the spirit of partnership and a more cordial relationship between the state and third sector, which prevailed in the early stages of New Labour's period in office (Bunyan, 2013: 121). But there is a clear tension between such beliefs and the new charity environment. A recognition that the sector has access to moral capital that politicians cannot or at least struggle to access is, in my view, a clear part of this. As Sir Stuart Etherington, Chief Executive of NCVO, put it in a letter to concerned charity leaders (cited in Smith, 2017), the implications of the Act's provisions may have been far bigger than the law's actual content sought to bring about. While one could easily argue that the political reaction to the Act's introduction was purposefully obtuse and ramped up, Etherington points out many reports of charities 'unduly stifling their voices ... a situation where fear and misunderstanding are doing far greater harm to charity campaigning than this legislation itself.' We can see echoes with the UK government's approach to the 'Go Home' vans (Jones et al, 2017: 141–7), where it was feared that a left-wing (over)reaction to a relatively small policy intervention may do more to advertise the policy, doing the government's work for them. Indeed, some leading sector figures claimed that charities were using the Lobbying Act as an excuse for other issues (Ricketts, 2017), and, in practice, we can never know what has not happened as a result of such legislation and gagging clauses in contracts. What is clear from such interventions, however, is that government is wary of criticism, recognises that charities have the symbolic credit to be able to point out policy flaws, and preventing such criticisms has become a standard part of winning the media war over policy. The Labour Party (2019) in opposition have pledged to ban gagging clauses from service delivery contracts with charities if elected, but one can doubt whether giving up a powerful tool would be a priority in office.

'We've got a minister who hates us ...'

Interviewees offered competing normative views of the sector as a political entity, and provided a diverse set of critiques of current practice within the sector, including issues of trust, legitimacy and relationships to power. But when asked whether politicians 'used' charities as ways to promote themselves or ingratiate themselves with people who may often have more of a claim to be legitimate community voices, such a view was pushed back on, or turned on its head:

> There's a number who have just, off their own back, said, "Can we come and have a look round?" and have been really supportive. We've had a few who have done that.... Honestly, on a local level, I think most of the politicians that we've seen don't want any press.... We want the press more than them really to push what we're doing.... I mean [our] Member of Parliament has been really supportive of us over the years. He's never wanted any press or anything like that.... We want publicity for fundraising things but

they've not really pushed it. (Chief executive, homelessness charity C, Sheffield)

We don't really have much to do with local MPs or councillors. A couple of councillors, but … I'm not sure how much influence…. God, this sounds really awful, but I'm not sure how much we'd get back. Because, you know, a photo op in the newspaper, we've got enough stories that can go in the paper without it being attached to [a politician]. (Chief executive, addiction support charity, Sheffield)

Similarly the idea that relationships between leading charities and the government had become too cosy over the years leading to a lack of independence and an inability to critique was pushed back on. The chief executive of a large national housing charity robustly countered the idea that large charities were beholden to the state, pointing out that, 'I last week accused the government of assisting the systematic attack on the poorest people in this country. I don't think that looks like I'm beholden.' But he did recognise that, as someone well connected in government, his social and political power gave him special privileges which may not exist at the local level:

I think it's a different thing at a very local relationship, which is a different thing. But nobody else funds those organisations. Nobody funds those small, local, mostly volunteer-led mental health social services. They get £40,000 a year from the council to pay for their one or two workers, keeps their building on…. People in those situations are worried that if they speak out, something will happen…. I think it's very difficult or much more challenging if you're a very small organisation.

Leaders of smaller, local charities had mixed views on whether this was an accurate view. The chief executive of a charity for people with disabilities in Sheffield spelt out the quandary she found her organisation in when it came to critiquing policy practitioners and local legislators:

The tricky thing about the relationships with that, though, is, once you start…. I mean, you know, we don't have any formal contracts with the council, but we have council run services, really, because everybody who comes here pays for their service with money from the council. So, and a lot of my colleagues in the sector are saying they feel like they're subcontracted to the council, and yet our role, historically, is to challenge and influence. And if we're going to challenge and influence, how are we going to do that, if the council feel we're contractors of theirs? It's very tricky.

The problems of this tightly bound relationship are exacerbated by austerity and budget cuts:

> A lot of charities are beginning to feel like they were cheaper extensions of local authority services. I know that we did and do and were being asked to do more than the local authority for less money. We're subsidising it. (Director of communications, homelessness charity A, London)

Hemmings (2017) finds that, in contrast to large-scale quantitative work in the US (Salamon, et al, 2008), dependent relationships between the voluntary sector and the state weaken political advocacy. Critical voices from the sector, he argues, have been limited as cuts force smaller organisations to weaken their lobbying and to focus on core functions: 'The fear of losing further funding in an austerity environment, and fear, in itself, can limit critical voice' (Hemmings, 2017: 62). From the point of view of the effective altruism movement (discussed later in Chapter 7), this may seem reasonable at first glance: why spend money on advocacy and awareness-raising campaigns, and political meetings, when beneficiaries need to be helped? But effecting long-term structural change may reduce need quicker and on a larger scale than individual interventions.

A frequently expressed way to engage policy practitioners and local councillors was to 'put myself about a bit' (chief executive, homelessness charity C, Sheffield), becoming known as one of 'the usual suspects', being willing to turn up to local forums and 'making sure you're sitting at the table'. While previous evidence suggests that less than a quarter of UK charities in a large national study felt that local statutory bodies involved their organisation in a constructive way in developing and carrying out policy (Cabinet Office, 2010; McGovern, 2017: 88–9), there was some feeling that, at a local level, where significant staff cuts had occurred since 2010 (unlike central government which has, amazingly, seen an increase in employment in the same time period), austerity had forced local authorities to open up a little to other voices, willing to deliver services differently and with partners in order to ameliorate cuts:

> One of the interesting things about the downturn, and austerity, and public sector cuts is there's been much more joined up work of statutory [and the] voluntary sector. (Chief executive, homelessness charity B, Sheffield)

The failure to 'let go' in the public sector had decreased, with the local council 'quite interested in exploring that a little bit more' (chief executive, charitable foundation), and interviewees did describe a situation where, after 'years of hammering away' (chief executive, disabilities charity, Sheffield), austerity had changed the charity–state relationship into what the sector wanted during a time of plenty (Parker, 2015).

While they may have a role to effectively persuade the government to introduce policies which will benefit the groups or issue that they represent, it was felt that politicians and policy practitioners generally lacked confidence in charity professionals as 'people that are good and know what they are talking about', commented a policy officer at an infrastructure charity. Yet despite this elitism, she also felt that government were somewhat 'scared' of charity's symbolic power. 'Whitehall and Westminster', she said, are 'pretty much terrified of anyone that's got more public support than they do', meaning that charities have an uphill struggle to with interventions like the Lobbying Act brought in to stem the tide of negative feedback. She saw this as a recent change:

Jon: Is there something about being a charity which means you are granted an audience or more respect from policy-makers?

Policy officer, voluntary sector infrastructure charity A, London:
Not any more.... I think if you asked me at the beginning of last Parliament then I think I would've said "Yes", and I still think that we have a level of public trust that Westminster is jealous of so I think that buys us a certain type or kind of audience. But we've got a minister [Rob Wilson MP, Minister for Civil Society, 2014–17] who hates us. We've got a minister who [wants to] restrict charities' ability to fundraise, which is a significant part of our income, and I'm like, well, that doesn't sound

like someone who likes or wants to support the sector. So, I don't think it necessarily gives us an audience.

So we find no consistent approach to thinking about politics and politicians across the sector, but certainly an increased feeling that the environment for the voluntary sector became tougher after the 2010 General Election, a situation charities made tougher in part by having to challenge increased poverty and derivation, but also by validating several long-existing critiques of the sector in terms of harmful fundraising practices. The final part of this chapter presents some recent cases where charity expertise is unquestioned yet can serve to simplify issues and narratives, and how interviewees reflect on how the charity world isn't always that great, and how pretending it is, is deeply problematic.

Assuming goodness

The leading LGBT rights charity Stonewall has come under criticism for presenting apparently shocking statistics about homophobia in the UK that rely on poor research methodology (McCormack, 2012, 2019). These methodologies are left to academics to unpick in largely ignored online blogs and articles, whereas national newspapers and broadcasters, those most likely to spread information about the studies, present the data uncritically in part *because* it comes from a respected charity (and in part because they themselves lack both the time and statistical skill to check [MacInnes and Cheung, 2013]). Homophobia is a stain on society, but in this case Stonewall's symbolic power as an historic champion of minority rights and liberal progress hampers society's ability to assess what's really going on. Similarly, when in 2017 several newspapers led with the headline that, building on new research from Girlguiding UK, girls were being turned off politics by the media's focus on appearance, the actual survey (Girlguiding, 2017) didn't seem to actually back this up at all. The survey highlighted lots of ways in which girls reported sexist attitudes and the lack of confidence that can come from stereotyping, all serious issues that need dealing with, but evidence for the central claim was absent (see Cowley, 2017). In another example, in 2017 a British autism charity, Autism Trust UK, was found to have promoted the infamous and unproven links between vaccines and autism, and a number of unscientific treatments (see Chivers, 2017), misappropriating the concept of a medical charity. All these examples may say more about the modern media: a lack of time and money, competition to publish as many stories as possible, headlines need to generate clicks – when a well-meaning and well-known charity comes along with a claim that sounds right and appeals to other media narratives, how many journalists are going to unpack the method and check the numbers? Very few. Is this a massive problem? Maybe not, but it does show how the symbolic notion of charity is a short-cut to credibility, and if the charity players have strategies and habitus that can, for want of a better word, take advantage of the media field, then it is in both parties' interests.

In parallel, food bank charities, given the high levels of food poverty in the UK, take a strategic approach to maximising their profile and opportunities, including how they operationalise charity's symbolic power to help with corporate 'brand polishing': as one Trussell Trust Corporate Relationships Manager told Lambie-Mumford (2017: 84), the charity sells itself to large supermarkets as both helping with their CSR agenda, and as a way to offer 'brownie points' in the eyes of the public. (The theory being, one supposes, that if a crisis or scandal hits, previously charitable activity acts as a minor bulwark against bad publicity or blowback.) On a different note, Strach's (2016) examination of the rise of breast cancer awareness organisations in the US shows how, not only are groups like Komen more recognisable to Americans than public and government-run groups that do far more research into tackling the disease, but that, in following a particular political strategy, breast cancer moved from being an ignored and unspoken issue *because* non-profit organisations branded it as pink, feminine, hopeful, and, most importantly from a political view, uncontroversial. She argues that cause-marketing campaigns for breast cancer are ubiquitous, portraying the disease as 'largely symbolic', represented by the fact that most Americans are familiar with pink ribbons but not the facts about lifetime risks, just like the symbol of the poppy (discussed later in Chapter 6) dominates over knowledge of mental health issues among military veterans. These material symbols are rewarded by *symbolic policy-making* at the expense of substantive policy-making, around issues like poverty and the environment. As King (2010: 108) puts it, breast cancer has been 'manufactured' over two decades of uncontroversial organising, suppressing conflict regarding what should be done about it, into a conservative and conformist issue: but because of its success, other campaigns follow its lead, even though it is not the most vital issue in terms of deadliness, commonality or fastest-growing (Strach, 2016: 13). This approach – finding 'the can in cancer' (a phrasing used by a cancer sufferer in

Strach's work) – does little to tackle structural issues which lead to such illnesses and prevent people from accessing proper treatment.

There is a question as to whether someone's contribution is put on a pedestal because they work for a charity. As Sean O'Neill, the *Times* journalist whose stories uncovered the Oxfam abuse scandal and cover-up (O'Neill, 2018; Charity Commission, 2019) said in the aftermath, 'What I'd like to see is [the international aid sector], which has been, if you like, cosseted and protected, face up to the culture that has festered in there and realise that that culture has to change. I think there is a political will in the UK but also overseas to make that happen … [but] there's an extraordinary code of silence around the whole place' (quoted in *Private Eye*, 2018). The lack of a profit motive provides an image of objectivity and perfection; the potentially voluntary nature provides an image of morality, able to 'influence from a moral sense' (policy officer, voluntary sector infrastructure charity A, London) and resultantly 'shape public opinion':

> We say it ourselves, there is the expectation of, "You are a charitable organisation. You are an expert in this area. You address this issue all the time so you must know what is good." Not always, let's be honest. (Policy officer, voluntary sector infrastructure charity A, London)

Jon: What does that badge, "charity", give you that being from either the public sector or the private sector doesn't give you?

Research director, youth volunteering charity, London:

> Well, the one thing you'll always get told whenever you introduce yourself as working for charity is that it's "noble". If I could have a £10 donation for every time they've said "noble", I could have probably funded one of [our] programmes. [Laughter]. [And] perhaps, people are more willing to listen from their own "guilt" perspective of, "Well, this poor lady works for charity. She's desperately trying to get some cash."

The chief executive of a charity for people with disabilities in Sheffield told me that when she was introduced to people as working for a charity, she was often faced with responses like, 'Oh, you should get something in the Queen's Birthday honours list'. She found this galling:

And I said, "Excuse me. I get paid to go to work, what on earth…?' "Yes, but you do great work." And I said, "Well, so does lots of other people." That's not, you know, in my mind, anyway, I think things like awards should go to people who don't get paid for doing what they're good at, or the things that they do. But there is that perception, isn't there, that you're doing a marvellous job? Somehow, when you're in a charity situation like I am, that you're doing a better job than someone who's working in something equally fantastic, in statutory services, and who's achieving fantastic things and changes for people, probably in a social care situation. Social workers, hospital managers, you know. I mean, my sister's a senior nurse manager and she's, you know, she's almost stoned on the way to work. And yet does a fabulous job and changes things for the better.

She finished with the obvious, yet rather sad, statement:

> There is, sometimes, an element of "you can do no wrong" in a charity setting, and you absolutely can.

None of this critique is to say that charities are not sites of objectivity and uplifting moral work, but automatic assumptions end up papering over a lot of cracks. But such assumptions are disappearing, with people less likely to listen:

> I think 10 years ago the perception of charities was possibly different. Politicians were more prepared to see charities as being on the side of the angels, for want of a better expression, as generally good and so on. (Director of policy, voluntary sector infrastructure charity B, London)

> Yes. I think it is disappearing.… It doesn't matter whether the spokesperson is a government minister, or the chief executive of G4S, or the chief executive of Barnardo's. They all present the same. They're mostly white men. They all wear suits. They speak the same language, and they present an image that they are all part of a largely invisible relationship with each other.… I think the sense of alienation of ordinary people, from anybody who sets themselves up as being in authority, or expert status, is pretty general really, and charities are included within that. (Andy Benson, NCIA)

One interviewee felt that charities 'have got away with it' for many years because they have been shielded from the 'depth of what people feel', because in general or until recently 'no one wants to criticise a charity' (Director of communications, international development charity, London):

> I think the charity sector, for a long time, has thought it is exceptional because it does good things, and therefore, it doesn't necessarily need to account [for itself].... I don't think it's okay for the charity sector to assume that, just because we work in charity and we're all really lovely, nice people doing nice things, we should be special. (Research director, youth volunteering charity, London)

The leaders of small charities found their expertise harder to parse at some points. At a local level, there was a feeling that the contractual nature of service delivery that the sector was now so wrapped up in meant the symbolic power was diminished:

> I don't think so, no. I think because there's contracts involved really, so we have a contract to provide accommodation and that's caught up in the tendering world, commissioning where it feels like we're seen often as just another provider of services. (Chief executive, homelessness charity B, Sheffield)

Similarly, the view of some organisations as 'brown rice and sandals' (chief executive, addiction support charity) meant it was harder to convince larger bodies of one's competence and expertise. The director of communications at an international development charity accounted for this as relating to the sector's lack of wider image:

> As charities have got more involved in service delivery, and therefore more involved in policy debates around that service delivery, the environments around that service delivery, campaigning and influencing policy around service delivery, more professional with paid staff, what a charity is in that context has grown far above people's consciousness of what their expectation would be. Because actually people don't think about charities from day to day. Why should they? So what happens is that when something big comes into the media they are confronted with an image that jars with their impression, and there's a dissonance. So,

there's no reason why they should be caught up-to-speed, but it's a dissonance that confronts them, and there is a discomfort with that dissonance. Of course, that's not to say that everyone working in every charity is a completely good person and no one who has ever worked for a charity hasn't run off with the money in the bank account, because we know from time-to-time it happens. But by and large, generally the charity sector doesn't have that consciousness-wrestling that some who work in the private sector have. (Director of communications, international development charity)

In one highly personal and revealing story, an interviewee who worked for a large advocacy charity (who I was speaking to on the phone and had never met) revealed to me the bullying she had experienced at a well-known organisation. 'I was scared of going to work', she told me. Working in universities, which are meant to be bastions of higher ideals but frequently are among the most unpleasant professional environments to work in, should leave me unsurprised that charities are similar, yet stories of the awfulness still shock. But the interviewee pointed out how it is the charities positioning as symbolically 'good' (and this is a charity to which I would be surprised if many people had a bad word) leads to avoiding responsibility for bad behaviour:

> I think that's sort of how they get away with it. I don't think that [her former employer] are the only ones, I think a lot of the bigger charities now, they sort of…. What's the phrase? It's hiding in plain sight, because people just wouldn't…. If I went to a journalist, say, and said, "Look, I want to tell the story of how terrifying it was working for [charity] and how awfully I was treated", they probably wouldn't believe me. People think, "It's nice, it's cuddly, it's well meaning, it's do-gooding, how can it possibly be true?" but I think that's how they get away with it.

This section has sought to outline charities' 'special' place in society as experts dealing with frequently horrific situations, how this feeds into their positioning within the delivery of welfare, and how an often unquestioning relationship between the public and charities is seen by those within it as sometimes propagating unhealthy ideals and expectations, as symbolic power works like a shield. Interviewees also noted a shift, however, that charities' special place may be being worn away, especially in the eyes of politicians, that they may not be 'heroes by default' anymore (Brittain, quoted in Birkwood, 2016).

Conclusions

Appeals for charities to do better are legion. In the *Evening Standard*, Anthony Hilton (2016) presents a list of the most egregious elements that need change: charities need to be 'authentic' and 'human', and 'explain unambiguously where the money goes'; they need to 'be clear not only about what they do, but about how it makes a difference', and 'more willing to merge with like-mined organisations to avoid duplication'; and charities must focus on 'explaining not just what worked but what was tried and did not work', while being 'honest about administration costs and able to justify them.' The point being that charities, like schools and universities (and unlike aeronautical engineering and space exploration) are a field where everyone (especially media commentators) feel they have something to say and that their insight is particularly astute. It's Hilton's next paragraph which seems to grasp this:

> But the rest of us need to lighten up too and accept that even if some charities occasionally lose the plot, the vast majority do a huge amount of good work which otherwise would not get done. (Hilton, 2016)

Acceptance that just because x or y charity or charity employee has done an awful thing doesn't mean the entire UK sector of over 160,000 organisations, 865,000 employees and 20 million volunteers (NCVO, 2019) needs reconfiguring. The 'losing of the plot' over Kids Company (discussed in the next chapter) in particular demonstrates how while growing mistrust of charity harms us all, those in the wrong are not the charity sector, but the people whose opinions are changing due to a tiny amount of malpractice. Charities can't be expected to be perfect all the time: they need to invest in strategy, including lobbying, and that lobbying has to take the form of that expected by the to-be-lobbied. When working in a voluntary capacity for various youth charities, I remember being invited to charity shindigs at both London's O2 arena and private boxes at the Lord's Cricket Grounds, in order to schmooze MPs and corporate funders. Food charities also see when they need to ride different horses in terms of CSR partnerships (Lambie-Mumford, 2017: 85), willing to move their symbolic beneficence around as it helps them. The charitable imperative means they frequently have to take the world as it is, and have little power to shift it to the world we want it to be, that being the politician's job.

But charities are not heroes by default anymore. As the then Chief Executive of Shelter Campbell Robb (2016) said, concerning a current external environment for the voluntary sector which was the most challenging he had known, trust had dropped in charities for good reason:

> If ever we had a right to tell people what to do, that's certainly not true now.

And as McDonnell and Rutherford (2017: 120) put it a year later:

> It is no longer sufficient (if indeed it ever was) to rely on charity status to convey trust and inspire confidence in the conduct of an organization.

And as an interviewee who worked for a youth volunteering charity in London told me:

> I don't think its okay for the charity sector to assume that, just because we work in charity and we're all really lovely, nice people doing nice things, we should be special.

State policy discourses which focus on a 'tougher entrepreneurial culture' undermine the moral public sphere (Milbourne, 2013: 224). The recent UK government *Civil Society Strategy* situates businesses that live up to their social responsibilities as the driving force of social transformation and builders of social value, assigning *expertise* to charities and social enterprises, but *power* to business (see Bennett et al, 2019). This chapter has shown how charity expertise can be both used and misused, but also how the environment for charities to operationalise such power of expertise has become much tougher, especially as their symbolic power for *being charities* has been reduced due to both internal and external factors.

5

The kids aren't alright: the collapse of Kids Company

This chapter tells the story of the summer 2015 collapse of Kids Company, the charity for disadvantaged young people, ostensibly situated in South London, but with smaller units in Bristol and Liverpool. Despite its relatively small geographic coverage, Kids Company received £46 million from central government between 2000 and 2015, at one time receiving over one-fifth of the Department for Education's grant budget (NAO, 2015: 13, 7). Much of the charity's reach was determined by the passion and talent of its founder and Chief Executive, Camila Batmanghelidjh. Batmanghelidjh was close to politicians from all parties, and hugely successful in encouraging politicians to keep Kids Company funded, a need made greater by her strategic and moral choice to allow children to self-refer themselves and to never turn a child she deemed in trouble away. The charity spent a great deal of public funds on some cases later deemed to be undeserving or at least not high priorities. Its collapse revealed Kids Company's over-reliance on its closeness to people at the top of government, symbolic power, and the charismatic authority of its founder rather than good governance and strategic planning. It challenged (some would say bullied) those who would talk it down, and used its access to Prime Ministers in order get special treatment. In the internet age, symbolic resonance can be disrupted in an instant. The decline of Kids Company was swift, showing how thin the veil of presentation can be. The collapse also reveals a story about the government's need for a narrative of social innovation, but the risks of losing control. By focusing in-depth on this case I want to demonstrate how symbolic power works in practice, through the prism of charismatic leadership, and through interview data reflect on how a sector comprising thousands of organisations felt about one charity causing so many problematic headlines for the field as a whole. It is a highly topical and charged case study, perhaps the most high-profile collapse of charity in recent times, and yet, barring a few short examinations (Foster, 2016; Macmillan, 2016; Molina, 2018), it has received scant attention academically.

The chapter will first provide an overview of what happened to Kids Company in 2015, and then move on to a discussion of the role of charisma within symbolic power, applying Max Weber's notion of charismatic authority both to charities as organisations and to charitable leaders. We see how charisma can be an otherworldly force of nature, vital for getting people on side, inspiring change and overcoming social injustice. But charisma has a problematic side, and in the case of Camila Batmanghelidjh's running of Kids Company, it's not enough to run a multi-million-pound charity, on which many rely, on charisma in the age of transparency and accountability. We will explore the notions of passion and professionalism within the charity sector, and how these two concepts are often thrown into opposition, and how charity leaders reflect on bridging this divide, and what the collapse of Kids Company, and the wider decline in trust in charity that we discussed in the previous chapter it was part of and helped engender, has meant for their work.

Kids Company: What happened

There are numerous news reports documenting what went on at Kids Company. The story was driven by Chris Cook of the BBC, Alan White of BuzzFeed and Miles Goslett of *The Spectator*, a story for which all three won press awards. The political and charity sector press also covered the story in detail (for the most detailed examples, see Cook, 2015a, b; Goslett, 2015, 2016; Payne, 2015; White and Curry, 2016; Weakley, 2017). There are also a number of official reports, such as those produced by the National Audit Office (NAO, 2015), the Public Administration and Constitutional Affairs Committee (PACAC, 2015) and the Public Accounts Committee (PAC, 2015). Documents do at times present a contradictory fog, and it seems that over the years many reports into Kids Company (such as auditor reports) were pushing complimentary narratives alongside raising significant warnings. This does mean that when the retribution flowed, everyone had material to back up their position. With that in mind, the following explanation of what happened is pieced together from these stories and reports, alongside Batmanghelidjh's (2017) memoir published in the wake of the closure.

In 1996, Camila Batmanghelidjh founded the charity Kids Company (it was registered with the Charity Commission in 1998). The charity served the young population of various boroughs in South London, providing counselling, arts therapy and wider social support to hard-to-reach young people, especially those experiencing multiple disadvantages, such as poverty, abuse, mental health problems, and those who may be at risk of involvement with gangs and drugs. These (occasionally controversial) interventions altered the traditional social worker relationship of detachment, instead taking a somewhat 'surrogate parent' approach to young people, but which also involved financial gifts to young people, serving as proto-pocket money and a way to keep them engaged. Batmanghelidjh argued that her interventions in young lives were much more cost-effective than either clinical therapy services or young offenders' institutions or prison, and pushed her model as the way to successfully turn dysfunctional young lives around.

The charity picked up the support of politicians from across the political spectrum, the support of well-known celebrity backers, and Batmanghelidjh herself became a national presence, appearing on political debate shows as a well-respected independent figure, someone with insight into the realities of young inner-city lives. Such support and attention led to rapid developments in the charity's remit, moving towards running campaigns, funding medical research, campaigning against public policy, alongside being contracted to deliver youth services. Its budget grew 10-fold in nine years. Batmanghelidjh dubbed herself the 'fat beggar', able to get money out of people through charisma and passion. And, surprisingly in hindsight, newspaper editors seemed loath to run stories that were critical of the charity. Despite the pressure on charities to professionalise and clearly demonstrate their impact (Carmel and Harlock, 2008; Hwang and Powell, 2009; King, 2017; Kim and Charbonneau, 2018), Kids Company remained loose about what they were achieving and how many people they were helping. As Cook (2015a) writes, many of Fleet Street's most courageous journalists didn't want to look into this inner-city charity for the dispossessed that had become part of the establishment, favoured by Princes and Prime Ministers:

> It helped that Kids Company was well connected. Its chair from 2003 until the end was Alan Yentob, the BBC's creative director. There are lots of archive photos of Batmanghelidjh in Technicolor gowns at society events – restaurant openings and art shows. The charity was embedded in that world – lots of staff members came from it too. Some celebrities even sought Batmanghelidjh's help as a therapist for their own children.

Kids Company also always lived close to the edge financially. Batmanghelidjh's principled decision to never turn a child in need away, and her belief that local authority social workers had too high a bar for which children required help, meant that the charity spent an awful lot of money: such a problem was exacerbated by reports of some children receiving incredibly large gifts to support them, such as rent payments, high-end trainers and educational scholarships. In retrospect, there are huge discrepancies in views of the extent of the client base. Social workers, journalists and the Deputy Children's Commissioner report very quiet centres and difficulty in speaking to actual children when they visited Kids Company, and the charity claimed to be helping many more children than they referred to local authority services when they closed. But the charity's safeguarding manager accounted for this gap by arguing that local authorities 'couldn't treat those without a significant mental-health diagnosis, didn't have the resources to help the ones who wouldn't engage, and wouldn't recognise the illegal ones (trafficked and migrant children) as even real' (Gee, quoted in Williams, 2015). Ultimately, reading about Kids Company, its work and its closure, is a thoroughly dispiriting experience, but one has to come to the conclusion that Kids Company may have been helping in a number of incredibly horrifying cases of neglect and disadvantage, but was not spending its money well, increasingly having trouble fundraising, and relying on a government in which significant figures ultimately lost faith in it. Auditor and central government reports were inconclusive, generally backing the charity while also questioning its financial management, but didn't bring about immediate change or challenge until 2015.

Things came to a head that summer, when civil servants in the Cabinet Office declined to provide £3 million worth of grants to Kids Company without express direction from ministers, a little-used process intended to definitively state that politicians are going against official advice. At the same time, the police opened an investigation into child safeguarding failures at Kids Company, with accusations that the charity, including Batmanghelidjh herself, encouraged a culture of silence around sexual assault and assault by clients against other clients and members of staff (BBC News, 2015). This investigation led to no charges (Laville, 2016), and Batmanghelidjh herself argued that many of these complaints were vexatious, driven by enemies in Whitehall, made because of the charity's tendency to speak out over dire child protection services locally, 'closed down malevolently and abruptly because Britain was unable to tolerate seeing its lack of welcome for vulnerable children reflected back on it' (Batmanghelidjh, 2017: xi).

When these accusations and those documenting financial mismanagement were put to Batmanghelidjh in media interviews during the summer of 2015, and in the now infamous PACAC enquiry into the relationship between Kids Company and government, it is a reasonable observation that Batmanghelidjh is undoubtedly passionate and caring, but not a detailed or precise responder to such questions, leading to a real lack of trust in Kids Company's previous ability to abide by high levels of safeguarding and financial probity. On 5 August 2015 Kids Company closed, with Batmanghelidjh decrying the 'trial by media' the organisation endured. It was later found that Alan Yentob had written to civil servants earlier that summer, arguing there would be a 'high risk' of arson attacks on government buildings, looting and rioting, and that communities would 'descend into savagery' if Kids Company were to close. Such ostentatious claims of widespread violence did not come to pass, and added to both a sense of ridicule around Yentob's role, and further evidence of Kids Company's over-stating of its impact on young lives. Yentob did raise a murder from stabbing and several suicide attempts linked to Kids Company's closure at the PACAC hearing to rebut this scorn, but this narrative was challenged by chair Bernard Jenkin MP, who reported the committee had been advised such incidents were related to ensuing drug-related conflict, as young people could no longer use Kids Company's money to pay dealers (Molina, 2018).

After the collapse and widespread media coverage, several official enquiries were launched into what had happened at Kids Company. The NAO (2015: 6) observed a pattern of behaviour which occurred six times between 2000 and 2015: that Kids Company, approaching the end of a grant term, would lobby the government for a new funding commitment; if officials resisted, the charity would write to ministers expressing fears of redundancies and the impact of service closures, and express the same concerns in the media. Ministers, perhaps as a result of these interventions, would then ask officials to review options for funding Kids Company, and officials would make the grants happen.

The NAO (2015: 7) report sets out the extent to which Kids Company was treated differently by the rest of the youth sector in terms of the Department for Education's budget, as the largest recipient of any departmental grant programme. This was true under both Labour and Conservative governments: in 2008, Kids Company received 20 per cent of the Department's grant programme with the remainder shared between 42 other charities; in 2011 it received more than twice the amount received by any other grant recipient. Whether the money was being used well is hard to determine. Numerous studies by audit firms, research consultancies and academics, and internal reports for funding purposes, provide a generally positive but still unclear picture of what Kids Company was achieving. There is no smoking gun, and Kids Company figures were always quick to challenge notions that they weren't dealing with an extensive client base. But the following summary from PACAC (2015: para 35) is quite damning in terms of evaluation:

> It has proved impossible to reconcile Kids Company's claims about its caseload with evidence from other sources. The evidence is that the figures were significantly over-inflated. This casts doubt on Kids Company's claims that overwhelming demand, rather than financial mismanagement, lay at the root of its financial difficulties. In addition, the charity's practice of calculating "reach", for example in counting a whole class of children as clients if they benefited from work with an individual student, was misleading to donors. Trustees were either ignorant of this exaggeration or simply accepted it, because it helped to promote the charity's fundraising.

When the story that the £3 million of extra government funding was conditional on Camila Batmanghelidjh stepping down as Chief Executive and the charity reorganising itself originally broke, it generated an enormous amount of online grief, instantly positioned on social media (admittedly not a good indicator of nuance) as the wicked Tories kicking a charity trying to help poor children, often from ethnic minorities. Batmanghelidjh herself said that she was being 'silenced' for speaking up against austerity. Two things struck here. First, it wasn't clear that Batmanghelidjh *had* been a particularly strident opponent of austerity compared to other elements of the sector: while she and Kids Company had launched the 'See the Child. Change the System' campaign in 2014 which aimed to investigate the crisis within children's services after Batmanghelidjh lost patience with political leadership on the issue, austerity wasn't particularly held up at the time as an explicit cause of the crisis, and the campaign was rather a damp squib after its launch (Weakley, 2015). Second, my reading saw an automatic assumption that the charity was in the right. Sociologically, I would argue that the charity's automatic (and rightfully) gained symbolic power, and Batmanghelidjh's dominant reputation, were preventing anyone thinking critically about it, echoing interviewee sentiments in the previous chapter. As Cook (2015a) concludes:

The story of Kids Company is a tale of the establishment espousing a cause, and that charity's success in leveraging that acclaim into donations. It definitely did good work. Many of its staff were very committed. But while everyone was supporting it, no one was checking whether the charity was a good investment.

The problem with charismatic leadership

The previous section has sought to provide readers with an overview of what happened at Kids Company. It is partial – the closure generated so much attention and column inches and inquiring reports and rebuttals and defences, that it is not all replicable here. But I now want to take a wider angle on what happened, looking at the prestige and symbolic authority we bestow on charismatic leaders such as Camila Batmanghelidjh. Charismatic authority rests 'on devotion to the exceptional sanctity, heroism or exemplary character of an individual person and of the normative pattern or order revealed or ordained by him [sic]' (Weber, 1968b: 212), and it is Batmanghelidjh's generally 'untouchable' heroic character (with admittedly the presence of some long-standing sceptics in the sector), wrapped in the good glow of charity, that may have led to many of the problems inherent at Kids Company and why they were missed.

In sociology, the place to start with charisma is Max Weber's examination, whose definition clearly extends far beyond its origin within analyses of the legitimacy of political authority. He sees charisma as 'a certain quality of an individual personality by virtue of which he is set apart from ordinary men and treated as endowed with supernatural, superhuman, or at least specifically exceptional qualities' (Weber, 1968a: 329), who attain 'personal devotion arising out of enthusiasm, despair or hope' (Weber, 1968a: 359). Charismatic and symbolic authority are at the centre of theoretical explorations of power in society, 'of how power was maintained and legitimated through specific cultural mechanisms' (Skeggs, 2015: 213), such as education, religion and other respected institutions, with the symbolic the key tool of legitimation in the conversion of culture to power. Charismatic authority, and wider Weberian theory, has been used to examine organisations in multiple ways, for instance McMillen (1978) uses the individual notion of charismatic authority to examine the leadership of trade unions. But the concept is less frequently applied to organisations. I would posit that society has a tendency to think of charities as organisations with charismatic authority, based on the idea that they have good intentions, volunteers who give their time unselfishly, work to tackle injustice and deprivation, all of which provide charities with a moral authority that public and private sector organisations cannot. These characteristics:

> ... are such as are not accessible to the ordinary person, but are regarded as of divine origin or as exemplary, and on the basis of them the individual concerned is treated as a leader. (Weber, 1947: 358)

This conceptualisation is of 'crucial importance for understanding of the process of institution building' (Eisenstadt, 1968: ix), with charisma a key part of the routine and continuous organised aspects of social institutions.

The term 'charisma' has been widely appropriated in contemporary Western culture (a Swiss rock band, a British record label, and a not uncommon first name in the US [Turner, 2003]), with empirical investigations into the concept emerging generally in management studies (Conger, 1993) examining the role of leadership. This focus on leadership qualities and not political power could be seen to be indicative of the difficulties Weber himself had in using the concept to explain social change:

> [I]t is unclear that it is an explanatory concept at all. It is a compelling description of a recognizable social phenomenon. But it is not the same as saying it explains the phenomenon. (Turner, 2003: 8)

Some figures such as Riesebrodt (2001) have argued that contemporary proliferation of the term 'charisma' positions it as something that can be developed in training rather than the theological roots of the heroic acts of Weberian authority (Adair-Toteff, 2005), which has led to an empty, almost banal, concept. Indeed, Adair-Toteff (2005) goes on to outline how it has been argued that Weber's concept is inherently contradictory, containing both power and weakness – a power which rests on only needing to be seen to perform 'heroic' acts; however, the fact that this authority rests on the perception of others is precisely its weakness and instability.

What are we able to say about how Weber formulates his concept of 'charismatic authority'? This formulation sees charisma as a highly personal, rather irrational and temporary or unstable form of political power, arising when particular socio-political conditions arise which facilitates the rise of individual authority (Weber, 1968b), as a captivating and extraordinary (or even daemonic) power (Jaspers, 1919) in contrast to the everyday impersonal, rational and everyday nature of traditional and legal-rational domination. Charismatic authority does not rest on compulsion (Weber, 1968b), and implies at least a minimum of voluntary compliance (Whimster, 2007), and intersects with the other forms of authority with unclear boundaries, recognising that one may not be compelled to act as a result of another's charisma – the figure may also have some legal or traditional power over you. Turner (2003) argues that the 'magic' of charisma is best summarised through the redefining of boundaries of risk, where the charismatic leader redefines what we thought was acceptable, both positively and negatively, and in making dangers more personal around a loss of face, where the leader imposes taboos (Steiner, 1967), and to violate norms or taboos professed by the leader is risky behaviour. This certainly has connotations to many themes evident in this book, whether it is ribbon culture (Moore, 2008) or poppy fascism, where the charismatic politician or (unwitting) charitable organisation imposes norms which it is then hard to transgress. 'The charismatic leader also inevitably provokes envy and is subject to destructive, envious attacks', writes Angela Foster (2016: 127), reasoning that resultantly 'there may be some truth in Ms Batmanghelidjh's claims of smear campaigns.'

In the creation of new and/or singular social institutions by innovators there is a 'continuous tension between what may be called the constrictive and creative aspects of institutions', which means that innovators try to keep control of their creations, limiting 'the attempts of other people or groups to participate in such creativity or extend its scope' (Eisenstadt, 1968: xvii). In such a formulation, entrepreneurs are natural hoarders of power and control. This inability to let go of control and open up an organisation to work with others or accept external criticism occurs in part because the innovations can engender 'hostility and alienation' among outside groups. When in operation in society, charisma has some inherent anti-institutional predispositions. As Eisenstadt (1968: xix) says in summary, charismatic leaders disavow rational scientific calculation, operate without 'elaborate systems of roles, rules, and procedures' to guide the performance of administrative functions, disdain the 'everyday economising' of setting a budget and meeting it through regular contracts, function with a 'lack of provision for succession', and because of their close relation to the very sources of social and cultural creativity, 'contain strong tendencies toward the destruction and decomposition of institutions'.

All of these elements can be seen in the way Batmanghelidjh ran Kids Company: the disavowal of institutions comes through in particular in Batmanghelidjh's view of the more bureaucratic and less personal ways local authority children's services operated, although many of her criticisms of child protection services are both valid and horrifying (see Batmanghelidjh, 2017: 115–42). Charismatics may be the bearers of great social and cultural innovation, as much as their charisma may lead to excesses of derangement and deviance. They have the potential to radically change society, and destroy it. Yet Eisenstadt wants to argue that these two forces are not as opposed as one thinks. Charisma's power is intensified by its relation to the centre of institutional life. As reported in *The Times*, 'A failing children's charity was propped up with public money because David Cameron was mesmerised by its charismatic founder', dismissing reports about financial problems because 'he was in thrall to Camila Batmanghelidjh' (Kenber et al, 2015). But it wasn't just Prime Ministers who were transfixed: as *Private Eye* was keen to point out at the time, *The Times*' own reporter Lydia Slater had only a few months earlier described Batmanghelidjh as 'the real patron saint of Christmas'.

'[A]mong the "egoistical" wishes of human beings a very important part is comprised by their quest for and conception of the symbolic order, of the "good society," and of the quest for participation in such an order' (Eisenstadt, 1968: xli). Charisma comes from a natural place: human beings' desire to participate in meaningful activities sits at the heart of social transformation. One reads Batmanghelidjh's book, and while many of the claims about Kids Company itself are disputable (for an overview, see Weakley, 2017), no one serious could doubt the picture painted about the terrible environments in which many young people are growing up in in Britain, the tremendous violence and harm being meted out to them, and the complete lack of interest in doing anything about it, especially as over-worked and under-funded social workers fail to maintain safe and loving homes for children. However, because Batmanghelidjh had relationships with politicians, and because those same politicians went against official advice, and because allegations of misconduct were raised at the same time, Britain completely failed in the summer of 2015 to have the debate it needed to have. In the wake of a general election where austerity had won, at that point few people wanted to stop and think deeply about why Kids Company was needed (although later in the year, former Primer Minister David Cameron [2015] did promise to step up state takeovers of failing children's services, a political challenge washed away in a swirl of Brexit), and why its founder may have thought it fair to stretch and break the limits of good practice rather than trust child protection services she thought weren't protecting children.

But the facts and stories emerging from Kids Company were too sexy – electricity bills not being paid so staff had to work in darkness (White, 2015); beneficiaries in their thirties (Batmanghelidjh, 2017); holding incredibly low reserves of 6 per cent of the recommended six months of cash (PAC, 2015: 9); most board members serving longer than average terms, with Alan Yentob having served as chair for 18 years (Laville, 2015); the policy of occasionally buying designer clothes and trainers for clients, or proving them with cash that was then spent on drugs (White, 2015). We find a litany of issues that are either widely agreed on within the sector as bad practice, or behaviour and decisions that just don't pass the smell test, or when viewed in total, add up to unacceptable failings. There's nothing wrong with charismatic leadership as long as a blend of skills exist within an organisation that can dampen its negatives.

There are four bases for legitimacy for voluntary sector leaders: legal, moral, political and technical (Buckingham et al, 2014: 61). Research from Taylor and Warburton (2003) and McGovern (2017) has shown that the moral legitimacy of leaders comes from their commitment to the values underpinning an organisation's social mission, and that political legitimacy comes from democratic accountability. McGovern (2017: 62) cautions that one of the big problems with establishing charitable organisations is oligarchy, 'that one group of individuals becomes so powerful that organisational democracy is threatened.' The problems of charismatic leadership that happened at Kids Company seem part of a narrative about 'founder syndrome', the idea that the initial leadership of organisations, the people who have often worked the hardest to get them off the ground, then struggle to take a step back, especially when different skills are needed as charities grow and professionalise. This concept is a problem in the charity sector where someone's moral values and principles drive their commitment to an organisation.

On a slightly different note, the lack of diversity in the upper echelons of the charity sector is also problematic (Charity Commission, 2017). Batmanghelidjh, as one of the few sector figures who cut through into mainstream debate, was the most high-profile woman of colour in the sector, but one where the complexities of her background (privately educated and fleeing to Britain after the Iranian revolution in 1979) meant that she could cut through to the establishment. As interviewees say below, many probably saw the powerful's support of *her*, this 'gregarious' and 'eccentric' woman, as a symbol of their goodness and commitment to diversity. But the lack of representation of people from diverse backgrounds in the sector is not solved by heroising or iconising the few people of colour in positions of leadership. Doing so not only takes an agential rather than structural approach to the issue, but, as in this case, it can blind everyone to bad practice, leading to a double injustice to minority communities and sector professionals. And using dramatic stories to tug at the heartstrings of politicians was a tactic employed by Batmanghelidjh. Spectacular fundraising results and force of personality meant ministers ignored warnings about the parlous state of the charity's finances:

> In this cut-throat atmosphere, it's easy to see why Kids Company cultivated friends in high places. Its success demonstrates how a single organisation, working with difficult children but without being able to show proper financial controls, was able to suck in publicity and public funds at a cost to others who were helping equally vulnerable people. (Smith, 2015)

As Macmillan (2016) says, Kids Company 'pursued a high risk political and media strategy, through its outspoken Chief Executive, in seeking to draw both attention and resources for supporting highly vulnerable and disadvantaged young people', and that things can turn awry very quickly when charities get too close to both government and the media. In the next section, interviewees reflect on Kids Company, and what it has meant for the wider charity sector. Moving on from this discussion, we then focus on a seemingly never-ending discourse in the voluntary sector about whether passion and professionalism need to be in balance in doing charitable work, and whether a perceived lack of balance in Batmanghelidjh's case (tilted strongly towards passion) shows how the symbolic power of doing good limits our desire to investigate bad practice.

Responsibility and impact

In the wake of Kids Company's collapse, ICSA, the Chartered Governance Institute in the UK, argued that the fall-out had tarnished the sector, with Head of Not-for-Profit Policy Louise Thomson (2015) strongly stating that the disaster 'smacks of an over-indulgent parent rewarding a favoured child for their inappropriate behaviour and giving in to emotional 'blackmail' demands. The charity was a cash-junkie and the government couldn't help but oblige despite its instincts and the evidence.' The consequences of the collapse of Kids Company were keenly felt by interviewees, who reported it led to a lot of 'pointing fingers' in their work. It must be said that very few individuals could point to a specific negative consequence for their organisation's own work, but more that the constant flow of damaging details, and the fact that it was an issue that they themselves would mull over with others in their field, meant it weighed heavy in many of the interviews. Some wanted to defend Batmanghelidjh:

> Yes. I met Camila. I haven't got anything bad to say about Camila. I met her and she was a passionate person ... nothing to make me think she was duplicitous in any way. She was just a very passionate caring woman. I think it is very easy to do a witch-hunt after the fact, to basically rubbish somebody's character without knowing the full facts. She is not the only person. She can't be the only person that is culpable in that scenario. (Chief executive, children's health charity)

Defences of Batmanghelidjh came either from this position of defending her character, or more commonly through critiquing the entire leadership of the organisation, and their incapacity to manage her approach. Wider criticisms were levelled at the Kids Company board of trustees, and their failure either to keep effective oversight of the charity's work and spending or Batmanghelidjh's ability to control the organisation:

> I can imagine she'll have recruited the board. She'd have got people on who were whatever, who she wanted. They were on it to support her as well, which is easily done. It's tempting. I think there's a few people I've recruited to our board. Obviously I've got people that I like and I think are good and are going to be supportive of my ideas but you can't really have everyone like that because it will fall apart. (Chief executive, homelessness charity C, Sheffield)

> I don't know how well run it was. I've not read their accounts. It is very difficult. Something must have gone wrong. Because if you put in a passionate director you are going to be incredibly blessed if they have got everything in terms of knowing how to run that business. (Chief executive, children's health charity)

I think that Kids Company is an example of a board being incapable of undertaking its governance duties, absolutely incapable because number one, they were too entrenched with the nice parts of their charity to believe that anything could be going wrong and they probably had a chief executive whose personality and persona was such that they felt they couldn't challenge. That is a very dangerous mixture. (Chief executive, hospice)

Not a great deal is known about the relationship between charity chief executives and the chair of the board of trustees, but there is some indication that relationship changes are triggered by organisational crises (Wood, 1992), and that chairs require both the 'skill' and the 'will' to use their sources of power in a contextually relevant way to shape the organisation (Cornforth and Macmillan, 2016). Trustees and boards must retain their independence, be willing to stand up to charismatic and powerful CEOs, and replace them if necessary (Micklethwait and Dimond, 2017). It feels a perfectly reasonable conclusion to make that Batmanghelidjh's entrepreneurial approach to leadership required a more careful and strict management than that provided by the laissez-faire board chair Alan Yentob.

These wider criticisms also focused on the government's relationship with the charity, both their desire to take advantage of Camila Batmanghelidjh's symbolic power:

I think that comes back again to the government giving, well, yes, it sounds like quite a bit of money. In the grand scheme of things it isn't and in the grand scheme of the other cuts that it had made to children's services it's easy to say, "Yes, but look, we give to Kids Company. Look at this eccentric women that the Tories [elevate]." (Director of policy and research, voluntary sector infrastructure charity C, London)

and their inability to treat the sector evenly:

Well that's probably the biggest failure, isn't it, that funding for that charity became the kneejerk reaction of a group of anonymous Whitehall staff members who were just told, "Save the charity." Now, if a minister came to us with a £3m payment, the rest of the hospice sector would be up in arms because they'd be saying, "Why should they get it?

What's so special about [them]? Why can't we all bid for it?" That was bypassed in this situation. No other charity was given the option of this funding. It was seen as being this is a charity that's too important and too high profile to fail, give them the money. That's entirely wrong. It can't be right. (Chief executive, hospice)

Such views echo those of sector bodies such as ACEVO (2015), which, in its response, lambasted the government for providing such 'preferment' to a charity without robust governance or widely recognised value for money. Such largesse and generosity were felt to have much wider effects, with interviewees struggling to countenance how such bad practices could not be picked up on at a senior level:

And, certainly, our funders would start to walk if we, kind of, tried to ask them to support us, and we'd got no money in the bank. So how on earth they got away with it, I've got no idea. But it's had deep and far-reaching effects on a lot of us.... I think Kids Company, across the sector, has harmed us. (Chief executive, addiction support charity, Sheffield)

This critique of structure and its relationship to personality came through in wider discussions about coverage of the collapse, and understanding that it was Batmanghelidjh's charismatic leadership in the first place that had got Kids Company to its pre-decline position – '[the government] just chucked money at them. It was just ridiculous!' (Chief executive, community foundation):

Why are we pointing fingers at the board and not necessarily pointing fingers at the government who were writing the cheques? So, I think there are a lot of lessons to learn, but I think, also, there was a risk, at the time.... I remember with my board, suddenly they were like, "Ah, do we know all this stuff?" It was like, "Yes, you do. It's fine, don't panic." I think there was a risk at the time that it's just viewed a little bit as if they were, I don't know, defrauding, and it wasn't defrauding. It was just bad governance, and there's a difference.... We all saw on the telly. We thought, "God, is it her again?" Especially the character, it was great for a tabloid, wasn't it, you know? This gregarious woman, and then.... (Chief executive, addiction support charity, Sheffield)

And ultimately, when a charity serving a disadvantaged population collapses, and as Batmanghelidjh herself constantly noted, who is it who suffers as a result? 'Now what's happened is it is the young people on the ground who have lost out…. [The leaders] will bounce back but the young people they helped won't will there? I think it is about not losing sight of that' (Chief executive, community foundation). Elite leadership is about sales, sweeping customers (or in this case, donors), off their feet, while expecting loyalty from those around them – yet ultimately leaving a trail of disappointment and loss behind as things turn out to be less than the sum of their parts (Davis, 2018). But does eliminating such behaviour mean we miss out on the passion and exuberance necessary to do the difficult work Kids Company was doing?

Passion and professionalism

> Just because we are called the voluntary sector, doesn't mean A, we're all volunteers, or B, that we're a bunch of sloppy-minded useless people who couldn't get a job anywhere else. (Chief executive, voluntary sector infrastructure charity D)

Within the charity sector, there is a long-standing debate about drawing a balance between passion and professionalism, or even if the two concepts need to be in conflict. We hold charities to a higher moral standard, and overwhelmingly they achieve it – that's why the stories when they fail can get so big. Should charities have to hold themselves to the same governance standards as government and the private sector? No, probably not, but through service delivery they are playing in the same pool as the other two, and the inherent difference of charity doesn't count for as much as it used to. I have spoken to many committed charity workers who are infuriated at bad practice in their sector – where being highly passionate about one's work can be seen as an excuse to do it badly, and that charities can use passion and voluntarism to cover for poor practice and low-quality services. Many feel the sector has been somewhat ruined because of the move towards professionalism; others that the sector doesn't understand the need for transparency and that a crisis of legitimacy is coming, to rival those that have spread through all our other institutions (see Rochester, 2013; NCIA, 2015; Wilding, 2016).

Breeze (2017: 1) tells the story of a fundraiser who, rushed off his feet, was approached in his office by an older woman who wanted a chat. Instead of perhaps doing what we could describe as the professional thing, and politely asking her to make an appointment, he made her a cup of tea and sat with her as he described the charity's relationship to her now deceased husband. She ended up becoming a significant donor for the charity. Sitting having a nice cup of tea and a chat is both allowing one's passion for talking to others to override traditional office practice, but also a deeply professional skill for a fundraiser, no different from wealthy financiers schmoozing clients at fashionable bars and restaurants (just with biscuits instead of bubbly).

There is, of course, no reason why you can't be both passionate about an issue or providing a service *and also* professional in the way you act and conduct yourself or your organisation. Yet within academic debates, and from my own experience of how people within the sector frequently talk about their work, it is still a burning issue for many (as revealed by King's [2017] autoethnography). And to ask interviewees about it, it was still an issue that they recognised as alive and problematic, particularly in managing the work of paid staff and the contribution of volunteers and how sector organisations carry themselves when performing functions in order to attract funders: '[A]ll of my staff are really passionate about what they do … but that can be taken advantage of if you are not careful. I think you can still be business-like and passionate about what you do' (Chief executive, charitable foundation). As the director of communications for a national homelessness charity told me, 'sometimes poor performance is excused because someone has a lot of passion', before going on to comment:

> I often don't think that's actually useful for the end beneficiary. We have young people who aren't actually benefitting from someone who is awful at their job but passionate about it. They're passionately awful. I'd much rather have somebody proficient, who cared but wasn't necessarily quite as passionate…. It's almost like a cruel to be kind approach where actually having someone, particularly in my area of work, where the difference between someone who is really, really good and someone who is average could affect the bottom line by £500,000, I would say. Then you think what that money could go and do, just having a really positive, passionate presence in the office, we've got a lot of that already. What we don't have a lot of is that expertise in terms of how to run a campaign or translate a Christmas appeal into a massive audience promotion. Yes, so I think I've answered my own question there. I think I would prefer someone who is slightly better at their job.

I asked the leader of a charity for people with disabilities whether she felt professionalism was seen as a persona non grata within the sector:

> I make no apologies for it whatsoever, and, I think, [professionalism] still is a dirty word. I think there is a lack of understanding. "Oh, we're losing why we're here." I've heard that once or twice. "We're losing our caring element because we're always out for the money." And, you know, that just shows a complete lack of understanding. I try and explain it by saying, "If we don't look for the money, there won't be a caring element, because we won't be here." So, you know, there's room for both, in terms of our role, I think. We've got to be professional. We've got to compete. We've got to price ourselves properly. We've got to operate full cost recovery. We've got to make sure that we don't rely too much on volunteers. We've got to make sure we get paid people in. And volunteers should also be the icing and the cherry, rather than the cake. We have to be able to function without them.

What professionalism meant in such contexts was an ability to measure impact, and account for how and why money was being spent:

> One of the things that charities and social enterprises, so the voluntary sector as a whole does very well, is that we can be quite innovative and we can sometimes take a risk on a way of doing things. I don't think we want to lose that ability, because, at the end of the day, we are independent. We're not part of the NHS or part of the local authority or government, and that's really, really important. So, you know, that doesn't mean that we can't be professional in what we do. When I mean "professional", I don't mean, you know, "corporate" or that everything has to be about paid staff, because I think volunteers in the voluntary sector do, you know, a vast amount of really, really good work. But, I think there's been a lot of money wasted in the voluntary sector, and I am shocked now if I speak to charities who aren't able to, say, give some form of measurement of the impact that they're having, whatever that may be, because I'd be arguing, "Well, how do you know what you're doing?" (Chief Executive, addiction support charity, Sheffield)

Interviewees identified areas such as fundraising and communications, the growth in the use of technology, extensions in fundraising activities and increased involvement in policy work as areas where the sector has undergone a certain transformation, 'but then that has also brought it head-butting up to political interests, more media scrutiny, political scrutiny' (Director of communications, international development charity, London). The charities that get talked about and receive media coverage fall into the 9 per cent of organisations that have paid members of staff, an observation that many *within* the sector fail to recognise, leading to wider misconceptions:

> I don't think as well, we don't necessarily *get* that picture within the charitable sector. So how is the rest of the society going to have that understanding that actually most charities are small, really local, depend on the dedicated work of just a few people and on incredibly slim resources? (Chief executive, youth volunteering charity, London)

But this move towards professionalism, including competing for money and contracts, has brought a different level of scrutiny. Charity has been changed in the process, less able to use its symbolic power, because it is too redolent of or similar to the wider public sector, echoing the discussion from Chapter 4:

> Are charities fair game? Yes absolutely. [The public] see us as just another set of big institutions. Even though the scale of charities is completely different to most big public bodies, and so on, I think they have a view of the voluntary sector that is about kitchen table voluntary action. It's not about large institutions with paid professional staff. (Director of policy and research, voluntary sector infrastructure charity C, London)

> Questions around public trust have become more acute. Because questions that get thrown at the public sector or the corporate sector around ethics, and behaviour, and operations, are more fair game. [Charities] are not just amateur organisations. The big ones, anyway. At the other end of the spectrum.... (Director of communications, international development charity, London)

The idea that the non-profit sector is a long-standing major vehicle for promoting and delivering social justice and fairness (Skocpol and Fiorina, 2004), engaged in 'moral work' that builds, upholds and reinforces the 'good society' (Garrow and Hasenfeld, 2010), is seen by many as under pressure from the need to professionalise. A pursuit of efficiency, and doing more with less in a difficult funding environment, means a move to hiring specialists with experience rather than well-meaning amateurs (King, 2017). They are caught between the need for dedication and sacrifice from (voluntary) employees and delivering 'professional' services. The shift from a largely volunteer workforce to paid professionals is well documented (Hwang and Powell, 2009), which can create more effective management and better 'customer' satisfaction (Kim and Charbonneau, 2018: 4), but has also been shown to threaten the sector's distinctiveness, resulting in increased bureaucratisation (see King, 2017: 242), rendering charities' 'social origins, ethos and goals absent, as if these are politically and socially irrelevant' (Carmel and Harlock, 2008: 156). There is also some indication that lower wages pervade in non-profits in the US, as there is a 'pervasive yet unspoken social expectation that those doing "lofty" or "meaningful" work should sacrifice the financial compensation that they deserve' (Kim and Charbonneau, 2018: 17).

Camila Batmanghelidjh was obviously hugely passionate about the work of Kids Company: 'She was just a very passionate caring woman' (Chief executive, children's health charity). It was her organisation, her approach to child welfare writ large, and that passion clearly enabled the organisation's work to be done and children to be helped. But the children aren't being helped any more, the kids aren't alright. Instead, 1,900 young people were referred for support to local authorities, out of the 36,000 reportedly reached and 18,000 reportedly offered intensive support by Kids Company, another controversial facet of the collapse (see PAC, 2015: paras 26–36; see also NAO, 2015). And given that local authority youth services budgets were slashed by £387 million from 2010/11 to 2015/16 (UNISON, 2016), as councils tried to push all their funding toward the even more essential services like social care and child protection, no one was being helped, with a 63 per cent increase in homelessness between 2010 and 2017 (DCLG, 2017), 4.1 million children living in poverty (DWP, 2019), and many other indicators of social degradation. No one wants the passion to be managed out of charities; no one wants charities to lose sight of their central mission in order to please abstract funder requirements (King, 2017); and no one wants children in need to be turned away because of artificial limits and the means-tested suffering of poverty plus a pound. But interviewees were aware of the balance they had to find, how bad practice breeds worse long-term conditions, and that waste ultimately leaves the children abandoned, which helps nobody and damages everybody.

Conclusions

The Kids Company story is not that singular. Charities frequently fail. Since Kids Company collapsed, we have seen other national charities, such as 4children, vinspired and the Lifeline Project, close in a similar way, although receiving only a scrap of the attention the collapse of Kids Company received. Given the precarious state of many organisations' finances, we can expect charities doing important, locally valued work to continue to close, especially if less is being donated to charity in the UK (CAF, 2019). But few stories hit home as much as this one. When a similar story unfurled – where the LGBT domestic abuse charity Broken Rainbow collapsed after receiving £1.4 million from the Home Office (Strudwick, 2017), with its leadership, the government and the Charity Commission all heavily criticised by the NAO (2017) – the story made barely a dent in the media, partly because of the surfeit of other news at the time, but also because of the lack of media pull: no deep connection to the decisions of Prime Ministers and Cabinet ministers, and a lack of high-profile leadership. What happened at Kids Company is both memorable and important to analyse, because of the profile of the characters involved, the connections to government and the elite which encouraged extensive media coverage, and the fact that there is so much material to explore, given it was a relatively quiet news summer after a general election. In some areas of the press and civil society, the demise of Kids Company brought *schadenfreude* masquerading as concern for abandoned children living in poverty, for negligent use of public money, or for an absence of good governance.

Applying the theoretical framework I've worked to develop here, Kids Company is a fundamental example of the problems with the symbolic authority that the charitable have, and has yet to receive significant critical analysis within academia. We can expect it to stick in the mind, as stories of 'worst charities' tend to stay with the public (Jones et al, 2018). But as we have seen with the mixed stories of declining trust in the charity sector, the worry for charity workers is always what happens if they get tarred with the same brush. How do they avoid being lumped in with the bad practice and failings happening at one, ultimately quite local charity that had very specific issues in its structure and the personalities behind it? What wider social impact occurs as a result of the public shaming of Batmanghelidjh, Yentob and others? Kant (1996), in *The Metaphysics of Morals*, cautions against kicking people for failing to do good well enough, and is worth quoting at length here:

> The intentional *spreading* (*propalatio*) of something that detracts from another's honor – even if it is not a matter of public justice, and even if what is said is true – diminishes respect for humanity as such, so as finally to cast a shadow of worthlessness over our race itself, making misanthropy (shying away from human beings) or contempt the prevalent cast of mind, or to dull one's moral feeling by repeatedly exposing one to the sight of such things and accustoming one to it. It is, therefore, a duty of virtue not to take malicious pleasure in exposing the faults of others so that one will be thought as good as, or at least not worse than, others, but rather to throw the veil of benevolence over their faults, not merely by softening our judgments but also by keeping these judgments to ourselves.... (1996: 212; original emphasis)

The combination of charisma and charity's symbolic power is a heady mix. When in 2019 the World Wildlife Fund was found to have funded paramilitary anti-poaching units that committed physical and sexual violence and murder (Warren and Baker, 2019), the Charity Commission's (rather understated) response was that, 'atrocities and human rights abuses ... are at odds with everything we associate with charity' (quoted in Warren et al, 2019). This central idea, however, that there are things we associate with charity and things we don't, and that those things we do are somewhat intangible and undefined but there's a common understanding of what they might be, means that recognising the realities of charity, and being inquiring rather than cynical, is tremendously important. It's important for democracy and the functioning of the welfare state at a time of austerity, inequality and need, because as Kant says, every scandal weakens the impulses of the morally good, increasing scepticism and eroding trust. Camila Batmanghelidjh used her charisma and the symbolic credit she got from the powerful for doing good, but while we expect charities to be given a little more opportunity and freedom to innovate and bend the rules, such power clearly only goes so far. This chapter has examined in-depth one case study that reveals how the *je ne sais quoi* of charity operates in practice, using an example that was once seen by many as beyond reproach. The next focus – the yearly debate over the remembrance poppy – is similarly contentious but reveals a lot about the social embeddedness of charity, and how it gets (mis)used symbolically, and weaponised in a culture war ordinarily far away from the charity world.

6

Poppy fascism

"Babs, what would you say to those who don't want to wear a poppy?"

"Well, they can go sod off for all I care." (Dame Barbara Windsor, Sky News, 2015)

You can set your watch by it. As the clocks go back, as we move from summer to autumn, and as birds start to plan their southerly migration, a distinct call can be heard across Britain. 'DISRESPECT!' it shouts, 'BETRAYAL OF OUR BRAVE WAR DEAD!' What that noise tells us is that Britain's tabloid press has got its teeth into its latest victim, usually a left-leaning public figure or media organisation or insufficiently supportive private company that has committed some imagined slight against the Poppy Appeal, the annual fundraising collection for The Royal British Legion, the voluntary organisation for war veterans, especially focused on commemorating service during the First and Second World Wars. Despite the Royal British Legion (2015) writing very clearly on its website that:

> There is no right or wrong way to wear a poppy. It is a matter of personal choice whether an individual chooses to wear a poppy and also how they choose to wear it.

such advice seems to struggle to enter public consciousness. 'Veterans urge boycott of motorway services after poppy ban', declares the *Daily Express* (Pilditch, 2014); 'BBC snubs official poppy appeal song by refusing to put it on radio playlist', contributes the *Daily Mirror* (Lines, 2014); and for balance, 'Cookie Monster wears a poppy on *The One Show* leaving BBC viewers baffled' (Gillett, 2016). To talk about the poppy is frequently to take a side in a culture war issue, that one side didn't realise it was fighting. People forgetting, or a broken pin, or a perfectly reasonable personal or practical choice are all held up as deep political statements, 'bans' and 'boycotts'. The poppy engenders a lot of conflict: even generally hagiographic books about the poppy (for example, McNab, 2018: 7–8) dwell on the social and cultural tensions around it, taking issue with the sentimentalisation of war, the rendering of war as poetic or of those who fight it as 'heroes'.

This chapter wants to explore the annual reaction to the Poppy Appeal, first, by providing a selection of the many examples of 'poppy fascism' that have appeared over recent years, then, by locating this yearly consternation within a wider discussion of nationalism and Britain's postcolonial identity. Data is then introduced from interviews on how those working in the charity sector view the poppy debate, the practicalities of having such a dominant charity symbol, and why this one symbol has such cultural and symbolic power. While the poppy is certainly not a traditional charitable symbol or icon, like a wristband or ribbon whose sales focus purely on fundraising and awareness, it is a fundraising tool, although one focused on remembrance and commemoration. In Sarah Moore's work on the awareness ribbon, her participants viewed such ribbons as 'charity symbols' akin to the remembrance poppy (Moore, 2008: 6), and the yearly poppy collections serve the purpose of raising much-needed funds for a population in need, under the auspices of a registered charity, with a fundraising income of £50.5 million in 2017/18 from the Poppy Appeal and more from other fundraising activities (The Royal British Legion, 2018a). While the poppy has singular symbolic characteristics and properties, I think it fair to discuss it in a wider exploration of charity symbols.

Just another grieving symbol?

Ironically, and we assume to the ignorance of many of those shouting the loudest, the remembrance poppy is not actually a British invention. An American university professor, Moira Michael, who, after reading John Alexander McCrae's poem 'In Flanders Fields', was motivated to convince the veterans' association of her home state of Georgia and then the American Legion to adopt the poppy as its symbol of remembrance, and Anna Guérin, a French YWCA member, who, as well as lobbying her own country, travelled to Australia, Canada, New Zealand and the UK to lobby the authorities there to adopt the poppy, are the true inspirations behind the symbol's adoption (McNab, 2018: 70–80). Since 1921 in England, the poppy has been sold to raise money for The Royal British Legion, with manufacturing taking place at a dedicated Poppy Factory in Richmond, followed by a Scottish Poppy Factory in Edinburgh (making a slightly differently designed poppy) in 1926. It is estimated that, adjusted for inflation, the Poppy Appeal has raised nearly £3 billion since its launch, about £1 every second (Kalia, 2018). It is one of the most recognisable symbols we have.

Poppy historian Chris McNab (2018: 8) is correct to say that the right way to think about war is carefully and, above all, soberly: buying the poppy gives us the chance to 'reflect upon our own social, historical and personal relationship to war', which is 'essential if we are to comprehend present and future threats properly.' Such seriousness of purpose is commendable, but it is a lack of seriousness which most aggravates in the behaviour of the poppy warriors: the turning of sober and meaningful reflection into a competitive game of one-upmanship does a disservice to those things that are lost in conflict. Such strife today operates under the banner of what has become known as 'poppy fascism', 'the modern trend which insists that everyone who appears on British TV must be seen wearing a poppy, or else be stigmatised as a cold non-patriot who cares nothing for the wartime dead, and it's a tendency that's very much alive, especially on social media' (Walsh, 2014).

In 2006 the Channel 4 newsreader Jon Snow (2006) wrote a blog in which he described his reasons for not wearing a Remembrance Day poppy on air. Explaining that 'typical' comments such as 'I'm disgusted at Jon Snow for refusing to wear a poppy' came regularly into the newsroom, Snow said that his decision was based on a desire not to wear political or politicised symbols while reading the news. He went on to say that charities and causes – such as AIDS awareness organisations, the Royal National Institute of Blind People, Marie Curie and others – regularly sent him symbolic tokens to wear, but he felt it was his duty as an impartial newsreader to refuse them all. Instead, Snow explained how he would wear the poppy off air, in his private life, but there was 'a rather unpleasant breed of poppy fascism out there – "he damned well must wear a poppy!"' Four years later, Snow (2010) had similar complaints levelled against him by an online commenter. Responding directly to this comment, Snow replied,

> Compelling people to wear poppies because YOU think they OUGHT to is precisely the Poppy fascism, or intolerance, that I have complained of in the past. On yer bike Stan [the commenter], with or without a poppy, it's all your own free choice…. Hitler lost the war!

This later interaction brought direct opprobrium from *The Daily Mail* newspaper, in which former Labour politician Roy Hattersley (2010) wrote an article highly critical of both Snow's use of the word fascism ('He should remember that many of the men and women to whose sacrifice we pay tribute on Remembrance Sunday died to save the world from fascist dictatorship'), and his choice to not wear a poppy.

Hattersley saw this as an abdication of responsibility by a public figure who may have viewers follow him ('How many young men, who ape the garish ties and exotic socks which he affects, are saying: "Jon Snow is right. Let us swim against the tide of public opinion and show that we cannot be bullied by convention. No poppies for us"'), potentially leading to lower donations to The Royal British Legion. (Whether Jon Snow's socks have inspired political campaigning among Britain's youth is unknown, but they definitely haven't.)

But Snow, despite coining the phrase poppy fascism in response to his critics, is far from the only public institution to receive such condemnation. *The Guardian* (Media Monkey, 2013) jokes over the annual drama 'BBC Poppywatch', when any perceived snub to war veterans was immediately jumped on by its foes in the media, or when the BBC acted pre-emptively to stop potential complaints. These included two occasions in 2003 (three years before Jon Snow coined the term 'poppy fascism') where a poppy was digitally superimposed on presenter Jonathan Ross (BBC News, 2003) – ironically, Ross only forgot to wear a poppy for this broadcast because the show was filming ahead for several episodes, some of which were to be broadcast after Remembrance Sunday, and he and the production crew kept putting on and taking off the poppy, and messed up one of the broadcast dates – and an occasion where newsreader Huw Edwards felt compelled to put on a poppy halfway through a news broadcast due to a viewer complaint received over the phone (Byrne, 2003). The notoriety of such stories leads to action by the BBC, which then falls over itself in showing respect: the corporation became criticised for having its presenters wear poppies *too early*, outside of the official two-week campaign period (Rowley, 2010), and led to accusations that these early poppies were recycled from the previous year, a situation which, according to one poppy seller, causes 'ill feeling' among sellers if people are already wearing them (Thomas, 2010). Whether poppies being pinned to Sesame Street characters appearing on anodyne chat shows causes similar feelings is not known. More recently, when the England cricketer Moeen Ali was pictured not wearing the poppy in a group photograph with his teammates all wearing one, social media users were quick to call him not fit to wear the shirt, and call for him to be dropped (Gani, 2017), many assuming his Muslim faith to be an impediment to his patriotism. The actual truth, which needed proving with other photographs, that he had been wearing one and it had fallen off, seems rather dull and prosaic by comparison. These stories are both funny and exasperating, but more importantly, are about much more than the poppy.

In an article for *The Telegraph*, Guy Walters (2010) expresses wariness at the 'growing culture that forces us, as individuals, to publicise our remembrance and our grief', which he links to populist calls to 'show us you care', most vividly flung at the Queen after Princess Diana died in 1997. Walters continues:

> [U]nfortunately for The Royal British Legion, its field of poppies has been overrun by grief flora and other sympathy junk.... It is in danger of being seen – sadly – as just another grieving symbol. How many of us really notice a newsreader wearing a poppy? And I hazard that most newsreaders give poppies no more thought than they give their ties – they are just part of the uniform.

This idea that people on television wearing poppies do not actually get a say or do not think about the act is brought home in a 2007 clip from the comedy panel show *Have I Got News For You*. The American comedian Reginald D. Hunter comments on a picture of former UK Prime Minister David Cameron that, 'He's wearing one of those things on his lapel like we got on!' (the clip is still available on YouTube). The other panellists clearly look uncomfortable, demonstrating that Hunter is not meant to say out loud that he does not know the nature or significance of what he is wearing. Perhaps a make-up artist or member of production staff has put it on him blindly to avoid complaints. Hunter's disarming statement, 'What's it supposed to mean? It's about AIDS or something?', demonstrates the extent to which the BBC's fear of criticism for looking unpatriotic has led them to act unreflexively and contributes to the diminution of the poppy, at the behest of the very patriots who claim to be upholding it:

> The BBC lives in terror of someone appearing on one of its programmes without a poppy and thus sparking a round of "BBC presenter in poppy snub" stories in the papers. If you appear on the BBC during this period you will find people on hand to pin a poppy on anyone not already sporting one. To my mind this slightly misses the charitable, not to mention voluntary, purpose of the exercise. (Murray, 2012)

In a lengthy article for *The Guardian*, commentator Michael White (2010) writes of a bullying media, led by *The Sun* and the *Daily Mail*, the 'armchair generals safe in our great newspaper offices', who engage in the 'habit of demanding ostentatious loyalty'. He continues:

> *The Sun* likes to present itself as the paper that supports
> our boys and it probably does so from a mixture of honest
> endeavour and commercial calculation. But it is one of
> nature's bullies; it can't help itself.

Similarly, conservative commentator Douglas Murray (2012) argues
that politicians try and 'out poppy' each other to appear more
empathetic and patriotic, and do so in order to ease their guilty
consciences, which Murray feels they must have due to low pay in the
armed forces and the appalling treatment of injured service personnel
once they return. Do the general public share in this guilt, buying a
poppy every autumn being enough to assuage such feelings?

These themes are attached to wider charity sector discussions and
sociological issues about the presentation of self in everyday life
(Goffman, 1959), and the role of spectacle on social media discussed
earlier in Chapter 3. There is no room for discussion here, but the 'Ice
Bucket Challenge' would be one such public display of charity which
both raised an incredible amount of money (over US$100 million)
for ALS, but also left some people uncomfortable with how it was
taken over as an act of social pressure and performance. In a similar
vein, Helene Snee's (2013) research on volunteering during gap
years presents the moral distinctions and 'worth' present in some
acts but not others – a hierarchy of giving or altruism, if you will.
As referenced earlier, Bekkers and Bowman (2009: 894) posit that
since 'volunteering involves a cost to the volunteer it constitutes a
credible sign that says, "You can believe I'm a good person because I
volunteer"', just as Jones (2006) argues that giving has the potential
to be seen as a demonstration of moral worth, and that participation
in such acts can be a way for individuals to gain such symbolic credit
(Bourdieu, 1984; Wilson and Musick, 1997).

The case of the poppy demonstrates the symbolic power of a
charitable cause. The Royal British Legion are not the 'fascists' in this
case; it is a certain section of the UK media and commentators and
below-the-line respondents with nothing better to do who take the
alleged snub of war veterans by various public personalities to further
their agendas of faux nationalism and outrage, and in order to attack
the national public broadcaster. In this case, the media are capable of
operationalising that symbolic power, and applying symbolic violence
and stigma to individuals who make private decisions with which they
disagree. This public morality spat is a vivid example of the shaming
ability of charity (as a concept, not of the organisations themselves).
As Walsh (2014) posits in a newspaper comment piece about the large

'river of poppies' art memorial displayed at the Tower of London in 2014 to commemorate 100 years since the start of the First World War, if an individual must be coerced or bullied into sympathy and remembrance, the act is rendered worthless. It is when thought of in such a way that the poppy is not part of the objective structures of society, but is determined by the subjective roles and actions of agents within it, becoming not a symbol of remembrance, but of moral worth.

In November 2016, the English Football Association (FA) and the UK government entered into a fight they symbolically couldn't lose, it being against one of the few organisations less popular than they – world football's governing body FIFA – and on a subject – the right for the England football team to wear poppies on their shirts – with broad public support. FIFA had decreed the poppy a 'political symbol' and therefore banned it from players' shirts, similar to how Swiss players of Albanian descent were fined for making pro-Kosovo gestures in a match against Serbia. In a match against Scotland, the English FA had requested the right to wear a poppy embroidered on armbands in tribute to the armed forces, many of whom would be represented at the match, and with a minute's silence. This was rejected and England, Scotland, Wales and Northern Ireland were fined for wearing the poppy symbol on armbands, although a year later the rules were changed so that 'commemorative symbols' would be allowed if both countries participating in a match agreed to the arrangement. The FA's hypocrisy was made clear, however, as they fined Manchester City manager Pep Guardiola for wearing a yellow ribbon in support of Catalan independence. 'If there's a real-world example of "virtue-signalling", it is surely having a shouting match over the right of 22 football players to wear a poppy they will soon forget, for the benefit of a crowd with other things on their mind', wrote Stephen Bush (2016) in the *Independent*, whereas actually putting measures in place to help ex-armed forces personnel would cost money, time and political capital, 'while shouting about poppies is practically cost-free.'

A spokeswoman for The Royal British Legion insisted at the time that the poppy is not 'a sign of support for war', but instead a symbol of 'remembrance and hope', telling the BBC, 'We see no reason why the poppy should be banned from players' shirts as it is not a political symbol' (BBC News, 2016). Others writing at the time of the dispute disagreed: poppies are a political symbol, argued Paul Breen (2016), an expert in national identities, who wrote that:

> Many Northern Irish unionists see the poppy as theirs, representing those who died for their freedom. Many

nationalists see the poppy as representing the army that denied them independence in the 1920s and that returned in the late 1960s, bringing with it such events as Bloody Sunday. For them and others, the poppy is not a universal or unifying symbol. It is seen as a celebration and remembrance of Britain's dead, Britain's victories, and Britain's freedom.

Writing about humanitarian relief agencies' desire to remain 'pure' as they aim to deliver their values without fear or favour, Krause (2014: 115) states that sacred symbols in political discussions (such as the nation, or the people) rub up alongside this aim and pollute this purity. The poppy sits at the intersection of charitable aims (to raise money and awareness for a deserving populace) and political aims (to remember the nation's conflicts and sacrifices). There is a reason that the Republic of Ireland footballer James McClean receives hideous abuse every year for his decision not to wear the poppy. While The Royal British Legion are at pains to rightly point out that it should not be an expectation to wear one, you cannot look at the abuse, the debate and the fact that Prime Minister Theresa May stood in Parliament to make the FA's case, and come to the conclusion that the poppy has not become deeply politicised. You might not think it should be, but it has.

A Britain deeply uneasy with itself

Paul Gilroy (2002: xxiv) writes of the downsizing of the symbols of Englishness and Britishness as the nation experiences the 'weird post-colonial pageantries of national decline'. Similar to the poppy, modern British nationalism has been reduced to symbols which cannot bear the weight of the complex colonial and violent narratives they need to:

> [T]he memory of World War II has been stretched so thin that it cannot possibly accomplish all the important cultural work it is increasingly relied upon to do. A generation for whom knowledge of that conflict arrives on a long loop via Hollywood are nonetheless required to use a cheaply-manufactured surrogate memory of it as the favoured means to find and restore their ebbing sense of what it means to be English. (Gilroy, 2002: xxv)

On an annual basis, nationalist figures and the media ask the poppy, and by extension The Royal British Legion, to do cultural work, serving a very narrow purpose. The poppy is, should be, primarily a memorialising and charitable fundraising tool, consumed to push money towards a worthy cause. But to pretend that's all it is, is disingenuous. It is a deeply political symbol, commemorating a deeply political act in which millions have died. By using it as a judgemental signifier, proponents of a certain form of Britishness use the purported concept of charity, and a depoliticised remembrance, to say there is only one way of being in this culture. To display any particular charity iconography is to say that that one is more important to you than another. While a subliminal peer pressure exhorting others to wear yellow AIDS ribbons or Make Poverty History wristbands may exist (Moore, 2008), commentators rarely write screeds demanding that other people wear them. If you believe that Bartholomew's (2015) previously discussed 'virtue signalling' is a thing (and to reiterate, for some this will merely be known as 'doing nice things' or 'believing in social justice'), then poppy fascism is its apotheosis. Remembrance becomes, in these circumstances, much like the need to be seen to give money to charity, the need to be *seen* to be remembering or for others to see you remembering (Liew, 2017), which isn't actually remembering.

George Orwell (2018), writing in 1945, argued that nationalism affects our thinking on nearly every subject. This was not just about nations, but is an inherent tendency to be against something, to classify 'like insects' entire issues, notions or peoples as good or bad. This leads people to place one's own nation 'beyond good or evil and recognizing no other duty than that of advancing its interests' (Orwell, 2018 [1945]: 2), a certainty of being right, and an ability to look past atrocities committed by one's own side:

> The smallest slur upon [the nationalist's] own unit, or any implied praise of a rival organization, fills him with uneasiness which he can only relieve by making some sharp retort.... He will show great sensitiveness about such things as the correct display of flags, relative size of headlines and the order in which different countries are named. (Orwell, 2018 [1945]: 9–10)

This sense of loyalty is so strong that 'pity ceases to function' (Orwell, 2018 [1945]: 29). Building on Orwell's problem with patriotism 30 years later, Rothman (1978: x) cautions that the claim to be acting benevolently has become suspect: 'if the last refuge of the scoundrel was once patriotism, it now appeared to be the activity of "doing good" for others, acting in the best interests of someone else.' Poppy watching requires the melding of patriotic fervour with the invasive regulation that only comes with pointing out other people are doing something wrong in the interest of 'the greater good'. There is an argument that Britain has staked its national sense of self on a partial myth of the Second World War, all fortitude, defiance and Blitz spirit that manages to overlook the horrors of Empire, foreign policy failures like Suez, and the fact that were it not for US and Russian intervention, that war would have been lost (Elledge, 2017). What matters in these 'very public exhibitions of "remembrance" is precisely that they be public: to be seen to be mourning the fallen is the loyalty oath of the contemporary British state … yet what sort of state is it that doesn't make adequate provision for those wounded, or the dependants of those killed in its service, out of the public purse' (Self, 2014).

Arguing against a conception of nationalism that somehow places it on the periphery of ideology and action, social scientist Michael Billig (1995) cautions that such thinking places nationalist tendencies as the property of 'others' rather than 'us'. In a time of Brexit, Trump, Putin and Modi, such a complaint feels slightly out of date – the largest countries in the world are pursuing avowedly nationalist policies, kicking back against globalism. But Billig points out that such eruptions of explicit nationalism don't come from nowhere, instead drawing on familiar images, clichés and symbols reproduced daily that reinforce one's sense of self-identity and of one's country. In trying to deconstruct the deeper meaning of the flag that is not waved on the top of a barricade but instead hangs limply in a Post Office or school hall, Billig talks of a 'banal nationalism' that enables the West to reproduce its ideology without having to frame it, or have others frame it, *as* ideological. The day-to-day reproduction of symbols helps establish a natural, moral order, where their unobtrusiveness stems from familiarity. This familiarity is because our identity is embedded in the routines of social life, and is something of which we have to be watchfully suspicious. The political imagination, he writes, is so bound up with such identity-building that nationhood is considered worth more than the individual life. We all, in little words and phrases, and little actions like cheering our county's Olympians or wearing certain tokens, prime ourselves, continually renewing our (national) identity. Ribbons, like poppies and flags, are a fundamentally conservative symbol, showing 'support for the "hard fought" status quo … a sense of belonging and a shared belief in the British way of life' (Moore, 2008: 150). Banal nationalism holds public approval not because of some overarching national project, but because of the tremendous trifles of blue passports, and penalty shoot-outs, and poppies.

Poppy fascism is symptomatic of what the author Douglas Coupland labels in *Generation X* 'legislated nostalgia', that forces people 'to have memories they do not actually possess' (Hatherley, 2017: 19). (It is not surprising that during the Brexit vote it was revealed that those UK citizens who either fought in or were alive during the Second World War were less Eurosceptic than the generation who came after them [Devine, 2019].) Some politicians are expert at using the past as a weapon (Hatherley, 2017: 12), expecting a 'patriotic correctness' (Nowrasteh, 2016) where politics 'becomes increasingly closed through an assumption or imposition of consensus in the name of management. Antagonistic interest cannot be voiced or even made visible' (Jones et al, 2017: 59). Writing about Orwell's critique of nationalism, Gilroy (2004: 26) outlines how (authoritarian) political actors seek to orchestrate nationalistic moods in order to 'close down every opportunity for a variety of reflection': dissent can have positive functions, yet we make it seem like 'low-grade treachery'.

For some reason it is the Blitz that has become the touchstone for Britain's sense of itself, held up as the right way to do community spirit. This sepia-tinged nostalgic view of the simpler (yet much more violent) times is all part of a lazy national narrative that happens to forget about both the myriad other wars British troops have fought in since, conflicts unable to command a similar 'mythological space' (Gilroy, 2004: 96), and the postcolonial atrocities that are much too negative for national consideration. 'Deluded patterns of historical reflection and self-understanding are not natural, automatic, or beneficial' (Gilroy, 2004: 3), but instead of reflating imperial myths and history, we need 'grim and brutal' exposure to colonial pasts and to critique the imperialist nostalgia that surrounds us today. In the last few years, a number of UK-based authors have engaged in such a debate within accessible books and the popular press (see, for example, Akala, 2018; Andrews, 2018; Eddo-Lodge, 2018; Hirsch, 2018). It should be possible to view the unhelpful reactions to the poppy, and not the poppy or the act of remembrance itself, as emblematic of the fact that empire is both part of Britain's history but also part of its day-to-day politics, where one gets to promote one's patriotic, altruistic virtue, but only in a pre-ordained way.

The poppy and today's charity

I don't think it is a good thing when you have these cultural phenomena like Remembrance Sunday, where then the organisations around them are seen as beyond reproach.

It's not work that I've done, or even looked at, but one of the things that I am aware of is that the number of charities that are about ex-servicemen, and military, is huge. It's thousands. I don't know to what extent they are accountable or held to account. They receive large amounts of money from the public on a rather unquestioning basis. (Director of policy and research, voluntary sector infrastructure charity C, London)

Of the 23 interviewees, 13 said that they wore a poppy pretty much every year, 2 said they generally wore one but 'not every year' (Director of policy, voluntary sector infrastructure charity B) or 'from time to time' (Director of communications, international development charity), and 6 said they never wore one (2 interviewees declined to answer the question). (One, prompted by our discussion being the first time she said she'd reflected on the poppy more widely, avowed not to buy one in the future.) This discussion was a fascinating part of the conversations: I left the simple question 'Do you wear a poppy?' until last, and then usually asked 'Why?' as a follow-up if the interviewee gave a short answer. These two simple questions, especially 'Why?', frequently led into a huge discussion about a eclectic range of topics: issues associated with the rise of veterans charities such as Help for Heroes ('[they] seem to have the more contemporary story' [Director of communications, international development charity]), the importance of family connections ('Both my grandfathers … one was in the Navy and one was in the Air Force' [fundraiser, homelessness charity C, Sheffield]), the difficulty in engaging younger generations (such as interviewees' own children) in discussions about the two World Wars ('the symbol of the poppy, how relevant is that to people who are 18 now?' [Andy Benson, NCIA]), and, principally in focus in this study, the role of social pressure and public displays of remembrance wrapped up in social debates about the poppy.

In my research career, I have done dozens of interviews with people who work in charities, often at a mid to high level within organisations. The principal observation I've taken is that the people who work for charities – ostensibly middle class, university educated, socially liberal, engaged in the world – like talking about wide-ranging topics, trying to locate what they do and experience in wider narratives. For a sociologist, seeking to tie charity trends to wider shifts within society and culture, this is amazingly helpful. The people I speak to generally have views about subjects wider than their professional purview – what's going on in the sector, how this relates to politics, what the big challenges facing people today are – which presents quite voluminous transcripts, and quite vivid discussions of the social context of the Poppy Appeal:

> No. No I don't [wear a poppy] because of what it's become.... I don't have a problem with people standing on the streets selling poppies. I don't have a problem with shops putting them in there if that's what they want to do and it's a thing that they're passionate it, but it's more that it's less about remembering the world wars anymore and it's about people that are serving now and fighting now in wars that I deem unnecessary.... Yes, it's more that it's now focusing on current conflicts and I don't want to hero worship people. I feel like that's what it's become. It's like, "Oh, but they're heroes." Even in the world wars, they're victims, not heroes. Does that make sense? (Policy officer, voluntary sector infrastructure charity A)

> I don't like enforced sentiment, I don't like this idea that we all must feel this way on this day. (Policy and communications officer, advocacy charity)

> There is an expectation that you will. Yes, it is almost a habit rather than thinking through the how and the why. It is a simple and effective way to give some money and show support. What is interesting for me personally is how it drives that – it ties into a narrative about veterans and soldiers which has an amazing power to drive guilt. And support because it ties into patriotism in a nationalistic sense which has seen a massive rise especially over the last few years. (Policy officer, voluntary sector infrastructure charity A, London)

This was an issue to which interviewees were knowledgeable. The head of one infrastructure charity, a proud poppy wearer who spoke movingly about his grandfather's rescue by a Gurkha in the Second World War, made a point that poppies shouldn't be pinned onto nice shirts just to please an imagined community watching on television:

> I think the notion of a bloke on Match of the Day, who is wearing a shirt having a poppy pinned to his shirt is absolutely ridiculous, absolutely ridiculous. No, I wear it

because I happen to believe in it, and as I say, for family reasons…. But I think pressuring people into wearing it is just fascism, because that's just stupid, but it's kind of – I don't like it. It's tasteless and it should be a personal thing. (Chief executive, voluntary sector infrastructure charity D)

Sarah Moore's (2008: 19) argument about the awareness ribbon culture from a political point of view is that the 'individualisation of symbolic meaning in late modern societies masks a creeping uniformity.' Behaviour is framed by social processes and institutions, and our individualism ends up a collective and socially determined endeavour, with a 'fundamental tension between the desire to be a unique individual, essentially different to others, and, on the other hand, the desire to receive validation from others, something that requires a subordination to conventions and norms that render the individual essentially similar to others. Asked whether they ever felt pressured to wear a poppy, some interviewees were quite frank in how they explained how the personal choice of wearing an awareness symbol would enter into their professional strategic thinking:

There is also a level of conformity, so it is expected of you…. I wouldn't go to a client meeting in the fortnight before Remembrance Sunday without a poppy just because it … if I got to the station and thought, "Oh shit [I'm not wearing one]", I would get another poppy because there is…. I think that showing solidarity with the troops is probably more of a big deal now than it was 10 years ago. (Chief fundraising consultant, private fundraising company, London)

To me, that's pointless. If I meet people here who don't wear poppies, I don't say, "Why haven't you got a poppy on?" We have no blanket policy on this. It is down to the individual. We don't sell them here. I sometimes buy half a dozen for the team so that if somebody is particularly conscious of the fact that they haven't got one and would like one, there's just a box they can [just get one]. (Chief executive, hospice)

Also, there is a feeling that as someone in my position, I feel almost as if some people I work with would frown me upon if I didn't wear a poppy. (Chief executive, children's health charity)

[Similar to the poppy] I'll always make sure my CEO or any spokespeople are wearing [my charity's] badge…. We're basically promoting our own charity and being pristine as well…. [But] I do feel like I would get castigated if I didn't wear [the poppy]. (Director of communications, homelessness charity A)

This need to demonstrate moral pristineness is a necessity for those competing for donations and attention, given that publicity is the lifeblood of charities (Deacon, 1999). It ends up being about managing risk, even though the risk in this case is widely interpreted as a personal choice. The fundraising consultant's story above has stuck with me quite unlike many other moments from interviews over the years. The image of him running around a train station in London, late for a meeting, trying to find a poppy seller, hoping he's got a quid, is an image that does speak to the way the ridiculousness of poppy fascism provides an embodied reaction and change of behaviour in some people. The hospice chief's decision to keep a box of poppies in the office to save his staff's embarrassment is a much more low key behaviour, but similarly speaks to the assumed lack of understanding. Why would anyone question your lack of a poppy? And even if they did, why would the simple human reaction of 'Oh, I just forgot today', or 'It's just on my other jacket', or 'I don't usually wear one' not be assumed to be enough of an answer? The vast majority of people – even if they are personally hugely connected to the Poppy Appeal – would obviously understand such an answer, because people are overwhelmingly reasonable. What the fear speaks to is the transition of online message board culture into real life: as we saw in Chapter 3, people accept that shaming and context collapse (Marwick and boyd, 2011) are parts of online life, but elements from this data about poppies indicates the permanent management of the presentation of self spills into how people feel they need to act offline as well. There was a feeling that the meaning of the poppy had changed due to its greater public appropriation:

They're almost becoming a bit of, like, a fashion thing, aren't they? Because you can buy proper pin ones, you can buy…. They're all sparkly. You know, when the X Factor is on, they're in their hair, they're on bobbles, they're rings…. It's not what it was. (Community engagement officer, students' union)

> I personally don't believe in wearing a fancy poppy that looks like it should be worth £50 or putting one on the front of my car, like people have started doing. (Chief executive, hospice)

There was some disagreement. Some interviewees were clear that they didn't think the poppy 'glorified' war in any way and that they 'had never felt' (director of communications, international development charity) any social pressure to wear one:

> No. I think everyone should have their own standpoint, just as in, "Do you want to wear a Marie Curie daffodil?" or, "Do you wear a daffodil for [etc]...?" I would never feel pressured into wearing one.... For me it's an "awareness" campaign. As with any awareness campaign, you opt in or you opt out, and that's fine and it's a personal choice. (Research director, youth volunteering charity)

But interviewees who felt that way did state that if the situation ever changed, that social rules changed to such an extent that wearing one was practically enforced, this would fundamentally alter the principle at stake, and they would stop wearing one:

> So, if the Poppy Appeal, if poppies became a symbol of our patriotism in that sort of way, I think I'd be ditching the poppy. (Chief executive, homelessness charity B)

> The defining characteristic of the voluntary sector is voluntarism, the fact that you are not compelled to do something. I would feel distinctly uncomfortable if social norms became such that you had to wear a poppy. Just moving this into a different area, if you look at something like Employer Supported Volunteering. If social norms in companies were created where you had to volunteer, I'd feel really uncomfortable about that. (Director of policy, voluntary sector infrastructure charity B, London)

Interviewees were generally aware of the wider public demonstration of emotion. Moore (2008) argues that it is not surprising that ribbon wearing is increasing at a time when other forms of mass participation are decreasing, as part of the reflexive turn in modernity, the move towards a Giddensian individualised biography. Ribbon wearing as a process is aimed at fostering reflexive self-identity, tied up with the growth of charity as a public act: 'The ribbon campaigns tell us much about the manner in which we conceive of victimhood and illness in contemporary society, and point to the development of a particular identity, rooted in emotion and self-expression' (Moore, 2008: 5). This 'culture of compassion' which has grown up over the 1990s and 2000s (often attached to the public mourning over the death of Princess Diana) has been exacerbated by technological developments such as social media:

Jon: Do you wear a poppy?
Policy officer, youth charity, Sheffield: No.... Umm.... I'm quite anti-military, and I suppose I don't agree with the "grief junkie" sentiment that we're, sort of, rapidly falling into, and we have been for quite a long time now. I think, recently, and, I suppose, over the past, sort of, five, ten years, a lot of the time, like, wearing a poppy has become more an opportunity for people to tap into someone else's grief, rather than show support for whatever cause they are wearing that poppy for, whether it's to support The British Legion, or to show support or solidarity for victims of World War II, or people who died in previous conflicts.

Much of this links back to the discussion in Chapter 3 about social media:

It's deeply, deeply conservative isn't it? "You must conform, you must do everything exactly right on the exact day, and if you don't you're some sort of heretic." It's really scary, it's similar to what Twitter is becoming, I think. Just one false move on Twitter, one wrong word, and you can end your career instantly, and be completely vilified and people can be turning up at your house and threatening to attack you, and it's just crazy, it's really crazy. (Policy and communications officer, advocacy charity, London)

When we've got younger runners for a marathon or whatever [our charity], they are clicking that and they are saying, "I've just raised £2,000", and they're posting it on Facebook or Twitter. I'm a little bit torn about that because are you doing it because you want to raise money or are you doing it for the kudos of doing that? It's almost like the poppy thing. Are you wearing it because you feel like you ought to or are you wearing it to respect the people or are you wearing it to show how social minds…? (Director of communications, homelessness charity A, London)

Without prompting, interviewees did attach ideas of nationalism and militarism to the Poppy Appeal:

Again for me I think part of it ties into that – the poppy one especially has a very nationalistic thing that ties into it. It ties into support for the forces which is, "Are you truly British?" Which again has been a rising issue in the last five, ten years that wasn't there before. Actually personally I find it quite scary…. I think that is more of a political tool rather than it is about the charity. It is used by others for reasons and they want to make a point. (Policy officer, voluntary sector infrastructure charity A, London)

Do I wear a poppy? Well, I'm an ex-serviceman, I always look for a white one but you can't find them anywhere. People that have fought in the past, I don't know, I have very complex feelings about that, because it's entirely at odds with my personal politics, but resonates with something inside me definitely…. I don't like the way that it's been hijacked for nationalistic purposes. The way that if you choose not to, that labels you. My partner refuses to wear one, and her son's just joined the army…. His photograph from him he was passing out on parade with his rifle, she's Pritt-sticked a feather duster over the rifle. (Policy officer, homelessness charity B, Sheffield)

I think a lot of their advertising has erred a bit more towards the glorifying war than remembering the dead. I know lots of people would disagree with that, and they would disagree with it too. I feel uneasy about something that has a hint of glorifying war, so that's why I do try to wear a white one if I can remember to get hold of one, but usually I can't. (Policy and communications officer, advocacy charity, London)

Some individuals realised they had no idea what the money raised from selling poppies was actually spent on, and that it was often interpreted as celebratory of catastrophic conflicts. The chief executive of an addiction support charity told me about how the Poppy Appeal intersected with some of the structural issues her charity faced, particularly within the hierarchy of need and popularity (Body and Breeze, 2016) that exist within the charity ecosystem. Drug and alcohol addiction services had been encouraged to set up veterans groups, she said, because 'that's where the money is, and the public is'. The deserving versus undeserving binary (Rosenthal, 2000) has always existed within systems (whether public or voluntary sector) that seek to tackle need, and within her part of the sector, this chief executive had identified that veterans with substance dependencies were deserving of help (because their addiction stemmed from their service), whereas the automatic assumption was that a civilian should take at least some, and perhaps all, of the 'blame' for their circumstances. Instead funders and donors 'want to know' that the person they are supporting needs help 'because they've had a trauma' or 'they've been damaged': 'People want a reason that they should feel sorry for someone – the deserving....' (Chief executive, addiction support charity)

Conclusions

There's a Siegfried Sassoon poem called 'Suicide in the Trenches', where a young soldier commits suicide on the front line because of the horrors of war he has witnessed. He and the truth of his death are forgotten about, just another consequence of brutal conflict. But the poem ends with an angry challenge to the 'smug-faced crowds' who 'cheer when soldier lads march by' who then 'sneak' home, avoiding the fight and sacrifice, praying they'll never know the 'hell' faced by youth and vitality in the trenches. It's a stark, 12-line lesson about the ease of glamorising war if you never have to fight in it.

I wear a poppy, and I don't feel pressured to wear one. But my status, as a white, middle-class man, although one whom would probably be dismissed as the liberal elite by someone much richer, more expensively educated and better connected to power than I, means that accusations of a lack of patriotism or support for the right causes rarely come my way. As someone who is proud to have carried the Scout flag on numerous Remembrance Day parades, and hung around enough Royal British Legion clubs, drinking a bottle of coke at the bar while veterans lined up to lead the parade and drop their flags while the Last Post was played, I do have deep and important memories of the importance of the Poppy Appeal. But the poppy fanaticism that rolls round every year does both these memories, and the actual memories of those who have served, a great disservice. Far better to get mad at others for not doing their bit, while feeling a pound in a tin allows you to think you've done yours. The treatment of veterans, in the UK and elsewhere, is often nothing short of a disgrace. No one ever seems to really consider what The Royal British Legion, the very charity that organises the Poppy Appeal and actually gets forgotten about in the middle of the poppy maelstrom, is actually raising the money for. They represent veterans at tribunals to overturn decisions where employment and disability benefits have been stopped, or where veterans have been sanctioned due to mental health issues (The Royal British Legion, 2018b). They provide short- and long-term care homes for ex-service personnel, including dementia care, and provide mobility aids for veterans who fall outside of Ministry of Defence jurisdiction. Their website details many more of the services that one can't quite believe aren't statutory duties covered by military covenant.

In conducting interviews with senior charity leaders, many couldn't remember the name of the charity behind the Poppy Appeal, and I'm sure a national survey would show the general public had even more of an issue linking the two. Neither the politicians nor commentators jumping on this bandwagon, on either side of the issue, nor many of the clickbait articles covering the ensuing poppy storm, mention The Royal British Legion and its work. 'Symbols represent the person, serving to make one's identity, emotions, and beliefs recognisable to others', writes Sarah Moore (2008: 12-13), yet often this use of symbols doesn't seem to correspond very closely to personal sentiments. This chapter has served to take one of the most recognisable items of charity in the UK, and examine how its symbolic power, its representation (in most eyes) of pure goodness gets operationalised, misrecognised and abused on a yearly basis. It becomes a token around which those without shame, like Donald Trump taking credit for a charitable donation he didn't make, can translate symbolic power into symbolic violence. And such violence creates awkward tensions for those trying to lead in the charity sector.

When he became Prime Minister, John Major stood on the steps of Downing Street and said that his vision was to 'see us build a country that is at ease with itself, a country that is confident and a country that is able and willing to build a better quality of life for all its citizens.' Major failed in many ways: a recession in 1992, sleaze and indecency in public life throughout his Party, and viscous splits over Conservative policy towards the European Union. And today Britain is certainly ill at ease with itself; Brexit, at a time of austerity, increased poverty, and flat-lining life expectancy, has left the country divided, confused and angry. While it is vital that current debates about the country's history as a colonial power and slave trader, and the deeply racist backgrounds of some British 'heroes' like Churchill are playing out, alongside efforts to decolonise the curriculum within education, no one who spent 10 minutes examining our national discourse would feel we were having this national conversation well – perhaps doing such public reflexive work is impossible at this conjuncture. But the yearly cataclysm over two small pieces of paper held together with two small pieces of plastic, all in the shape of a poppy, is quite distressing. To have the charitable symbol of the best of us – the defeat of fascism, and today our willingness to give to those who risked their lives – ruined by those who would claim to love it the most, shows how well the symbolic glow of charity and goodness can be weaponised.

7

Effective altruism and ignoring charity's symbolic power

Our discussion of the inherent symbolic power of doing good and being seen and widely acknowledged as a good person because you do things for charity demonstrates intangible power relations that shape the world around us and require sustained theoretical analysis. We have seen how the act of fundraising can manipulate the symbolic power of charity to bounce people into giving donations to certain causes; we have seen how young people struggle to negotiate the symbolic power of charity online, witnessing both their friends take advantage of their good deeds to present themselves one way, and how individuals themselves are wary about how their own charity may look to others and be misinterpreted, suffering context collapse. We have seen how the position of charities in society as bodies we once automatically saw as right and just, giving them sway in terms of lobbying, are seeing their position as experts come under threat, and their opportunity to take advantage of symbolic power diminishing because of both sector scandals and a general social malaise, alongside growing distrust of mega-philanthropy. We have seen how the symbolic power of charity leaders was instrumental in the collapse of the Kids Company, as the right motivations became impossible to say no to, and passion becomes a cover for bad practice. And we have seen how a yearly outrage over an otherwise respectful fundraising symbol in the poppy demonstrates how the power of charity becomes weaponised, erupting with a quasi-nationalistic demand for enforced participation.

What this shorter penultimate chapter wants to do is introduce an alternative way of thinking about charity – the effective altruism movement – and explore how its proponents deal with the concept of the symbolic power of doing good, when that movement's central desire is for us to see past the symbolic power of charity, to be able to ignore it, so we can throw off the shackles of clumsy emotion, and really focus on putting charity to work, for as much good as it can muster.

Effective altruism has at its core a simple idea, which is that when doing good we have a duty to do 'the most good we can' (Singer, 2015: vii). The philosopher Peter Singer (2010: 3–12, 2016a), the biggest name behind the push for effective altruism, uses a famous allegory for why we should all give more: if you see a small boy drowning in a pond, and to save him would cost you only getting your shoes a bit wet, then anyone decent would agree that you have a moral obligation to save him. Therefore, if a boy or girl is dying of a preventable disease halfway round the world, and we have identified a medical intervention that would save them, and to do so would cost you only a small amount, it would be equally immoral not to do so. And just as, if there were hundreds of children drowning in shallow pools that were easy to rescue you would not rest until you had pulled them all out, equally you should continue to donate to life-saving treatments in developing nations until the amount of money you've given starts to have a seriously deleterious effect on your life. To do otherwise is immoral. Singer asks quite simply, why do we not think of giving as something we have to do?

There is a traditional distinction between duty and charity: giving money to a charitable cause gets you thanked for your generosity, but generally not looked at negatively if you choose not to do it. It is not a duty, but a choice. Singer (2016a: 14–15) has problems with this:

> Because giving money is regarded as an act of charity, it is not thought that there is anything wrong with not giving. The charitable man [sic] may be praised, but the man who is not charitable is not condemned.… This way of looking at the matter cannot be justified … we ought to give money away and it is wrong not to do so.

People (including myself) make excuses about why we don't give more to charity, often saying that either it's up to governments to increase aid spending, or we already give a 'decent' amount, or our 'fair share'. Singer argues that it is morally wrong not to give more than your 'fair share' if you can. Your 'fair share' is not a percentage of your income, or flat-rate amount determined elsewhere, it is how much you can afford to give without causing detriment to yourself. The idea that the charitable can use 'Well, I do my bit' as a defence is punctured any time we buy something we don't really need, because your purchase proves 'your bit' could be larger.

Alongside Singer, it is William MacAskill who has done the most to set out the practical and symbolic impediments to effective giving. He tells the story of PlayPump (MacAskill, 2015: 1–6), a water pump that used a child's roundabout to draw water to the surface rather than the more common hand pump or wind-powered pump, which could be either labour-intensive or relied on certain weather conditions. It seemed a fantastic innovation, and hit a nerve with the public, business and politicians, collecting sponsorship and celebrity endorsements; 1,800 PlayPumps were installed across Africa, until events turned sour. The PlayPump was exhausting for children to constantly push, demeaning for local women to use, and dangerous, with reports of children suffering vomiting and broken limbs. It collected less water and required more maintenance than the old-fashioned hand pumps that many villagers preferred: no one had asked them whether they wanted a PlayPump installed, with backers assuming that what was currently sexy and in vogue was what was best. This story explains the mission for effective altruism, to take emotion, trends and celebrity out of charitable endeavour, and to focus simply on 'what works', and more specifically asks where one's donation can do the most good. MacAskill (2015: 12) argues that we need to remove the 'thrill' from charity because 'relying on good intentions alone to inform your decisions can be potentially disastrous'. This feeds into a critique of the consequences of 'moral licensing', where people who perform good or charitable actions 'often compensate by doing fewer good actions in the future', showing that 'people are often more concerned about looking good or feeling good rather than actually doing good' (MacAskill, 2015: 180). Instead, by applying data and rationality to a charitable endeavour, we don't rob the act of virtue but instead do the more virtuous thing, which is to act on more than virtue. There is a need to basically bypass the social norms and symbolic rewards offered by charity and doing good. In sum, the effective altruists' argument is boiled down to Singer's (2016b: 161) hard truths:

> We tend to think of charity as something that is "morally optional" – good to do, but not wrong to fail to do. As long as one does not kill, maim, steal, cheat, and so on, one can be a morally virtuous citizen, even if ones spends lavishly and gives nothing to charity. But those that have enough to spend on luxuries yet fail to share even a tiny fraction of their income with the poor, must bear some responsibility for the deaths they could have prevented. Those who do not meet even the minimal 1 percent standard should be seen as doing something that is morally wrong.

Effective altruism meets people

MacAskill (2015: 10–11, 60) writes of how efforts to de-worm children in Sub-Saharan Africa are much more cost-effective in tackling school absenteeism and raising test scores than other methods, such as scholarships, free uniforms or extra textbooks or even teachers. But you can see how a campaign centred on school uniforms, with cute children dressed up smartly, has more symbolic resonance and looks better in marketing materials than having to communicate the horrors of worms to an audience who may not want to know. Teachers, textbooks and uniforms are relatable policies that rich Westerners can see translated from their own lives, but our own frames limit the quality of our donation. In the prosperous Global North, we may think that the way we might 'save' a life would be to give first aid at the scene of an accident or emergency, or pull someone from a burning car or house. Yet MacAskill (2015: 63–4), drawing on well-developed estimates, reasons that it costs approximately US$3,400 to save a life in the developing world: 'Donating to charity is not nearly as glamorous as kicking down the door of a burning building, but the benefits are just as great.' The benefits to others in either scenario are as great, both save one life. But the effective altruists would be wrong to suggest that the benefits to the saver are the same. One brings hero status, stupendously positive local news coverage, a row of drinks left behind the bar in a nearby pub, and the ceaseless gratitude of a loving family. The other may get you (if you choose to tell anyone) a slap on the back, or a supportive, 'Oh well done you, that's really impressive', but it may equally result in quizzical looks, and the suspicion that you've got money to burn. MacAskill (2015: 70–2) also cautions that we should be wary of giving to disaster relief. The earthquake in Japan in 2011 caused 15,000 deaths, but raised so much money the Japanese Red Cross and Red Crescent societies asked the public to stop donating; US$330,000 was raised for each death, yet for each poverty-related death worldwide, only US$15,000 is raised through philanthropy or government foreign aid budgets. It is immoral that funding is allocated by individual donors depending on how evocative and widely publicised a disaster is and where it is, rather than the severity of the issue. Disasters seem bad as they explode onto our news screens, but the continuing daily disaster that is poverty in Sub-Saharan Africa does not have the same immediacy and is not capable of pulling us out of our daily routines in the same way.

One could argue that it is unfair to expect ordinary people to make decisions in the same way privileged Oxbridge or Ivy League professors like MacAskill or Singer do: not everyone, in fact barely anyone, has had training in moral philosophy. There is a certain privilege that enables one to write a book, as Paul Bloom (2016) does, entitled *Against Empathy*, because perhaps going without empathy is a luxury only some can afford. Bloom argues that empathy – the act of putting yourself in someone else's shoes and feeling what they feel – is not always good, kind or moral, often a disaster, and that we are better off without it. Noting that we often feel more empathy for people like us, in terms of race or ethnicity, for instance, or people who are more attractive, and that empathy can be used by unscrupulous politicians to set one group off against another, Bloom sees empathy as a poor moral guide. He instead makes a case for a rational and deliberative compassionate reasoning in everyday life, arguing quite persuasively and in line with the central theory of this book, that '[e]mpathy is used as a tool by charitable organizations, religious groups, political parties, and governments … it can be strategically used to motivate people to do good things' (Bloom, 2016: 45). Empathetic distress at someone else's distress may be very human, for instance, but it is quite useless: there is no point being stymied by others' suffering.

I think there are problems with Bloom's argument: in examples where empathy is shown to be useful he categorises it differently, as compassion, for instance, a purposeful definitional blurring that Bloom complains of in his critics. He also ends up arguing that empathy tilts us too much towards violent actions such as war, as we try to avenge those who have suffered, which seems abstracted from both the symbolic power of strength in international relations, and the realpolitik of calculations of advantage. Bloom (2016: 30) argues that 'empathy drives people to treat others' suffering as if it were their own, which then motivates action to make the suffering go away', but that this action can actually be unhelpful or cause more problems. He provides an example: after the tragedy of Newtown, where a gunman entered Sandy Hook Elementary School and murdered 20 children and 6 adults, the town was inundated with both condolences and forms of charity, especially the donation of gifts and toys for local children, and millions of dollars. This relatively affluent community, of which Bloom is a member, struggled to cope with the influx of goods, cramming a warehouse with plush toys. 'There was a dark comedy here', Bloom (2016: 32) writes, 'with people from far poorer communities sending their money to much richer people, guided by the persistent itch of empathetic concern.' But this is where, for me, Bloom's argument falls down: this is not a problem with empathy per se, but people taking an action as a result of empathising with those in distress that is not necessarily helpful. It wasn't wrong for them to feel empathetic for the people of Newtown who'd just suffered a devastating loss, but just that they could have done it in a different way. It does feel that the effective altruists, the rationalists, and those who want to reduce decisions about generosity to an algorithm, live in a non-reality where people are blank slates, who, in economic game theory terms, have perfect information and can see every event and the consequences of their actions. *Of course* Bloom cares more about Newtown – it's his community. It's what makes close communities such useful, rewarding and joyous places to be. Community is a thing that makes life worth living and it falls down if you don't care more about things that happen around you than things that happen far away. The social contract we sign when we choose to live somewhere requires it. (This is not to say don't care about people far away, but just that it is not immoral to prioritise suffering close to home.) All of us, I am sure, would want to live in a world where Sandy Hook survivors got too many toys and donations than not enough. Yes, we would want there to be a more even spread of caring about issues, and a less convoluted spread of charitable resources, but events have power (Rojek, 2013), and people's knowledge of events is not in their own control but filtered through media and education, and their emotional connection to events is affected by personal experience. If people's pre-existing bias leads them to be unequally empathetic, the solution isn't to reduce the empathy; it's to reduce the bias.

This notion of rallying round a cause, and whether it's something we would risk losing along with the bathwater, is common in the effective altruism literature. Singer (2010: 47–8) tells the story of Jessica McClure, an 18-month old Texan girl who fell into a well in 1987. It was national news, became a *cause célèbre* (and was parodied on *The Simpsons*) and led to Americans from across the country sending both prayers, but also money: McClure reportedly now has a million dollar trust fund. As Singer points out, obviously no one would wish ill-will on McClure, and it is imperative she was saved by the rescue teams, but why donate to her? What would that achieve but present her with a millionaire life she neither deserved nor needed? In the two and a half days she was in the well, Singer estimates, over 67,000 children died worldwide from avoidable poverty-related causes. 'The identifiable person moves us in a way more abstract information does not' (Singer, 2010: 48), a well-known concept in charity marketing which often seeks to tell individualised stories, because while writing off 'the homeless' is easy, ignoring one young woman who became homeless for a list of specific and sympathy-arousing reasons is harder. A similar story can be told in the UK, of Bradley Lowery, a young boy who was diagnosed with and later died from an aggressive form of childhood cancer called neuroblastoma (see BBC News, 2017b). Before he died, Bradley's story was widely publicised, with Bradley himself given a number of high-profile experiences, including being a mascot for the England team and being given the Premier League Goal of the Month award for a penalty he took before a match. A foundation in his name was later set up to provide support to families who required treatment not available on the NHS. Bradley Lowery's story clearly touched a lot of people – he received 250,000 Christmas cards from around the world and received over £1 million in donations. How does one balance Singer's (2010: 69) view here, that 'giving money to individual children isn't a particularly effective way of helping the poor', and the absolute heartbreak that Bradley Lowery's family will have gone through his suffering, and the genuine groundswell of empathy and compassion generated by knowledge of his cause? Should newspaper campaigns focused on charity malfeasance and waste instead bring their ire down on the Make-A-Wish foundation, who, in 2013, gave Miles Scott, a five-year-old boy suffering with leukaemia, a once-in-a-lifetime experience of running around San Francisco dressed as 'Batkid', working with an actor dressed as Batman, spending the day capturing bad guys and saving the city? On that day 12,000 people volunteered to cheer Miles on and make the day an event – the documentary made of the event shows an extraordinary gift. But as Singer (2015: 6) and Nick Cooney (2015: 50–8) point out, the US$7,500 approximate cost could have saved the lives of at least three children and perhaps many more. Effective altruists have made the comical but straightforward point that perhaps we should talk in terms of 'Dead Child Currency': 'If it cost $800 to save a child's life, each $800 spent on anything else…' (Wise, 2015: 9). Similarly, the 11,000 people (including my dad) who donated to buy J.M.W. Turner's painting 'The Blue Rigi' for the Tate Gallery (and thereby the nation) are classed as not having 'the right mental habits' by Alexander (2015) because the £550,000 they raised could have saved the lives of about 300 people from disease. Basically your personal preferences don't matter. Your personal preferences are stupid and immoral. You are stupid and immoral. Think again. Think better. Yet we can't treat human nature and social realities like switches to be turned off or variables to be amended. We can't ignore the symbolic resonance of some stories and not others, *even if* there is a perfectly valid argument that the symbolic power of collective grief and associated charity doesn't always lead to rational decisions about resource allocation.

Smith and Davidson (2014: 114–79) speak to ungenerous Americans, both self-defined and when compared to the giving of others, who classify being a good person as being about what one does not do (commit crime, avoid tax, trouble other people) rather than what one does. While obviously this is completely opposite to the effective altruists approach – where giving as much as you can afford is seen as an obligation – there is an interesting parallel. In Smith and Davidson's work, the ungenerous are aware that their lack of generosity may be socially undesirable, but they do not see their actions as having a ripple of influence: keeping oneself to oneself is enough. The effective altruists are aware that they will be seen as miserabilists, people who are down on people's emotions, sympathies and philanthropic enthusiasm, but argue that it is wrong to privilege the needs of some groups just because you've met them, because that would mean being led by emotion rather than morality. It is arbitrary to have seen a problem at close quarters. '[T]he sadness we feel at the loss of a loved one should be harnessed in order to make the world a better place', MacAskill (2015: 49) writes, but the motivation should be focused on saving lives per se, not a specific way.

Non-profit sector commentator Nick Cooney (2015) writes about Oscar Schindler, the Second World War hero, depicted in the film *Schindler's List* who, by employing over a thousand Jews in his factory in Poland, saved their lives from the Holocaust. Cooney focuses on Schindler's regret that he did not save more lives. Part of Schindler's tactic was to use his own money (over US$1 million) to support his factory, just so his Jewish workers would be protected. As Schindler says in the film, if he had sold his car, or more jewellery, he could have saved more people, and Cooney uses this example to demonstrate how even the best among us, as Schindler undoubtedly is, 'overlook the opportunities' to do more, to help more, to save more. While I do not doubt Schindler's own truly felt sense of failure, Cooney's simplified use of this example to argue for effective altruism is quite problematic and a bit gross. We will never know if Schindler had acted slightly differently what the outcome would have been: if he'd sold his car or his gold Nazi pin, perhaps more questions would have been asked – perhaps he needed his car and his pin to demonstrate his commitment to Nazism and diminish suspicion. For Cooney (2015: xiv) to write, 'like Schindler, we often fall short of our potential in the charity work we do' is a horrible reach: we don't know that Schindler fell short. He felt he did, but that doesn't mean he did. The hero's remorse will always kick in after victory, and he or she has a right to that remorse – we don't.

My view is that the effective altruists need a healthy dose of realism – we give to the things we are asked to give to. It's why the quality of the ask is so important (Breeze, 2017). Instead, perhaps effective altruists should focus on two things: encourage the charities they find are the most effective per dollar (as on sites like givewell.org) to invest in better fundraising techniques and asks, and focus energies on large corporations, charitable foundations and governments to make sure these large amalgamations of (taxpayer) donations are used as well as possible without worrying about individuals' personal conflicts about where to put their relatively tiny donation. Not every act of charity seeks to do the most it can: when I give a quid to a homeless man on my way to work, I do not think this is the most effective thing I could do; the greater issue may be combining the instinctive and the small, with the systematic and large. Individual donations of a fiver may be 'wasted' in effective altruists' eyes if they don't go either to the number one ranked charity on givewell.org, or at least the best charity in that field; but many large projects – such as the Gates' Foundation's $100 million InBloom Inc educational charity (Raventós and Wark, 2018: 89) and quick establishment and closure of small schools (Aschoff, 2015: 123), or Mark Zuckerberg's US$100 million donation to Newark schools – don't work brilliantly either, but dominate because of the non-profit industrial complex (INCITE!, 2007). Effective altruists do sometimes recognise the practical barriers offered by the symbolic power of charity (such as MacAskill's close connection to a fistula clinic he visited), but generally they seem to think it is something we can, as rational beings, move past.

Ignoring charity's symbolic power is hard, and evidence suggests that people don't want to do it. While some studies have shown that those who take a utilitarian approach to life are likely to be less emotional when making decisions (Navarette et al, 2012), hard-wired perhaps to avoid the issues of the symbolic plane of experience, this is rare. In a series of experiments, Berman and colleagues (2018) show that even when people are given detailed information about charity effectiveness, it has a limited impact on how they make choices about where to donate. Donors are found to prefer giving to a cancer research organisation, widely and intuitively seen as the most pressing cause, rather than an arthritis research unit, even when they were told that the cancer research centre was much less effective in its use of the money. Investing in financial products or buying a new mobile phone were both seen as areas where evaluating objective measures were seen as more important than choosing where to donate: choosing a charity was considered as much of a subjective decision (that is, one not to be viewed as a rational, effectiveness-led decision) as choosing a restaurant in which to eat. Ergo, this leads to effective altruism's central problem, that people don't give to the right things because charity is viewed as a relatively personal or subjective decision that shouldn't be made using objective information. People are more likely to prefer donating to single victims than to groups of victims (see, for example, Small et al, 2007), and rely on their feelings to guide choice. Reading the effective altruism literature, one often gets the feeling its proponents can't believe people have the temerity to do such a thing. The effective altruism movement may have identified a problem but seem to think that pointing out that problem might be enough to overcome it. As we find in many current political debates – Brexit, Trump – bringing facts to an emotional subjective field has only limited potential (Baumberg Geiger and Meueleman, 2016; Ball, 2017), and maximising social welfare instead requires a complete refiguring on a much wider scale of how people think of themselves as donors (Berman et al, 2018: 843). Those with expectations about changing charitable behaviours – both charities themselves trying to convince people to make new donations, and the effective altruists who want charitable decisions to be effectiveness-driven – have underestimated the fact that donation decisions are supply-driven, not demand-driven (Breeze, 2017): it's about what donors are close to, affected by and care about. People think it is moral to give to those issues that they care about rather than those that have the most 'effective' impact. There is a pot of money that exists that people don't get to decide how it gets spent called tax – they get a decision over who gets to decide how to spend that money but no exact say over how it is spent, and that's absolutely right. Ordinary people's giving (not mega-giving funded by generous tax breaks [Reich, 2018]) is their own decision, and when we start moving into an arena where people are criticised for having personal opinions and preferences about how their own money should be spent, we are arguing for expanding the tax base wider and spending it better. Berman and colleagues (2018) demonstrate that people are much more likely to 'think effectively' when coming from an organisational paradigm (when asked to imagine they are the head of a research institute, for instance), reinforcing the idea that the effective altruists should focus on governments' aid spending rather than making people feel guilty for caring about sick dogs. It is government that should be most encouraged to take effectiveness issues seriously, before pathologising individual giving. Reason has to be the servant of the passions (Hume, 2012 [1738]), and being able to not care about things you care about is a luxury few can afford.

Conclusions

As Asheem Singh (2018: 103) puts it in his work on social enterprise:

> Social impact measurement was supposed to liberate philanthropic organisations from the caprice of the philanthropist; from the agendas of old-style donors, often the rich and the privileged. If you have a measurement, you can no longer be pushed around by the whims of the agenda-driven rich person to build a statue in their honour or ward in their name.

The problem of the 'caprice of the philanthropist' is something those making anti-charity arguments from the political left (for example, Raventós and Wark, 2018) and the effective altruists have in common: both see people with spare money (who are likely to be among the wealthiest on the planet) donating to causes they believe in *as an issue*, one because social issues get to be the playthings of the rich, who coincidentally never propose structural reforms which would limit their own power, and the other because personal peccadillos are driven by emotion rather than good judgement, which is a terrible waste. It is the solutions that are different: the anti-privatisation or contracting out left would prefer higher taxes, particularly on the rich, and democratically elected governments to replace the voluntarily provided functions of charities with fully funded and sustainable statutory services. The effective altruists are generally fine with the concept of wealthy philanthropists, as long as they focus their resources on the right things – those that will save the most lives and tackle the most need per dollar.

If we desire a better welfare state and a fundamentally fairer economy, as well as social policy that is rational, evidence-driven, and that treats people decently, it is challenging to simultaneously recognise that we can't ignore the emotional side of charity. What feels to me to be the right way of solving social problems, and avoiding the symbolic power of giving, is for the left-wing desire for a larger state and more intervention to be led by the principles of effective altruism. Government, state and media institutions and their occasional nostalgia and nationalism (as exemplified in the last chapter) need to be driven much more by technocratic evidence, rather than, for example, creating a National Cancer Drugs Fund which provides some funding to non-statutory funded medicines to tackle that most emotional of diseases, *and sounds good*, but is incredibly ineffective when compared to early diagnosis interventions and practitioner training (Health Policy Insight, 2010). Asking for politicians to speak to evidence rather than the narrow particulars of what will play well with voters and their base is, I know, pie in the sky, but more locally this seems an obvious place where competing ideologies over the right way for altruism to operate could come to a semblance of agreement.

8

Conclusions: the good glow

This has been a sociology of the act of charity, the institution of charity and the notion of charity. Sociology and social theory, after much anthropology devoted to the gift and the informal helping that exists between people, have largely left charity alone, instead considering it a field for social policy or public administration studies to cover, despite the work of charities and the people who work for them being central figures in providing expert social commentary and contributing to sociological studies concerned with inequality, disadvantage and injustice. In this Conclusion I want to summarise what we have learned through this examination of how charity works, about what it means for charity and what it means for people.

The first thing to note is that the idea that charity, gift-giving and kindness are imbued with a certain symbolic goodness that improves the actor's image is not a new observation. Mauss' work on the power of the gift, Shapely's, Ostrander's and other historical demonstrations of the use of charity for social status, and many examinations of the ways in which businesses use CSR to alleviate some reputational damage, demonstrate that researchers and charity professionals have been thinking about these issues for a long time. Possible cynicism around the veracity of the motivation for charitable deeds is almost instrumental to the doing of charity. From white students taking a gap year before university in former colonial states so they can pose for photos with people of colour and demonstrate their enthusiasm for 'otherness' (Snee, 2014; Kallman, 2020), demonstrating their goodwill in Indonesian orphanages that exist principally as places for 'voluntourism', and not places to alleviate suffering (Flaherty, 2016: 47), to *parents who purchase orphanages in Botswana so that their children have places to spend their summers volunteering in order to bulk up their applications to Harvard* (yes, really; see Bruni, 2016), because suffering is bad and alleviating suffering is good, such actions can be manipulated and taken advantage of. But the point of this book has not been to undercut people who do great work for others and the charities that serve so many vulnerable people and communities, but to recognise instead that the symbolic plane of charity always exists, and so our choice is not about whether we agree with it or make normative judgements about how it should work. The fact that doing charity provides an aura of goodness exists, and so our choice is to recognise it or not, think about it or not, and analyse it or not.

What is interesting is how the presence of such a symbolic plane affects individuals' interpretation of others' actions. As Bourdieu (1990) says, a certain misrecognition is central to how charity and gifts operate in everyday social interactions, with the potential for charity to act as a form of social dominance, between giver and receiver. Symbolic power exists in potentia in all charitable acts. It is in the purview of the actor or the observer to operationalise it or not, to take advantage of it or not. But with social media and other public witnessing of charity, we add a third part into this relationship – the observer. Throughout this book it has frequently not been recipients or beneficiaries who have been central to understanding how charity's symbolic power can provide kudos to the charitable; it has been third party observers – the audience at Trump's ribbon-cutting event, acquaintances looking at your social media feed, passers-by seeing the poppy on your lapel – who have been the participants in the recognition and legitimisation of the charitable act as good. Charity works because people get to get something out of it, and part of that reward is 'getting and keeping a lasting hold over someone' (Bourdieu, 1990: 126), both in terms of being owed a gift in return, but also because of the glow of goodness that will continue to surround you, energised by those around you who knew you did the good deed. Whereas Andreoni (1990) wrote of the warm glow that exists in all genuine giving, the completely human internalised response to doing something kind for someone else, a more problematic 'good glow' is bestowed on and around the charitable by recipients and observers in wider society who benefit from or witness a gift. Such a glow can be used or not, and may be misrecognised as boastful or troublesome, but either way, its effects can be powerful. Whether it was actually a good deed or not (on either level, a Trumpian fake deed, or a decent but not the best deed you could have done, à la effective altruism) is where observers' misrecognition comes in.

Symbolic power exists in all charitable behaviour. Such power is not necessarily negative, but is generally understood as such. People's everyday understandings of charity frequently posit this secondary realm as bragging or showing off, or an indication of having too much money, or of looking to get something in return, thereby undercutting the gift. The good glow does present something of a bind for the charitable, because to stay anonymous induces assumptions of selfishness. On social media, where the 'context collapse' (Marwick and boyd, 2011) of misinterpretation works both ways (genuinely good acts seen as humblebrags, manipulative statements seen as genuine) a slight push back on the inherent power of charity's goodness comes from its role in the larger swirl of fakery and mistrust that young people are facing online, the desire to go, 'Look, I'm a great human being' (as Lucy puts it in Chapter 3) is a known and enacted behaviour, so the edifice of charity crumbles a little. The fact that genuinely charitable acts may be inaccurately judged – 'they pretend they've donated' (Irma) – is par for the course for charity. A theme of this book has been that charity has to be considered part of the social world, not outside it, subject to the same rules and sociological examinations and theories or explanations as any other realm, even if we would maybe want to live in a world where charity is always special. If people are individualistic and focused on instrumental reward for their behaviour, such behaviours will be present in charitable activity *even if* such behaviours cut across the logic of charity. If patriarchal structures and sexual violence exist outside of the voluntary sector, they damn sure exist within it as well. If people like being close to power, and have trouble letting go of their creation in the private or public sectors, such behaviours will be seen in charities. The act of charity is special and different, but that doesn't mean it is unique: by applying sociological ideas throughout, and demonstrating that previous interpretations and applications of such theories can be applied to charity as well, this book has hopefully started distilling a sociology of charity, not as a cynical venture, but to be inquisitive in a way that connects thinking about charity to wider thinking about society. Because charity is a socially constructed phenomenon. There are no objective good deeds, just those that we mostly agree are good. Charity exists in a larger social, political and cultural swirl that defines the rules of what is seen as good or selfless. Even charities, as legally defined organisations, act in ways according to laws that control them: different jurisdictions have different laws for charities to follow, and different conceptions of what a charity is. Even charities that are legally established and follow the rules will be viewed differently, and individuals will have multiple views on whether they *should* be charities, whether they deserve that label. This is important because we still think that charity is a label that people and organisations must *deserve* – something that means something, that people would want to be associated with, and don't want to become devalued. Yet of course the reality is that most people have an understandably narrow view of what charity is, how charities work and what they do. It's something people can have extremely strong opinions on, with an incredibly thin depth of knowledge. Terms like 'do-gooder' can be thrown around at will, without interrogating the term. It is the hidden but always present symbolic power of charity which has turned 'do-gooder' – someone who literally *does good* – into a negative. If we apply the Bourdieusian notion of the two plains of social life, we can see how do-gooder ends up in this situation. Taken materially, at face value, the do-gooder is an unabashed social hero, someone who steps up to give back. Yet symbolically, the label is inherently aligned with the worst sort of interfering busybody, unsuited to a rather cynical and individualist modern age, and is why some movements rejected calling themselves charities in order to avoid the do-gooder tag (Lockyer, 2016). The critiqued, stereotypical roles of do-gooder and saviour come from different ideological perspectives, but both contribute to a (frequently merited) critique that individuals are aware of what being unthinkingly charitable can do for them.

The cultural theorist Stuart Hall (quoted in Giroux, 2016) once said that the university must be a critical institution or it is nothing. Similarly, as we look on at a moneyed elite using foundational philanthropy as a way to cement privilege and power (Giridharadas, 2018), we have to take a critical eye towards outwardly altruistic activity. As researchers we must consistently ask whether this non-profit endeavour is supporting or stymieing human flourishing and equality. This book is published just as we hopefully – *hopefully* – approach the end of the Trump presidency. Donald Trump's abuse of the charitable imperative and the socially known fact that charitable actors are automatically in credit is far from the worst thing about him. But critical philanthropy studies need to document how charity has become an unwitting pawn in extending the social structures that make everything worse. Recognising the realities of charity – and the ease with which its symbolic power can be taken advantage of – should make us all pause. Philanthropy can be used to launder bad reputations, moving policy discussions away from solutions that would cost big donors, with Giridharadas (2018) documenting Wall Street financiers' use of charity after the financial crisis of 2008 as a screen in order to continue taking on a massive level, promoting their charitable initiatives after critical news stories. Reputation laundering through good deeds is as far away from the altruistic basis of charity as could be imagined, and yet they can march in lockstep, cementing the bastardisation of public life through donations, plaques, naming rights and 'philanthropic graffiti'. It speaks to a thin and hollowed-out culture and civil society when the giving that is truly the best of us is so easily manipulated against society's interests. However, while reputation laundering would be an unfair statement to use about an 18-year-old slightly manipulating a Facebook status, the principle is very similar, and comes from the same place. Whereas Giridharadas

(2018), McGoey (2015) and Reich (2018) are talking about today's super-rich, and historians like Shapely (1998) are applying symbolic power to the Victorian elite, I have argued and hopefully demonstrated that symbolic power's inherent existence in charity means everyone is able to take advantage of it locally in their own milieu, as a way to boost capitals and effectiveness as a multi-positional agent within fields of power (Harvey et al, 2011: 425). The benefits, however, increase exponentially the further we go up the social class ladder.

A final story. When I was about 14, I was home one summer's day, and answered a knock at the door to find a smartly dressed man in his twenties with a clipboard. 'Hello', he said, 'are you interested in donating to the RSPCA?' I replied that I wasn't interested. I will never forget what happened next, because in hindsight it sounds so unbelievable. Changing his voice to imitate the way one would speak to a baby or toddler, he tilted his head, and asked, 'Oh, so don't you like likkle kittens and puppies then?' Stunned that he would take such a tactic, or maybe fearing that wearing a suit on a hot summer's day had addled his brain, I just said 'No', and slowly closed the door in a state of bemusement.

This door-to-door direct debit collector has stayed with me, the perfect illustration of what we've covered in this book. He was totally aware of the symbolic power of charity – especially the power associated with cute, fluffy, and above all, *helpless*, animals, but was surprised at my unwillingness to take advantage of it, both my desire to make other charitable choices, to give up the ability to stand proud and claim I was the one saving 'likkle kittens and puppies', but also the rejection of his manipulative practices. This can help us assess some conclusions about the nature of symbolic power. Just as symbolic power is the ability to take advantage of cultural and social capital, the symbolic power of charity is similarly a resource that, while ever present in potentia, needs operationalising. Donald Trump is willing to do it, Larry David is annoyed that someone else has taken advantage of it in a way that makes him look like *he* was trying to take advantage of it, and the young people interviewed in Chapter 3 were so frequently wary of being seen to take advantage of it, the notion became quite stymieing for them. But symbolic power is one of the reasons charity works – society has deemed it reasonable, if someone is being truly charitable and decent, that they should be able to be seen as a little better than others who (ceteris paribus) choose to be selfish.

One of the purposes of this book has been to contribute to wider ongoing debates about how charity is politicised, abused and generally thought about socially. Rather than focusing on the material powers involved – who sits on what board, how much is given to what – it has aimed to generate deeper thinking about the power generated by charity atmospheres that is invisible. The very act of demystifying the workings of power, and revealing the secrets that create the illusion of authority (Jones et al, 2017: 51), allows us to think theoretically and practically about what charity does at both the elite level and in people's everyday lives. Throughout this book we have seen countless examples of the ways in which our accelerated, cynical 'didn't happen' post-truth world means charity is no longer an automatic good, and any halo of the good weighs heavier than ever.

We have seen how the symbolic power of charity can make the uncharitable look charitable, the ineffective philanthropic gift be forgotten about, the innocent social media post become viewed as craven, illegal or corrosive acts be swept under the carpet, bad management be justified as passionate charisma, and the memory of those who gave their lives in conflict be weaponised in a culture war. The charities that are trying to do good in this maelstrom are caught between a rock and a hard place: 'NGOs are either said to serve human dignity and channel the voices of the oppressed, or they are described as a tool of the interests of donor governments or imperial systems of domination' (Krause, 2014: 16). The symbolism of doing good deeds, and the wide recognition that such social processes exist, means that we are free to make judgements on others – spy on their morals – according to our own continuing subjectivities. But the symbolic power of charity also enables guilt: guilt that others are trying to do something when you are not. They should get socially rewarded for thinking of others. The fact that people are not robots, and are affected by emotional appeals, and visuals of suffering, is a good thing.

Those things we assume to be unarguably good are contentious and complex (Pettinger, 2019), with 'profoundly buried' (Bourdieu, 1996) power and tensions, which we should want to reveal. But doing good *is* good. No one would want to live in a world where people do less good, and those of us engaged with studying and explaining voluntary action are generally on the side of charities and seek to affect policy in ways that will improve things for the voluntary sector. If a charity exists to help the needy, we can want to both increase funds going to and improve the work of such organisations, but to do so does not preclude asking hard questions about why there are needy in the first place, or whether charity is the best way to solve that problem and make people's lives better, or whether the act of charity is generating social impacts far beyond the giver and receiver, placing halos on certain heads.

References

ACEVO (Association of Chief Executives of Voluntary Organisations) (2015) 'PAC Report on Kids Company', News, Available at: www.acevo.org.uk/news/pac-report-kids-company

Adair-Tottef, C. (2005) 'Max Weber's charisma', *The Classical Journal of Sociology*, 5(2): 189–204.

Agnew, J. (2009) *Globalization and Sovereignty*, Lanham, MD: Littlefield Publishers.

Akala (2018) *Natives: Race and Class in the Ruins of Empire*, London: Two Roads.

Alexander, S. (2015) 'Efficient Charity: Do Unto Others', in R. Carey (ed) *The Effective Altruism Handbook*, Oxford: The Centre for Effective Altruism, 15–20.

Allred, A.T. and Amos, C. (2018) 'Disgust images and nonprofit children's causes', *Journal of Social Marketing*, 8(1): 120–40.

Anderson, P. and Green, P. (2012) 'Beyond CV building: The communal benefits of student volunteering', *Voluntary Sector Review*, 3(2): 247–56.

Andreoni, J. (1989) 'Giving with impure altruism: Applications to charity and Ricardian equivalence', *Journal of Political Economy*, 97(6): 1447–58.

Andreoni, J. (1990) 'Impure altruism and donations to public goods: A theory of warm-glow giving', *The Economic Journal*, 100(401): 464–77.

Andrews, K. (2018) *Back to Black: Retelling Black Radicalism for the 21st Century*, London: Zed Books.

Ariely, D., Bracha, A. and Meier, S. (2009) 'Doing good or doing well? Image motivation and monetary incentives in behaving prosocially', *American Economic Review*, 99(1): 544–55.

Aschoff, N. (2015) *The New Prophets of Capital*, London: Verso.

Asthana, A. (2017) 'Charities say "gag law" stops them speaking out on Tory social care plans', *The Guardian*, 29 May, Available at: www.theguardian.com/politics/2017/may/29/charities-gag-law-stops-them-speaking-out-tory-social-care-plans

Auger, G. (2014) 'Rhetorical framing: Examining the message structure of nonprofit organizations on Twitter', *International Journal of Nonprofit and Voluntary Sector Marketing*, 19(4): 239–49.

Back, L. and Puwar, N. (2012) *Live Methods*, Oxford: Blackwell.

Ball, J. (2017) *Post-Truth: How Bullshit Conquered the World*, London: Biteback.

Banks, J. (2017) 'Multimodal, multiplex, multispatial: A network model of the self', *New Media & Society*, 19(3): 419–38.

Barkan, J. (2013) 'Plutocrats at work: How big philanthropy undermines democracy', *Social Research*, 80(2): 635–52.

Bartholomew, J. (2015) 'The awful rise of "virtue signalling"', *The Spectator*, 18 April, Available at www.spectator.co.uk/2015/04/hating-the-daily-mail-is-a-substitute-for-doing-good

Basil, D., Ridgway, N. and Basil, M. (2006) 'Guilt appeals: The mediating effect of responsibility', *Psychology & Marketing*, 23(12): 1035–54.

Basil, D., Ridgway, N. and Basil, M. (2008) 'Guilt and giving: A process model of empathy and efficacy', *Psychology & Marketing*, 25(1): 1–23.

Batmanghelidjh, C. (2017) *Kids: Child Protection in Britain: The Truth*, London: Biteback.

Baumberg Geiger, B. and Meueleman, B. (2016) 'Beyond "mythbusting": How to respond to myths and perceived undeservingness in the British benefits system', *Journal of Poverty and Social Justice*, 24(3): 291–306.

BBC News (2003) '"Virtual poppy" for TV host Ross', 11 November, Available at: http://news.bbc.co.uk/1/hi/entertainment/3260277.stm

BBC News (2015) 'Kids Company accused of mishandling sexual assault allegations', 7 August, Available at: www.bbc.co.uk/news/uk-33813048

BBC News (2016) 'Is the poppy a political symbol?', 1 November, Available at: www.bbc.co.uk/news/magazine-37834224

BBC News (2017a) 'UK charities fined for data law breaches', 5 April, Available at: www.bbc.co.uk/news/technology-39502258

BBC News (2017b) 'Bradley Lowery: Sunderland fan dies after long illness', 7 July, Available at: www.bbc.co.uk/news/uk-england-39883344

BBC News (2019) 'Amber Rudd links universal credit to rise in food bank use', 11 February, Available at: www.bbc.co.uk/news/uk-politics-47203389

Bekkers, R., and Bowman, W. (2009) 'The relationship between confidence in voluntary organizations and volunteering revisited', *Nonprofit and Voluntary Sector Quarterly*, 38(5): 884–97.

Bekkers, R. and Wiepking, P. (2011) 'A literature review of empirical studies of philanthropy: Eight mechanisms that drive charitable giving', *Nonprofit and Voluntary Sector Quarterly*, 40(5): 924–73.

Bennett, E., Coule, T., Damm, C., Dayson, C., Dean, J. and Macmillan, R. (2019) 'Civil society strategy: A policy review', *Voluntary Sector Review*, 10(2): 213–23.

Bennett, R. (2015) 'Individual characteristics and the arousal of mixed emotions: Consequences for the effectiveness of charity fundraising advertisements', *International Journal of Nonprofit and Voluntary Sector Marketing*, 20(2): 188–209.

Berman, J., Barasch, A., Levine, E. and Small, D. (2018) 'Impediments to effective altruism: The role of subjective preferences in charitable giving', *Psychological Science*, 29(5): 834–44.

Billig, M. (1995) *Banal Nationalism*, London: Sage.

Billis, D. and Glennerster, H. (1998) 'Human services and the voluntary sector: Towards a theory of comparative advantage', *Journal of Social Policy*, 27(1): 79–98.

Binns, A. (2014) 'Twitter City and Facebook Village: Teenage girls' personas and experiences influenced by choice architecture in social networking sites', *Journal of Media Practice*, 15(2): 71–91.

Birkwood, S. (2015) 'Tory MPs dislike charity campaigning because so many staff are Labour, says MP Sarah Wollaston', *Third Sector*, 8 October, Available at www.thirdsector.co.uk/tory-mps-dislike-charity-campaigning-so-staff-labour-says-mp-sarah-wollaston/communications/article/1367109

Birkwood, S. (2016) '"Charities aren't villains but we're not heroes by default anymore – the onus is on us to prove ourselves" – @KateBrittain4 of @ACEVO #wspfe', Available at: https://twitter.com/SusannahBirkwoo/status/692646308952285184

Bishop, M. and Green, M. (2010) *Philanthrocapitalism: How Giving Can Save the World*, London: Bloomsbury.

Black, E. (2003) *War against the Weak: Eugenics and America's Campaign to Create a Master Race*, Washington, DC: Dialog Press.

Bloom, P. (2016) *Against Empathy*, London: Vintage.

Body, A. and Breeze, B. (2016) 'What are "unpopular causes" and how can they achieve fundraising success?', *International Journal of Nonprofit and Voluntary Sector Marketing*, 21(1): 57–70.

Bolduc, V.L. (1980) 'Representation and legitimacy in neighborhood organizations', *Nonprofit and Voluntary Sector Quarterly*, 9(1–4): 165–78.

Bourdieu, P. (1979) 'Symbolic power', *Critique of Anthropology*, 4(13–14): 77–85.

Bourdieu, P. (1984) *Distinction: A Social Critique of the Judgment of Taste*, Cambridge, MA: Harvard University Press.

Bourdieu, P. (1985) 'The social space and the genesis of groups', *Information*, 24(2), 195–220.

Bourdieu, P. (1986) 'The Forms of Capital', in J. Richardson (ed) *Handbook of Theory and Research for the Sociology of Education*, New York: Greenwood Press, 241–58.

Bourdieu, P. (1989) 'Social space and symbolic power', *Sociological Theory*, 7(1), 14–25.

Bourdieu, P. (1990) *The Logic of Practice*, Cambridge: Polity.

Bourdieu, P. (1991) *Language and Symbolic Power*, Cambridge, MA: Harvard University Press.

Bourdieu, P. (1994) *The Field of Cultural Production*, New York: Columbia University Press.

Bourdieu, P. (1996) *The State Nobility*, Stanford, CA: Stanford University Press.

Bourdieu, P. (1997) 'Marginalia – Some Additional Notes on the Gift', in A. Schrift (ed) *The Logic of the Gift*, London: Routledge, 231–2.

Bourdieu, P. (2014) *On the State: Lectures at the Collège de France, 1989–1992*, Cambridge: Polity.

Bourdieu, P. and Wacquant, L. (1992) *An Invitation to Reflexive Sociology*, Cambridge: Polity.

Breen, P. (2016) 'Poppies are a political symbol – both on and off the football pitch', *The Conversation*, 3 November, Available at: https://theconversation.com/poppies-are-a-political-symbol-both-on-and-off-the-football-pitch-68113

Breeze, B. (2017) *The New Fundraisers: Who Organises Charitable Giving in Contemporary Society?*, Bristol: Policy Press.

Breeze, B. and Dean, J. (2012a) *User Views of Fundraising: A Study of Charitable Beneficiaries' Opinion of their Representation in Appeals*, London: Alliance.

Breeze, B. and Dean, J. (2012b) 'Pictures of me: User views on their representation in homelessness fundraising appeals', *International Journal of Nonprofit and Voluntary Sector Marketing*, 17(2): 132–43.

Brennan, L. and Binney, W. (2010) 'Fear, guilt, and shame appeals in social marketing', *Journal of Business Research*, 63(2): 140–6.

Brown, R. (1973) 'The emergence of voluntary associations in Massachusetts, 1760–1830', *Journal of Voluntary Action Research*, 2(2): 64–73.

Browne, J., Jochum, V. and Paylor, J. (2013) *The Value of Giving a Little Time: Understanding the Potential of Micro-volunteering*, London: Institute for Volunteering Research.

Bruni, F. (2016) 'To get to Harvard, go to Haiti?', *The New York Times*, 13 August, Available at: www.nytimes.com/2016/08/14/opinion/sunday/to-get-to-harvard-go-to-haiti.html

Buckingham, H., Paine, A., Alcock, P., Kendall, J. and Macmillan, R. (2014) *Who's Speaking for Whom? Exploring Issues of Third Sector Leadership, Leverage and Legitimacy*, Birmingham: Third Sector Research Centre, Available at: www.birmingham.ac.uk/Documents/college-social-sciences/social-policy/tsrc/working-papers/working-paper-121.pdf

Bullen, E. and Kenway, J. (2005) 'Bourdieu, subcultural capital and risky girlhood', *Theory and Research in Education*, 3(1): 47–61.

Bullingham, L. and Vasconcelos, A.C. (2013) '"The presentation of self in the online world": Goffman and the study of online identities', *Journal of Information Science*, 39(1): 101–12.

Bunyan, P. (2013) 'Partnership, the Big Society and community organizing: Between romanticizing, problematizing and politicizing community', *Community Development Journal*, 4(1): 119–33.

Bush, S. (2016) 'Criticising FIFA is literally the very least Theresa May can do to help ex-soldiers', *iNews*, 3 November, Available at: https://inews.co.uk/opinion/criticising-fifa-literally-least-theresa-may-can-help-ex-soldiers

Byrne, C. (2003) 'BBC pinned "virtual poppy" on Jonathan Ross', *The Guardian*, 11 November, Available at: www.theguardian.com/media/2003/nov/11/bbc.broadcasting1

Cabinet Office (2010) *National Survey of Charities and Social Enterprises, 2010*, London: Ipsos Mori/Cabinet Office.

Cabinet Office (2016) 'Government announces new clause to be inserted into grant agreements', Press release, 6 February, Available at: www.gov.uk/government/news/government-announces-new-clause-to-be-inserted-into-grant-agreements

Caesar, T. (2008) '"Larry David is anonymous": Anonymity in the system', *symplokē*, 16(1/2): 37–42.

CAF (Charities Aid Foundation) (2017) *CAF UK Giving 2017: An Overview of Charitable Giving in the UK*, London: CAF.

CAF (2019) *CAF UK Giving Report 2019: An Overview of Charitable Giving in the UK*, London: CAF.

Cameron, D. (2015) 'My vision for a smarter state', Speech, 11 September, Available at: www.gov.uk/government/speeches/prime-minister-my-vision-for-a-smarter-state

Carmel, E. and Harlock, J. (2008) 'Instituting the "third sector" as a governable terrain: Partnership, procurement and performance in the UK', *Policy & Politics*, 36(2): 155–71.

Charity Commission (2017) *Taken on Trust: The Awareness and Effectiveness of Charity Trustees in England and Wales*, London: Charity Commission.

Charity Commission (2018a) 'Recent charity register statistics: Charity Commission', Available at: www.gov.uk/government/publications/charity-register-statistics/recent-charity-register-statistics-charity-commission

Charity Commission (2018b) *Trust in Charities, 2018*, London: Charity Commission.

Charity Commission (2019) *Statement of the Results of an Inquiry: Oxfam*, London: Charity Commission.

Chivers, T. (2017) 'This British autism charity has promoted "dangerous" unlicensed treatments', BuzzFeed.News, 11 February, Available at: www.buzzfeed.com/tomchivers/this-british-autism-charity-has-promoted-dangerous-unlicense

Cnaan, R., Handy, F. and Wadsworth, M. (1996) 'Defining who is a volunteer: Conceptual and empirical considerations', *Nonprofit and Voluntary Sector Quarterly*, 25(3): 364–83.

Conger, J. (1993) 'Max Weber's conceptualization of charismatic authority: Its influence on organizational research', *The Leadership Quarterly*, 4(3/4): 277–88.

Cook, C. (2015a) 'The fall of Kids Company', BBC News Magazine, 12 November, Available at: www.bbc.co.uk/news/magazine-34676281

Cook, C. (2015b) 'Kids Company warned its closure could cause "rioting"', BBC News, 25 August, Available at: www.bbc.co.uk/news/uk-34043725

Cooney, N. (2015) *How to Be Great at Doing Good*, Hoboken, NJ: John Wiley & Sons.

Cooney, R. (2015) '"Pretend to collude with ministers while you actually oppose", Lord Blunkett tells charities', Available at: www.thirdsector.co.uk/pretend-collude-ministers-actually-oppose-lord-blunkett-tells-charities/policy-and-politics/article/1370658

Cornforth, C. and Macmillan, R. (2016) 'Evolution in board chair–CEO relationships: A negotiated order perspective', *Nonprofit and Voluntary Sector Quarterly*, 45(5): 949–70.

Cowley, P. (2017) 'This study got widespread coverage last week. But I can't actually find the data referred to anywhere – can anyone help?', Available at: https://twitter.com/philipjcowley/status/862334323579637760

Cox, J., Oh, E.Y., Simmons, B., Graham, G., Greenhill, A., Lintott, C., et al (2018) 'Getting connected: An empirical investigation of the relationship between social capital and philanthropy among online volunteers', *Nonprofit and Voluntary Sector Quarterly*, 48(2), doi:0899764018794905

Crewe, E. (2015) *The House of Commons: An Anthropology of MPs at Work*, London: Bloomsbury.

Cutcher, L. and Achtel, P. (2017) '"Doing the brand": Aesthetic labour as situated, relational performance in fashion retail', *Work, Employment and Society*, 31(4): 675–91.

Dahl, R. (1957) 'The concept of power', *Behavioural Science*, 2(3): 201–15.

Davies, J. (2018) '"We'd get slagged and bullied": Understanding barriers to volunteering among young people in deprived urban areas', *Voluntary Sector Review*, 9(3): 255–72.

Davis, A. (2018) *Reckless Opportunists: Elites at the End of the Establishment*, Manchester: Manchester University Press.

Dayson, C., Baker, L. and Rees, J. (2018) *The Value of Small*, Sheffield: Centre for Regional Economic and Social Research (CRESR).

DCLG (Department for Communities and Local Government) (2017) *Statutory Homelessness and Prevention and Relief, April to June (Q2) 2017: England*, London: DCLG.

DCMS (Department for Digital, Culture, Media and Sport) (2017) 'Tampon Tax Fund application form: 2018–2019 funding round', Available at: www.gov.uk/government/publications/tampon-tax-fund-application-form-2018-2019-funding-round

DCMS (2018) *Civil Society Strategy: Building a Future that Works for Everyone*, London: Cabinet Office.

De Wit, A., Bekkers, R., Karamat Ali, D. and Verkaik, D. (2015) 'Welfare Impacts of Participation', Deliverable 3.3 of the Project: 'Impact of the Third Sector as Social Innovation' (ITSSOIN), European Commission – 7th Framework Programme, Brussels: European Commission, DG Research.

Deacon, D. (1999) 'Charitable Images: The Construction of Voluntary Sector News', in B. Franklin (eds) *Social Policy, The Media and Misrepresentation*, London: Routledge, 51–68.

Deacon, M. (2017) 'Why it's time to stop jeering at "virtue signalling"', *The Telegraph*, 11 February, Available at: www.telegraph.co.uk/opinion/2017/02/11/time-stop-jeering-virtue-signalling/

Deakin, N. (2001) *In Search of Civil Society*, Basingstoke: Palgrave.

Dean, J. (2014) 'How structural factors promote instrumental motivations within youth volunteering: A qualitative analysis of volunteer brokerage', *Voluntary Sector Review*, 5(2): 231–47.

Dean, J. (2015a) 'Drawing what homelessness looks like: Using creative visual methods as a tool of critical pedagogy', *Sociological Research Online*, 20(1): 2.

Dean, J. (2015b) 'Volunteering, the market, and neoliberalism', *People, Place and Policy*, 9(2): 139–48.

Dean, J. (2016a) 'Class diversity and youth volunteering in the UK: Applying Bourdieu's habitus and cultural capital', *Nonprofit and Voluntary Sector Quarterly*, 45(1S): 95–113.

Dean, J. (2016b) 'Recruiting young volunteers in an area of selective education: A qualitative case study', *British Journal of Sociology of Education*, 37(4): 643–61.

Dean, J. (2017) *Doing Reflexivity: An Introduction*, Bristol: Policy Press.

Dean, J. (2020) 'Student perceptions and experiences of charity on social media: The authenticity of offline networks in online giving', *Voluntary Sector Review*, 11(1): 41–57.

Dean, J. and Verrier, D. (2018) 'Defining Who Is a Volunteer: Motivations and Principles from a New Generation', Paper presented at Voluntary Sector Studies Network (VSSN) Conference, London.

Dean, J. and Wood, R. (2017) '"You can try to press different emotional buttons": The conflicts and strategies of eliciting emotions for fundraisers', *International Journal of Nonprofit and Voluntary Sector Marketing*, 22(4): e1603.

Dean, J., Honeywell, C. and Price, A. (2019) 'Volunteering: From Social Control to Prefigurative Participation', in A. Eikenberry, R. Mirabella and B. Sandberg (eds) *Reframing Nonprofit Organizations: Democracy, Inclusion, and Social Change*, Irvine, CA: Melvin & Leigh, 193–202.

Dean, J., Furness, P., Verrier, D., Lennon, H., Bennett, C. and Spencer, S. (2018) 'Desert island data: An investigation into researcher positionality', *Qualitative Research*, 18(3): 273–89.

Devine, K. (2019) 'Not all the "over 65s" are in favour of Brexit – Britain's wartime generation are almost as pro-EU as millennials', LSE Comment, Available at: https://blogs.lse.ac.uk/europpblog/2019/03/21/not-all-the-over-65s-are-in-favour-of-brexit-britains-wartime-generation-are-almost-as-pro-eu-as-millennials/

Durkheim, E. (1982) *The Rules of Sociological Method*, New York: Free Press.

DWP (Department for Work and Pensions) (2019) *Households Below Average Income: An Analysis of the UK Income Distribution: 1994/95–2017/18*. London: DWP.

Eayrs, C. and Ellis, N. (1990) 'Charity advertising: For or against people with a mental handicap?', *British Journal of Social Psychology*, 29(4): 349–60.

Eddo-Lodge, R. (2018) *Why I'm No Longer Talking to White People about Race*, London: Bloomsbury.

Eikenberry, A. (2009) *Giving Circles: Philanthropy, Voluntary Association, and Democracy*, Indianapolis, IN: Indiana University Press.

Eikenberry, A. and Breeze, B. (2015) 'Growing philanthropy through collaboration: The landscape of giving circles in the United Kingdom and Ireland', *Voluntary Sector Review*, 6(1): 41–59.

Eikenberry, A. and Mirabella, R. (2018) 'Extreme philanthropy: Philanthrocapitalism, effective altruism, and the discourse of neoliberalism', *PS: Political Science & Politics*, 51(1): 43–7.

Eisenstadt, S.N. (1968) 'Introduction', in M. Weber (ed) *On Charisma and Institution Building: Selected Papers*, Chicago, IL: Chicago University Press, ix–lvi.

Elder-Vass, D. (2010) *The Causal Power of Social Structures: Emergency, Structure and Agency*, Cambridge: Cambridge University Press.

Elder-Vass, D. (2016) *Profit and Gift in the Digital Economy*, Cambridge: Cambridge University Press.

Elder-Vass, D. (2018) 'Bourdieu, art and financial value', *Materially Social*, 4 July, Available at: http://materiallysocial.blogspot.com/2018/07/bourdieu-art-and-financial-value.html

Eliasoph, N. (2013) *The Politics of Volunteering*, Cambridge: Polity Press.

Elledge, J. (2017) 'Britain has built a national myth on winning the Second World War, but it's distorting our politics', *New Statesman*, 18–24 August, 36.

Ellis Paine, A., McKay, S. and Moro, D. (2013) 'Does volunteering improve employability? Insights from the British Household Panel Survey and beyond', *Voluntary Sector Review*, 4(3): 355–76.

Elster, J. (2011) 'The Valmont Effect: The Warm-glow Theory of Philanthropy', in P. Illingworth, T. Pogge, and L. Wenar (eds) *Giving Well: The Ethics of Philanthropy*, Oxford: Oxford University Press, 67–83.

Eranti, V. and Lonkila, M. (2015) 'The social significance of the Facebook Like button', *First Monday*, 20(6).

Evans, B., Glass, J. and Wellstead, A. (2017) 'Policy Analysis and the Voluntary Sector', in M. Brans, I. Geva-May and M. Howlett (eds) *Routledge Handbook of Comparative Policy Analysis*, London: Routledge, 291–306.

Evans, M. (2015) *Artwash: Big Oil and the Arts*, London: Pluto Press.

Falco, N., Fopma, W., Maxwell, S., Stoller, M. and Turrell, N. (1998) 'Is philanthropy a learned behavior?', *Fund Raising Management*, 29(7), 36–7.

Farenthold, D. (2016) 'Trump boasts about his philanthropy. But his giving falls short of his words', *The Washington Post*, 29 October, Available at: www.washingtonpost.com/politics/trump-boasts-of-his-philanthropy-but-his-giving-falls-short-of-his-words/2016/10/29/b3c03106-9ac7-11e6-a0ed-ab0774c1eaa5_story.html

Farenthold, D. (2017) 'The Daily 202: What Trump's giving to charity – or lack thereof – foreshadowed about his presidency', *The Washington Post*, 21 April, Available at: www.washingtonpost.com/news/powerpost/paloma/daily-202/2017/04/21/daily-202-what-trump-s-giving-to-charity-or-lack-thereof-foreshadowed-about-his-presidency/58f9b8abe9b69b3a72331eaf/

Farenthold, D. (2018) 'New York files civil suit against President Trump, alleging his charity engaged in "illegal conduct"', *The Washington Post*, 14 June, Available at: www.washingtonpost.com/politics/new-york-files-suit-against-president-trump-alleging-his-charity-engaged-in-illegal-conduct

Flaherty, J. (2016) *No More Heroes: Grassroots Challenges to the Saviour Mentality*, Edinburgh: AK Press.

Flannagan, M. (2017) 'The charity sector lacks political capital', *Third Sector*, 13 March, Available at: www.thirdsector.co.uk/mark-flannagan-charity-sector-lacks-political-capital/policy-and-politics/article/1426996

Fluskey, D. (2019) 'Why fewer people are giving to charity and what we can do about it', Civil Society Media, 8 May, Available at: www.civilsociety.co.uk/voices/daniel-fluskey-why-fewer-people-are-giving-to-charity-and-what-we-can-do-about-it.html

Foster, A. (2016) 'How can we understand the demise of Kids Company?', *British Journal of Psychotherapy*, 32(1): 125–31.

Foucault, M. (1988) *Technologies of the Self: A Seminar with Michel Foucault*, Amherst, MA: University of Massachusetts Press.

Fowler, A. (2000) 'NGDOs as a moment in time: Beyond aid to social entrepreneurship or civic innovation?', *Third World Quarterly*, 21(4): 637–54.

Gallagher, B. (2018) 'Larry David and the game theory of anonymous donations', *Nautilus*, 8 June, Available at: http://nautil.us/blog/larry-david-and-the-game-theory-of-anonymous-donations

Gani, A. (2017) 'This England cricketer's poppy fell off in a photoshoot and people have a lot of thoughts', BuzzFeed.News, 30 October, Available at: www.buzzfeed.com/aishagani/a-poppy-fell-off-and-the-poppy-police-are-out

Garrow, E. and Hasenfeld, Y. (2010) 'Theoretical Approaches to Human Service Organizations', in Y. Hasenfeld (ed) *Human Services as Complex Organisations*, Thousand Oaks, CA: Sage, 33–60.

Garthwaite, K. (2016) *Hunger Pains: Life inside Foodbank Britain*, Bristol: Policy Press.

Giddens, A. (1998) *The Third Way: The Renewal of Social Democracy*, Cambridge: Polity.

Gillett, F. (2016) 'Cookie Monster wears a poppy on *The One Show* leaving BBC viewers baffled', *Evening Standard*, 8 November, Available at: www.standard.co.uk/news/uk/bbc-viewers-baffled-as-cookie-monster-wears-a-poppy-on-the-one-show-a3389846.html

Gilroy, P. (2002) *There Ain't No Black in the Union Jack* (2nd edn), London: Routledge.

Gilroy, P. (2004) *After Empire: Melancholia or Convivial Culture?*, Abingdon: Routledge.

Giridharadas, A. (2018) *Winners Take All: The Elite Charade of Changing the World*, London: Allen Lane.

Girlguiding (2017) *Girls' Attitudes Survey 2017*, London: Girlguiding.

Giroux, H. (2016) 'Writing the public good back into education: Reclaiming the role of the public intellectual', in J.R. Di Leo and P. Hitchcock (eds) *The New Public Intellectual*, Palgrave Macmillan: New York, 3–28.

Goffman, E. (1959) *The Presentation of Self in Everyday Life*, Harmondsworth: Penguin.

Goffman, E. (1963) *Stigma: Notes on the Management of Spoiled Identity*, New York: Simon & Schuster.

Gold, T. (2017) 'The rise of the euphemistic slur', *New Statesman*, 10–16 February, 17.

Goslett, M. (2015) 'The trouble with Kids Company', *The Spectator*, 14 February, Available at: www.spectator.co.uk/2015/02/the-trouble-with-kids-company

Goslett, M. (2016) 'Kids Company: How *The Spectator* first blew the whistle', *The Spectator*, 1 February, Available at: https://blogs.spectator.co.uk/2016/02/kids-company-how-the-spectator-first-blew-the-whistle

GOV.UK (2019) 'Set up a charity: Step by step', Available at: www.gov.uk/set-up-a-charity

Graeber, D. (2004) *Fragments of an Anarchist Anthropology*. Chicago, IL: Prickly Paradigm Press.

Grattan, L. (2012) 'Pierre Bourdieu and populism: The everyday politics of outrageous resistance', *The Good Society*, 21(2): 194–218.

Gunstone, B. and Ellison, G. (2017a) *Insights into Charity Fundraising: Changes in Knowledge, Attitude and Action as a Result of Donating*, London: YouGov.

Gunstone, B. and Ellison, G. (2017b) *Why People Give and their Experience of Donating*, London: YouGov.

Guo, C. and Musso, C. (2007) 'Representation in nonprofit and voluntary organizations: A conceptual framework', *Nonprofit and Voluntary Sector Quarterly*, 36(2): 308–26.

Guo, C. and Saxton, G. (2014) 'Tweeting social change: How social media are changing nonprofit advocacy', *Nonprofit and Voluntary Sector Quarterly*, 43(1): 57–79.

Harden, J., Jukes, I. and Joyce, P (2015) *An Insight into the Charitable Giving of Young Adults and Students*, London: Reason Digital.

Harper, D. (2002) 'Talking about pictures: A case for photo elicitation', *Visual Studies*, 17(1): 13–26.

Harrison, P. (1960) 'Weber's categories of authority and voluntary associations', *American Sociological Review*, 25(2): 231–7.

Hart, M. (2017) 'Being naked on the internet: Young people's selfies as intimate edgework', *Journal of Youth Studies*, 20(3): 301–15.

Harvey, C., Maclean, M., Gordon, J. and Shaw, E. (2011) 'Andrew Carnegie and the foundations of contemporary entrepreneurial philanthropy', *Business History*, 53(3): 425–50.

Hatherley, O. (2017) *The Ministry of Nostalgia*, London: Verso.

Hattersley, R. (2010) 'Poppy fascists? Does Jon Snow realise how offensive he is being to the loved ones of those who died fighting real fascism?', *The Daily Mail*, 5 November, Available at: www.dailymail.co.uk/debate/article-1326408/Jon-Snow-poppy-fascism-row-Does-know-offensive-hes-being.html

Health Policy Insight (2010) Editor's blog, Wednesday 22 December 2010: 'DH cancer czar – Cancer Drugs Fund "extremely unlikely" to alter survival difference', Available at: www.healthpolicyinsight.com/?q=node/898

Healy, K. (2017) 'Fuck nuance', *Sociological Theory*, 35(2): 118–27.

Heckler, N. (2018) 'Critical Whiteness and Masculinity Studies Are Needed in NPO Research', Paper presented at ARNOVA (Association for Research on Nonprofit Organizations and Voluntary Action) Conference, Austin, Texas.

Hemmings, M. (2017) 'The constraints on voluntary sector voice in a period of continued austerity', *Voluntary Sector Review*, 8(1): 41–66.

Hibbert, S., Smith, A., Davies, A. and Ireland, F. (2007) 'Guilt appeals: Persuasion knowledge and charitable giving', *Psychology & Marketing*, 24(8): 723–42.

Hillier, A. (2015) 'Charity pay study: Who are the highest earners?', *Third Sector*, 26 February, Available at: www.thirdsector.co.uk/charity-pay-study-highest-earners/management/article/1335060

Hilton, A. (2016) 'Growing mistrust of charity could harm us all', *Evening Standard*, 8 December, Available at: www.standard.co.uk/business/anthony-hilton-growing-mistrust-of-charity-could-harm-us-all-a3415531.html

Hilton, M., McKay, J., Crowson, N. and Mouhot, J. (2013) *The Politics of Expertise: How NGOs Shaped Modern Britain*, Oxford: Oxford University Press.

Hirsch, A. (2018) *Brit(ish): On Race, Identity and Belonging*, London: Jonathan Cape.

Hogan, B. (2010) 'The presentation of self in the age of social media: Distinguishing performances and exhibitions online', *Bulletin of Science, Technology & Society*, 30(6): 377–86.

Hogg, E. (2017) 'What regulation, who pays? Public attitudes to charity regulation in England and Wales', *Nonprofit and Voluntary Sector Quarterly*, 47(1): 72–88.

Hogg, E. and Baines, S. (2011) 'Changing responsibilities and roles of the voluntary and community sector in the welfare mix: A review', *Social Policy and Society*, 10(3): 341–52.

Holdsworth, C. (2017) 'The cult of experience: Standing out from the crowd in an era of austerity', *Area*, 49(3): 296–302.

Holdsworth, C. and Brewis, G. (2014) 'Volunteering, choice and control: A case study of higher education student volunteering', *Journal of Youth Studies*, 17(2), 204–19.

Home Office (1998) *Compact on Relations between Government and the Voluntary and Community Sector in England*, London: Home Office.

Hume, D. (2012 [1738]) *A Treatise of Human Nature*, CreateSpace Independent Publishing Platform.

Hustinx, L. and Meijs, L. (2011) 'Re-embedding volunteerism: In search of a new collective ground', *Voluntary Sector Review*, 2(1): 5–21.

Hustinx, L., Cnaan, R. and Handy, F. (2010) 'Navigating theories of volunteering: A hybrid map for a complex phenomenon', *Journal for the Theory of Social Behaviour*, 40(4): 410–34.

Hwang, H. and Powell, W. (2009) 'The rationalization of charity: The influences of professionalism in the nonprofit sector', *Administrative Science Quarterly*, 54(2): 268–98.

INCITE! Women of Color Against Violence (2007) *The Revolution Will Not Be Funded: Beyond the Non-Profit Industrial Complex*, Cambridge, MA: South End Press.

Independence Panel (2015) *An Independent Mission: The Voluntary Sector in 2015*, Panel on the Independence of the Voluntary Sector, Available at: https://cdn.baringfoundation.org.uk/wp-content/uploads/2015/02/IP-Mission.pdf

Ipsos MORI (2014) *Public Trust and Confidence in Charities 2014*, Available at: www.ipsos.com/ipsos-mori/en-uk/public-trust-and-confidence-charities-2014

Isherwood, C. (2007) 'The graffiti of the philanthropic class', *The New York Times*, 2 December.

Isidore, C. and Schuman, S. (2018) 'New York attorney general sues Trump Foundation', CNN, 14 June, Available at: https://edition.cnn.com/2018/06/14/politics/new-york-lawsuit-trump-foundation/index.html

Jaspers, C. (1919) *Psychology of Worldviews*, Berlin: Springer Press.

Jessop, B. (2016) *The State*, Cambridge: Polity.

Jones, A. (2017) 'Band Aid revisited: Humanitarianism, consumption and philanthropy in the 1980s', *Contemporary British History*, 31(2): 189–209.

Jones, H., Gunaratnam, Y., Bhattacharyya, G., Davies, W., Dhaliwal, S., Forkert, K., et al (2017) *Go Home? The Politics of Immigration Controversies*, Manchester: Manchester University Press.

Jones, J., Cantrell, R. and Lindsey, A. (2018) 'America's worst charities: The effect of bad press on philanthropic giving behavior', *International Journal of Nonprofit and Voluntary Sector Marketing*, 24(1): e1616.

Jones, K. (2006) 'Giving and volunteering as distinct forms of civic engagement: The role of community resources and personal integration in forming helping', *Nonprofit and Voluntary Sector Quarterly*, 35(2): 249–66.

Kalia, A. (2018) 'Poppy appeal has raised £1 every second since first world war', *The Guardian*, 10 November, Available at: www.theguardian.com/world/2018/nov/10/poppy-appeal-has-raised-1-every-second-since-first-world-war

Kallman, M. (2020) *The Death of Idealism: Professionalization as Anti-Politics in the Peace Corps*, New York: Columbia University Press.

Kant, I. (1996) *The Metaphysics of Morals*, Cambridge: Cambridge University Press.

Kapoor, I. (2013) *Celebrity Humanitarianism: The Ideology of Global Charity*, London: Routledge.

Karlan, D. and McConnell, M. (2014) 'Hey look at me: The effect of giving circles on giving', *Journal of Economic Behavior & Organization*, 106: 402–12.

Kedrowski, K.M. and Sarow, M.S. (2007) *Cancer Activism: Gender, Media, and Public Policy*, Chicago, IL: University of Illinois Press.

Kenber, B., Sherman, J. and Bannerman, L. (2015) 'Cameron accused as charity fails', *The Times*, 6 August, 6.

Kendall, J. (2003) *The Voluntary Sector: Comparative Perspectives in the UK*, London: Routledge.

Kendall, J. and Knapp, M. (1995) 'A Loose and Baggy Monster', in J. Davis Smith, C. Rochester and R. Hedley (eds) *An Introduction to the Voluntary Sector*, London: Routledge, 66–95.

Khan, S. (2011) *Privilege: The Making of an Adolescent Elite at St Paul's School*, Oxford: Princeton University Press.

Kim, M. and Charbonneau, E. (2018) 'Caught between volunteerism and professionalism: Support by nonprofit leaders for the donative labor hypothesis', *Review of Public Personnel Administration*, doi:10.1177/0734371X18816139

King, D. (2017) 'Becoming business-like: Governing the nonprofit professional', *Nonprofit and Voluntary Sector Quarterly*, 46(2): 241–60.

King, S. (2010) 'Pink Ribbons Inc: The Emergence of Cause-related Marketing and the Corporatization of the Breast Cancer Movement', in L. Reed and P. Saukko (eds) *Governing the Female Body: Gender, Health, and Networks of Power*, New York: State University of New York Press, 85–111.

Klein, N. (2001) *No Logo: Taking Aim at the Brand Bullies*, London: HarperCollins.

Klekar, C. (2009) 'Obligation, Coercion, and Economy: The Deed of Trust in Congreve's *The Way of the World*', in L. Zionkowski and C. Klekar (eds) *The Culture of the Gift in Eighteenth-Century England*, New York: Palgrave Macmillan, 125–41.

Koffman, O., Orgad, S. and Gill, R. (2015) 'Girl power and "selfie humanitarianism"', *Journal of Media & Cultural Studies*, 29(2): 157–68.

Konrath, S., Ho, M.-H. and Zairns, S. (2016) 'The strategic helper: Narcissism and prosocial motives and behaviors', *Current Psychology*, 35(2): 182–94.

Kranish, M. and Fisher, M. (2016) *Trump Revealed: The Definitive Biography of the 45th President*, London: Simon & Schuster.

Krause, M. (2014) *The Good Project: Humanitarian Relief NGOs and the Fragmentation of Reason*, London: University of Chicago Press.

Kropotkin, P. (1914) *Mutual Aid: A Factor of Evolution*, London: Porter Sergeant.

Labour Party, The (2019) *From Paternalism to Participation: Putting Civil Society at the Heart of National Renewal*, London: The Labour Party.

Lambie-Munford, H. (2017) *Hungry Britain: The Rise of Food Charity*, Bristol: Policy Press.

Lange, P. (2014) *Kids on YouTube: Technical Identities and Digital Literacies*, Walnut Creek, CA: Left Coast Press.

Laville, S. (2015) 'Pressure on Alan Yentob over Kids Company shows as he loses cool on TV', *The Guardian*, 7 August, Available at: www.theguardian.com/media/2015/aug/07/pressure-alan-yentob-kids-company-loses-cool-on-channel-4-news

Laville, S. (2016) 'Police drop Kids Company abuse investigation', *The Guardian*, 28 January, Available at: www.theguardian.com/uk-news/2016/jan/28/police-drop-kids-company-abuse-investigation

Lawler, S. (2008) *Identity: Sociological Perspectives*, London: Polity Press.

Leftwich, A. (2004) 'The Political Approach to Human Behaviour', in A. Leftwich (ed) *What Is Politics?*, Cambridge: Polity, 100–18.

Liew, J. (2017) 'Tedious annual poppy circus reminds us that, for some, remembrance isn't about remembering, it's being seen to remember', *Independent*, 30 October, Available at: www.independent.co.uk/sport/football/premier-league/remembrance-day-moeen-ali-jonathan-liew-james-mcclean-poppies-royal-british-legion-a8028301.html

Lim, M. and Moufahim, M. (2015) 'The spectacularization of suffering: An analysis of the use of celebrities in "Comic Relief" UK's charity fundraising campaigns', *Journal of Marketing Management*, 31(5–6): 525–45.

Lines, A. (2014) 'BBC snubs official poppy appeal song by refusing to put it on radio playlist', *Mirror*, 9 November, Available at: www.mirror.co.uk/news/uk-news/bbc-snubs-official-poppy-appeal-4600035

Littlejohn, G. (2018) 'Homeless charity boss "told she won't get Lottery funding unless she stops criticising Universal Credit"', *iNews*, 27 October, Available at: https://inews.co.uk/news/homeless-charity-boss-claims-she-was-told-she-wont-get-lottery-funding-unless-she-stops-criticising-the-government/

Littler, J. (2011) 'What's Wrong with Ethical Consumption?', in T. Lewis and E. Potter (eds) *Ethical Consumption: A Critical Introduction*, London: Routledge, 27–39.

Lloyd, T. (2004) *Why Rich People Give*, London: Philanthropy UK.

Lockyer, B. (2016) 'The early women's movement resisted the charity label', *Third Sector*, 29 December, Available at: www.thirdsector.co.uk/early-womens-movement-resisted-charity-label/article/1376938

Longmore, P. (2016) *Telethons: Spectacle, Disability, and the Business of Charity*, New York: Oxford University Press.

MacAskill, W. (2015) *Doing Good Better: Effective Altruism and a Radical New Way to Make a Difference*, London: Guardian Books/Faber & Faber.

MacInnes, J. and Cheung, S.Y. (2013) 'Creating public attitudes to immigration by mis-counting', *Discover Society*, 5 November, Available at: https://discoversociety.org/2013/11/05/creating-public-attitudes-to-immigration-by-mis-counting/

Macmillan, R. (2013) '"Distinction" in the third sector', *Voluntary Sector Review*, 4(1): 39–54.

Macmillan, R. (2016) 'The collapse of Kids Company – A settling of accounts', University of Birmingham, Perspectives, Available at: www.birmingham.ac.uk/research/perspective/kids-company.aspx

Marwick, A. and boyd, d. (2011) 'I tweet honestly, I tweet passionately: Twitter users, context collapse, and the imagined audience', *New Media & Society*, 13(1): 114–33.

Mason, R. (2014) 'Charities should stick to knitting and stay out of politics, says MP', *The Guardian*, 3 September, Available at: www.theguardian.com/society/2014/sep/03/charities-knitting-politics-brook-newmark

Mauss, M. (2011) *The Gift: Forms and Functions of Exchange in Archaic Societies*, Eastford, CT: Martino Fine Books.

McCormack, M. (2012) 'Stonewalling progress', OUPblog, 25 August, Available at: https://blog.oup.com/2012/08/stonewalling-progress/

McCormack, M. (2019) 'Advocacy research on homophobia in education: Claims-making, trauma construction and the politics of evidence', *Sociology*, doi:0038038519858585

McDonnell, D. and Rutherford, A. (2017) 'The determinants of charity misconduct', *Nonprofit and Voluntary Sector Quarterly*, 47(1): 107–25.

McGarvey, D. (2017) *Poverty Safari*, Edinburgh: Luath Press.

McGhee, D., Bennett, C. and Walker, S. (2016) 'The combination of "insider" and "outsider" strategies in VSO–government partnerships: The relationship between Refugee Action and the Home Office in the UK', *Voluntary Sector Review*, 7(1): 27–46.

McGoey, L. (2012) 'Philanthrocapitalism and its critics', *Poetics*, 40(2): 185–99.

McGoey, L. (2015) *No Such Thing as a Free Gift: The Gates Foundation and the Price of Philanthropy*, London: Verso.

McGovern, P. (2017) *Small Voluntary Organisations in the 'Age of Austerity': Funding Challenges and Opportunities*, London: Palgrave.

Mckenzie, L. (2015) *Getting By: Estates, Class and Culture in Austerity Britain*, Bristol: Policy Press.

McMillen, D.B. (1978) 'The UMW as a social movement', *Nonprofit and Voluntary Sector Quarterly*, 7(3): 106–19.

McNab, C. (2018) *The Book of the Poppy*, Stroud: The History Press.

Media Monkey (2013) 'BBC acts to stem poppy row', *The Guardian*, 16 October, Available at: www.theguardian.com/media/mediamonkeyblog/2013/oct/16/bbc-poppy-row

Micklethwait, A. and Dimond, P. (2017) *Driven to the Brink: Why Corporate Governance, Board Leadership and Culture Matter*, London: Palgrave Macmillan.

Mikołajewska-Zając, K. (2018) 'Terms of reference: The moral economy of reputation in a sharing economy platform', *European Journal of Social Theory*, 21(2): 148–68.

Milbourne, L. (2013) *The Voluntary Sector in Transition: Hard Times or New Opportunities?*, Bristol: Policy Press.

Mohan, J. (2016) 'Series Editor's Foreword', in J. Rees and D. Mullins (eds) *The Third Sector Delivering Public Services: Developments, Innovations and Challenges*, Bristol: Policy Press, vi–vii.

Mohan, J. and Breeze, B. (2016) *The Logic of Charity: Great Expectations in Hard Times*, Basingstoke: Palgrave Macmillan.

Molina, J. (2018) 'The end of Kids Company: Making sense of closure', *Youth & Policy*, Available at: www.youthandpolicy.org/articles/the-end-of-kids-company/

Moll, J., Krueger, F., Zahn, R., Pardini, M., de Oliveira-Souza, R. and Grafman, J. (2006) 'Human fronto–mesolimbic networks guide decisions about charitable donation', *Proceedings of the National Academy of Sciences*, 103(42), 15623–8.

Moore, S. (2008) *Ribbon Culture: Charity, Compassion and Public Awareness*, Basingstoke: Palgrave Macmillan.

Morgan-Bentley, P. (2018) 'Charities under gagging clauses will be allowed to speak out against government', *The Times*, 6 December, Available at: www.thetimes.co.uk/article/charities-will-be-allowed-to-speak-out-against-government-kb6hcp2wn

Morris, D. (2016) 'Legal limits on campaigning by charities: Drawing the line', *Voluntary Sector Review*, 7(1): 109–15.

Murray, D. (2012) 'The politics of poppies', *The Spectator*, 1 November, Available at: http://blogs.spectator.co.uk/douglas-murray/2012/11/the-politics-of-poppies/

Murray, U. (2006) 'To what extent is the voluntary sector colonised by neo-liberal thinking?', National Coalition for Independent Action, Available at: www.independentaction.net/wp-content/uploads/2013/09/Voluntary-Sector-Neo-Liberal-thinking-Ursula-Murray.pdf

Najan, A. (2003) 'The four-C's of third sector–government relations', *Nonprofit Leadership and Management*, 10(4): 375–96.

Nakamura, L. (2002) *Cybertypes: Race, Ethnicity, and Identity on the Internet*, London: Routledge.

NAO (National Audit Office) (2015) *Investigation: The Government's Funding of Kids Company*, London: NAO.

NAO (2017) *Report on the Funding and Governance of Broken Rainbow*, London: NAO.

Navarrete, C.D., McDonald, M.M., Mott, M.L. and Asher, B. (2012) 'Virtual morality: Emotion and action in a simulated three-dimensional "trolley problem"', *Emotion*, 12(2), 364–70.

NCIA (National Coalition for Independent Action) (2015) *Fight or Fright: Voluntary Services in 2015*, Available at: www.independentaction.net/wp-content/uploads/sites/8/2015/02/NCIA-Inquiry-summary-report-final.pdf

NCVO (National Council for Voluntary Organisations) (2019) *UK Civil Society Almanac 2019*, Available at: https://data.ncvo.org.uk/

Neville, S. (2016) 'Tories accused of pushing for sympathisers to be handed key public posts', *Financial Times*, Available at: https://next.ft.com/content/245d20e2-fc1a-11e5-b5f5-070dca6d0a0d

nfp Synergy (2017) *Trust in Charities and Other Public Institutions*, London: nfp Synergy.

Nowrasteh, A. (2016) 'The right has its own version of political correctness. It's just as stifling', *The Washington Post*, 7 December, Available at: www.washingtonpost.com/posteverything/wp/2016/12/07/the-right-has-its-own-version-of-political-correctness-its-just-as-stifling

NYA (National Youth Agency) (2007) *Young People's Volunteering and Skills Development*, London: NYA.

O'Neill, M. (1994) 'Fundraising as an ethical act', *New Directions for Philanthropic Fundraising*, 6: 3–13.

O'Neill, S. (2018) 'How the Oxfam sex scandal unfolded', *The Times*, 16 February, Available at: www.thetimes.co.uk/article/one-week-on-how-the-oxfam-sex-scandal-unfolded-rdq6qhzgh

Orben, A., Dienlin, T. and Przybylski, A. (2019) 'Social media's enduring effect on adolescent life satisfaction', *Proceedings of the National Academy of Sciences*, 116(21): 10226–8.

Orwell, G. (2018 [1945]) *Notes on Nationalism*, London: Penguin.

Ostrander, S. (1984) *Women of the Upper Class*, Philadelphia, PA: Temple University Press.

Ostrander, S. (1989) 'Why Philanthropy Neglects Poverty: Some Thoughts from History and Theory', in V. Hodgkinson and R. Lyman (eds) *The Future of the Nonprofit Sector*, San Francisco, CA: Jossey-Bass, 219–36.

Ostrander, S. and Schervish, P. (1990) 'Giving and Getting: Philanthropy as Social Relation', in J. van Til (ed) *Critical Issues in American Philanthropy: Strengthening Theory and Practice*, San Francisco, CA: Jossey-Bass, 67–98.

Owen, D. (1964) *English Philanthropy, 1660–1960*, Cambridge, MA: Harvard University Press.

PAC (Public Accounts Committee) (2015) *The Government's Funding of Kids Company: Eighth Report of Session 2015–16*, London: The Stationery Office, Available at: https://publications.parliament.uk/pa/cm201516/cmselect/cmpubacc/504/504.pdf

PACAC (Public Administration and Constitutional Affairs Committee) (2015) *The Collapse of Kids Company: Lessons for Charity Trustees, Professional Firms, the Charity Commission, and Whitehall*, Available at: https://publications.parliament.uk/pa/cm201516/cmselect/cmpubadm/433/43302.htm

Parker, S. (2015) *Taking Power Back: Putting People in Charge of Politics*, Bristol: Policy Press.

Payne, S. (2015) 'Britain's "fat beggar" scandal', POLITICO, 11 February, Available at: www.politico.eu/article/britains-fat-beggar-scandal-wormald-heaton-kids-company

Pellandini-Simányi, L. (2014) 'Bourdieu, ethics and symbolic power', *The Sociological Review*, 62(4): 651–74.

Pettinger, L. (2019) *What's Wrong with Work?*, Bristol: Policy Press.

Phillimore, J. and McCabe, A. (2015) 'Small-scale civil society and social policy: The importance of experiential learning, insider knowledge and diverse motivations in shaping community action', *Voluntary Sector Review*, 6(2): 135–51.

Pilditch, D. (2014) 'Veterans urge boycott of motorway services after poppy ban', *Daily Express*, 29 October, Available at: www.express.co.uk/news/uk/528656/Boycott-motorway-services-who-banned-poppy-sales

PKF Littlejohn (2016) *Annual Fraud Indicator 2016 (Research Report)*, London: PKF Littlejohn.

Plummer, J. (2019) 'Olive Cooke case enabled fundraising reform despite charities not being responsible, says former minister', *Third Sector*, 20 September, Available at: www.thirdsector.co.uk/olive-cooke-case-enabled-fundraising-reform-despite-charities-not-responsible-says-former-minister/fundraising/article/1660206

Private Eye (2018) 'Footy footy footy', Page 94 Podcast, Episode 34, Available at: www.private-eye.co.uk/eyeplayer/play-342

Pulitzer Prizes, The (2017) 'David A. Farenthold of *The Washington Post*', Available at: www.pulitzer.org/winners/david-fahrenthold

Rai, S. (2015) 'Political performance: A framework for understanding democratic politics', *Political Studies*, 63(5): 1179–97.

Raventós, D. and Wark, J. (2018) *Against Charity*, Chicago, IL: AK Press.

Reay, D. (2006) 'The Zombie stalking English schools: Social class and educational inequality', *British Journal of Educational Studies*, 54(3): 288–307.

Rees, J., Macmillan, R. and Buckingham, H. (2015) 'The Voluntary and Faith Sector: "Stepping Up" or "Waving but Drowning" in the Age of Austerity?', in L. Foster, A. Brunton, C. Deeming and T. Haux (eds) *In Defence of Welfare 2*, Bristol: Policy Press, 117–20.

Reich, R. (2018) *Just Giving: Why Philanthropy Is Failing Democracy and How It Can Do It Better*, Princeton, NJ: Princeton University Press.

Reyniers, D. and Bhalla, R. (2013) 'Reluctant altruism and peer pressure in charitable giving', *Judgment and Decision Making*, 8(1): 7–15.

Riches, G. (1997) *First World Hunger: Food Security and Welfare Politics*, Basingstoke: Macmillan.

Richey, L. and Ponte, S. (2011) *Brand Aid: Shopping Well to Save the World*, Minneapolis, MN: University of Minnesota Press.

Ricketts, A. (2017) 'Sector too ready to use lobbying act as an excuse, says JRRT chief', *Third Sector*, 11 October, Available at www.thirdsector.co.uk/sector-ready-use-lobbying-act-excuse-says-jrrt-chief/policy-and-politics/article/1447104

Ridley-Duff, R. and Bull, M. (2019) *Understanding Social Enterprise: Theory and Practice* (3rd edn), London: Sage.

Riesebrodt, M. (2001) 'Charisma', in H.G. Klippenberg and M. Risebrodt (eds) *Max Weber's 'Religionssystemtik'*, Tubingen: J.C.B. Mohr, 151–66.

Robb, C. (2016) Speech at the Voluntary Sector and Volunteering Research Conference, Nottingham, 8 September.

Robinson, L. (2012) 'Putting the charity back into charity singles: Charity singles in Britain 1984–1995', *Contemporary British History*, 26(3): 405–25.

Rochester, C. (2013) *Rediscovering Voluntary Action: The Beat of a Different Drum*, Basingstoke: Palgrave.

Rochester, C., Howlett, S. and Ellis Paine, A. (2010) *Volunteering and Society in the 21st Century*, Basingstoke: Palgrave Macmillan.

Rojek, C. (2013) *Event Power: How Global Events Manage and Manipulate*, London: Sage.

Ronson, J. (2016) *So You've Been Publically Shamed*, London: Picador.

Rose-Ackerman, S. (1990) 'Competition between non-profits and for-profits: Entry and growth', *Voluntas: International Journal of Voluntary and Nonprofit Organizations*, 1: 13–25.

Rosenthal, R. (2000) 'Imaging homelessness and homeless people: Visions and strategies within the movement(s)', *Journal of Social Distress and the Homeless*, 9(2): 111–26.

Rosenthal, S. (2015) 'Philanthropy: The capitalist art of deception', *Socialist Review*, May, Available at: http://socialistreview.org.uk/402/philanthropy-capitalist-art-deception

Rothman, D. (1978) 'Introduction', in W. Gaylin, I. Glasser, S. Marcus and D. Rothman (eds) *Doing Good: The Limits of Benevolence*, New York: Pantheon, ix–xv.

Rowley, T. (2010) 'BBC criticised over premature poppy wearing', *Independent*, 25 October, Available at: www.independent.co.uk/arts-entertainment/tv/news/bbc-criticised-over-premature-poppy-wearing-2115647.html

Royal British Legion, The (2015) 'How do you wear your poppy?', London: The Royal British Legion, Available at: www.britishlegion.org.uk/community/stories/remembrance/how-do-you-wear-your-poppy/

Royal British Legion, The (2018a) *The Royal British Legion Annual Report & Accounts*, London: The Royal British Legion.

Royal British Legion, The (2018b) 'Help with disability benefits', London: The Royal British Legion, Available at: www.britishlegion.org.uk/get-support/financial-and-employment-support/finance/help-with-disability-benefits

Russakoff, D. (2015) *The Prize: Who's in Charge of America's Schools?*, Boston, MA: Houghton Mifflin Harcourt.

Salamon, L.M., Geller, S.L. and Lorentz, S.C. (2008). *Nonprofit America: A Force for Democracy?*, Baltimore, MD: Johns Hopkins University Center for Civil Society Studies.

Sales, N.J. (2016) *American Girls: Social Media and the Secret lives of Teenagers*, New York: Vintage Books.

Sampson, S. (1996) 'The Social Life of Projects: Importing Civil Society to Albania', in C. Hann and E. Dunn (eds) *Civil Society: Challenging Western Models*, New York: Routledge, 121–42.

Sapiro, G. (2010) 'Introduction', in G. Sapiro (ed) *Sociology Is a Martial Art: The Political Writings of Pierre Bourdieu*, New York: New Press, iv–xxi.

Sargeant, A., Ford, J. and West, D. (2000) 'Widening the appeal of charity', *International Journal of Nonprofit and Voluntary Sector Marketing*, 5(4): 318–32.

Sargeant, A. and Woodliffe, L. (2007) 'Gift giving: An interdisciplinary review', *International Journal of Nonprofit and Voluntary Sector Marketing*, 12(4): 275–307.

Saxton, G.D. and Wang, L. (2014) 'The social network effect: The determinants of giving through social media', *Nonprofit and Voluntary Sector Quarterly*, 43(5): 850–68.

Schervish, P. (1992) 'Adoption and altruism: Those with whom I want to share a dream', *Nonprofit and Voluntary Sector Quarterly*, 21(4): 327–50.

Scherz, C. (2014) *Having People, Having Heart: Charity, Sustainable Development, and Problems of Dependence in Central Uganda*, Chicago, IL: University of Chicago Press.

Schokkaert, E. (2006) 'The Empirical Analysis of Transfer Motives', in S.-C. Kolm and J.M. Ytheir (eds) *Handbook of the Economics of Giving, Altruism and Reciprocity*, Amsterdam: Elsevier, 127–81.

Self, W. (2014) 'Public mourning is the loyalty oath of the modern British state – and a deflection for our cock-ups', *New Statesman*, 14–20 November, 70.

Shapely, P. (1998) 'Charity, status and leadership: Charitable image and the Manchester man', *Journal of Social History*, 32(1): 157–77.

Sharman, A. (2017) 'DCMS attacked for gagging charities using Tampon Tax Fund', Civil Society Media, 8 December, Available at: www.civilsociety.co.uk/news/dcms-attacked-over-clause-prohibiting-tampon-tax-funding-campaigning.html

Sherrington, M. (2015) 'Our mission is to solve the unsolvable – so it's important that we learn from our failures', *Third Sector*, 23 July, Available at: www.thirdsector.co.uk/mission-solve-unsolvable-so-its-important-learn-failures/management/article/1356402

Sherry Jr, J., McGrath, M. and Levy, S. (1993) 'The dark side of the gift', *Journal of Business Research*, 28(3): 225–44.

Singer, P. (2010) *The Life You Can Save*, New York: Random House.

Singer, P. (2015) *The Most Good You Can Do*, London: Yale University Press.

Singer, P. (2016a) *Famine, Affluence, and Morality*, Oxford: Oxford University Press.

Singer, P. (2016b) *Ethics in the Real World: 82 Brief Essays on Things that Matter*, Oxford: Princeton University Press.

Singer, T., Seymour, B., O'Doherty, J., Kaube, H., Dolan, R. and Frith, C. (2004) 'Empathy for pain involves the affective but not sensory components of pain', *Science*, 303(5661): 1157–62.

Singh, A. (2018) *The Moral Marketplace*, Bristol: Policy Press.

Skeggs, B. (1997) *Formations of Class and Gender: Becoming Respectable*, London: Sage.

Skeggs, B. (2004a) *Class, Self, Culture*, London: Routledge.

Skeggs, B. (2004b) 'Exchange, Value and Affect: Bourdieu and "the Self"', in L. Adkins and B. Skeggs (eds) *Feminism after Bourdieu*, Oxford: Blackwell Publishing, 75–96.

Skeggs, B. (2015) 'Introduction: Stratification or exploitation, domination, dispossession or devaluation?', *The Sociological Review*, 63(2): 205–22.

Skocpol, T. and Fiorina, M. (2004) *Civic Engagement in American Democracy*, Washington, DC: Brookings Institution Press.

Sky News (2015) 'Windsor: "Sod off" if you won't wear a poppy', Sky News, 29 October, Available at: https://news.sky.com/story/windsor-sod-off-if-you-wont-wear-a-poppy-10341450

Small, D., Loewenstein, G. and Slovic, P. (2007) 'Sympathy and callousness: The impact of deliberative thought on donations to identifiable and statistical victims', *Organizational Behavior and Human Decision Processes*, 102(2): 143–53.

Smith, C. and Davidson, H. (2014) *The Paradox of Generosity*, Oxford: Oxford University Press.

Smith, D. (2017) 'Helpful clarification from @NCVO @SEtherington. #LobbyingAct will NOT stop most charities from campaigning. @ACEVO', Available at: https://twitter.com/david3012/status/869951700626542595

Smith, D.H. (2000) *Grassroots Associations*, London: Sage.

Smith, J. (2015) 'Charities have to play Whitehall's game', *Independent on Sunday*, 1 November, 42.

Smith, J.D. (1995) 'The Voluntary Tradition: Philanthropy and Self-help in Britain 1500–1945', in J.D. Smith, C. Rochester and R. Hedley (eds) *An Introduction to the Voluntary Sector*, London: Routledge, 9–39.

Smith, J.D. (1999) 'Poor Marketing or the Decline of Altruism? Young People and Volunteering in the United Kingdom', *International Journal of Nonprofit and Voluntary Sector Marketing*, 4(4): 372–7.

Smith, S. and Grønbjerg, K. (2018) 'Introduction to special issue of NVSQ: Nonprofits and public policy', *Nonprofit and Voluntary Sector Quarterly*, 47(4S): 5–10.

Snee, H. (2013) 'Doing something "worthwhile": Intersubjectivity and morality in gap year narratives', *The Sociological Review*, 62(4): 843–61.

Snee, H. (2014) *A Cosmopolitan Journey? Difference, Distinction and Identity Work in Gap Year Travel*, Farnham: Ashgate.

Snow, J. (2006) 'Why I don't wear a poppy on air', Channel 4 News, 8 November, Available at: http://blogs.channel4.com/snowblog/wear-poppy-air/16514

Snow, J. (2010) 'Bonkers to be missing a money saving, time saving trick', Channel 4 News, 28 October, Available at: http://blogs.channel4.com/snowblog/bonkers-to-be-missing-a-money-saving-time-saving-trick/13989

Spade, D. (2011) *Normal Life: Administrative Violence, Critical Trans Politics and the Limits of Law*, New York: South End Press.

Stannard-Stockton, S. (2008) 'Why do people really give to charity?', *Stanford Social Innovation Review*, 25 June, Available at: https://ssir.org/articles/entry/why_do_people_really_give_to_charity

Steiner, F. (1967) *Taboo*, Baltimore, MD: Penguin.

Strach, P. (2016) *Hiding Politics in Plain Sight: Cause Marketing, Corporate Influence, and Breast Cancer Policymaking*, Oxford: Oxford University Press.

Strudwick, P. (2017) 'The Home Office missed repeated warning signs that an LGBT charity was about to collapse', BuzzFeed.News, 27 April, Available at: www.buzzfeed.com/patrickstrudwick/the-home-office-missed-repeated-warning-signs-that-an-lgbt

Suler, J. (2004) 'The online disinhibition effect', *Cyberpsychology & Behavior*, 7(3): 321–6.

Sulik, G.A. (2010) *Pink Ribbon Blues: How Breast Cancer Culture Undermines Women's Health*, Oxford: Oxford University Press.

Svensson, P., Mahoney, T. and Hambrick, M. (2015) 'Twitter as a communication tool for nonprofits: A study of sport-for-development organizations', *Nonprofit and Voluntary Sector Quarterly*, 44(6): 1086–106.

Swan, P. (2018) 'Charging, accessibility and legitimacy: A case study of a third sector "arts and health" charity', *Voluntary Sector Review*, 9(2): 177–95.

Swartz, D. (2013) *Symbolic Power, Politics, and Intellectuals: The Political Sociology of Pierre Bourdieu*, Chicago, IL: University of Chicago Press.

Sweney, M. and De Liz, A. (2018) '"Parents killed it": Why Facebook is losing its teenage users', *The Guardian*, 16 February, Available at: www.theguardian.com/technology/2018/feb/16/parents-killed-it-facebook-losing-teenage-users

Tait, A. (2017) 'Hetty Douglas and how 15 minutes of fame became 15 minutes of hate', *New Statesman*, 7 September, Available at: www.newstatesman.com/science-tech/social-media/2017/09/hetty-douglas-and-how-15-minutes-fame-became-15-minutes-hate

Tate, A. (2018) 'Are vloggers exploiting homeless people?', *New Statesman*, 4 July, Available at: www.newstatesman.com/science-tech/2018/07/are-vloggers-exploiting-homeless-people

Taylor, M. and Warburton, D. (2003) 'Legitimacy and the role of UK third sector organizations in the policy process', *Voluntas: International Journal of Voluntary and Nonprofit Organizations*, 14(3): 321–38.

Taylor-Collins, E. (2019) *Working-class Girls and Youth Social Action: 'Hope Labour'?*, Working Paper 144, Birmingham: Third Sector Research Centre, Available at: www.birmingham.ac.uk/Documents/college-social-sciences/social-policy/tsrc/hope-labour.pdf

Tester, K. (2010) *Humanitarianism and Modern Culture*, University Park, PA: Penn State University Press.

Thomas, L. (2010) 'BBC's blooming error: Charity collectors criticise presenters for wearing poppies too early', *Daily Mail Online*, 26 October, Available at: www.dailymail.co.uk/news/article-1323540/BBC-presenters-criticised-charities-wearing-poppies-early.html

Thompson, C. (2014) 'Philanthrocapitalism: Appropriation of Africa's genetic wealth', *Review of African Political Economy*, 41(141): 1–17.

Thomson, L. (2015) 'Kids Company has tarnished the charity sector', *ICSA: The Governance Institute*, Available at: www.icsa.org.uk/blog/kids-company-has-tarnished-the-charity-sector

Thorup, M. (2014) *Pro Bono?*, Winchester: Zero Books.

Timming, A. (2015) 'Visible tattoos in the service sector: A new challenge to recruitment and selection', *Work, Employment and Society*, 29(1): 60–78.

Timming, A., Nickson, D., Re, D. and Perrett, D. (2017) 'What do you think of my ink? Assessing the effects of body art on employment chances', *Human Resource Management*, 56(1): 133–49.

Tonkiss, K. (2018) 'The narrative assemblage of civil society interventions into refugee and asylum policy debates in the UK', *Voluntary Sector Review*, 9(2): 119–35.

Turkle, S. (2011) *Alone Together: Why We Expect More from Technology and Less from Each Other*, New York: Basic Books.

Turner, S. (2003) 'Charisma reconsidered', *The Journal of Classical Sociology*, 3(1): 5–26.

Tweedie, N. (2013) 'Bill Gates interview: I have no use for money. This is God's work', *The Telegraph*, 18 January, Available at: www.telegraph.co.uk/technology/bill-gates/9812672/Bill-Gates-interview-I-have-no-use-for-money.-This-is-Gods-work.html

UNISON (2016) *A Future at Risk: Cuts in Youth Services*, London: UNISON.

United Nations Volunteers (2011) *State of the World's Volunteerism Report: Universal Values for Global Well-being*, New York: United Nations.

Urban Dictionary (2011) 'Humble Brag', Available at: www.urbandictionary.com/define.php?term=Humble%20Brag

v (2008) *Youth Volunteering: Attitudes and Perceptions*, London: v

Valkenburg, P.M., Schouten, A.P. and Peter, J. (2005) 'Adolescents' identity experiments on the internet', *New Media & Society*, 7(3): 383–402.

Vickers, T. (2014) 'Developing an independent anti-racist model for asylum rights organizing in England', *Ethnic and Racial Studies*, 37(8): 1427–47.

Wagner, D. (2001) *What's Love Got to do With it? A Critical Look at American Charity*, New York: New Press.

Wahhab, I. (2016) *Charity Sucks*, London: Biteback.

Walker, D. (2015) 'David Cameron's love affair with the voluntary sector is over', *The Guardian*, 30 September, Available at: www.theguardian.com/society/2015/sep/30/david-camerons-love-affair-voluntary-sector-over

Walsh, J. (2014) 'Is Remembrance Day being undermined by "poppy fascism"?', *Independent*, 5 November, Available at: www.independent.co.uk/voices/comment/is-remembrance-day-being-undermined-by-poppy-facism-9842084.html

Walters, G. (2010) 'No one should be obliged to wear a poppy', *The Telegraph*, 4 November, Available at: www.telegraph.co.uk/news/uknews/defence/8109510/No-one-should-be-obliged-to-wear-a-poppy.html

Wardell, F., Lishman, J. and Whalley, L.J. (2000) 'Who volunteers?', *British Journal of Social Work*, 30(2): 227–48.

Warren, T. and Baker, K. (2019) 'WWF funds guards who have tortured and killed people', BuzzFeed.News, Available at: www.buzzfeednews.com/article/tomwarren/wwf-world-wide-fund-nature-parks-torture-death

Warren, T., Baker, K. and Bradley, J. (2019) 'Britain's Charity Regulator Will Grill WWF Over "Appalling Atrocities"', BuzzFeed.News, Available at: https://www.buzzfeed.com/tomwarren/wwf-charity-regulator-serious-incident

Weakley, K. (2015) 'Kids Company's See the Child campaign failed to secure any funding or launch promised task force', Civil Society Media, 28 July, Available at: www.civilsociety.co.uk/news/kids-company-s-see-the-child-campaign-failed-to-secure-any-funding-or-launch-promised-task-force.html

Weakley, K. (2016) 'Who is really in charge at the Charity Commission?', Civil Society Media, Available at: www.civilsociety.co.uk/finance/who-is-really-in-charge-at-the-charity-commission-.html

Weakley, K. (2017) 'Fact check: Separating truth from fantasy in the Kids Company book', Civil Society Media, 24 October, Available at: www.civilsociety.co.uk/voices/fact-check-separating-truth-from-fantasy-in-the-kids-company-book.html

Weber, M. (1947) *The Theory of Social and Economic Organization*, New York: Oxford University Press.

Weber, M. (1968a) *The Theory of Social and Economic Organization*, New York: Free Press.

Weber, M. (1968b) *Economy and Society*, New York: Bedminster Press.

Whimster, S. (2007) *Understanding Weber*, London: Routledge.

White, A. (2015) 'Clients and workers describe "havoc" at Kids Company', BuzzFeed.News, 6 August, Available at: www.buzzfeed.com/alanwhite/clients-and-workers-describe-havoc-at-kids-company

White, A. (2016) 'Kids Company scandal is being used to silence charities, campaigners claim', BuzzFeed.News, 9 March, Available at: www.buzzfeed.com/alanwhite/charities-say-government-is-using-kids-company-scandal-to-si

White, A. and Curry, P. (2016) 'The full story of Kids Company's fall', BuzzFeed.News, 3 February, Available at: www.buzzfeed.com/alanwhite/the-full-story-of-kids-companys-fall

White, K. and Peloza, J. (2009) 'Self-benefit versus other-benefit marketing appeals: Their effectiveness in generating charitable support', *Journal of Marketing*, 73(4), 109–24.

White, M. (2010) 'Remembrance Day: No one should be given a white feather for not wearing a poppy', *The Guardian*, 5 November, Available at: www.theguardian.com/politics/blog/2010/nov/05/michael-white-poppy-white-feather

Wilding, K. (2016) 'Why "show and tell" is so important for charities', Charity Bank, 16 March, Available at: https://charitybank.org/news/charityis-our-greatest-strength-and-our-biggest-weakness

Williams, Z. (2015) 'Camila Batmanghelidjh: "I'm actually quite rigorous. I'm just not wearing a suit"', *The Guardian*, 14 August, Available at: www.theguardian.com/society/2015/aug/14/camila-batmanghelidjh-interview-im-actually-quite-rigorous

Wilson, J. (2000) 'Volunteering', *Annual Review of Sociology*, 26(1): 215–40.

Wilson, J. and Musick, M. (1997) 'Who cares? Toward an integrated theory of volunteer work', *American Sociological Review*, 62: 694–13.

Wise, J. (2015) 'Tradeoffs', in R. Carey (ed) *The Effective Altruism Handbook*, Oxford: The Centre for Effective Altruism, 9–11.

Wood, M. (1992) 'Is governing board behavior cyclical?', *Nonprofit Management & Leadership*, 3(2): 139–63.

Wood, T. (2017) 'Moved to horrible tears by the poignancy of this charity appeal', Available at: https://twitter.com/trevwood/status/852236256604041217

Wu, C. (2002) *Privatising Culture: Corporate Art Intervention since the 1980s*, London: Verso.

Young, H., Osman, A.M.K., Aklilu, Y., Dale, R., Badri, B. and Fuddle, A.J.A. (2005) *Darfur: Livelihoods under Siege*, Medford, MA: Feinstein International Famine Center.

Žižek, S. (2009) *Violence: Six Sideways Reflections*, London: Profile Books.

Methodological appendix

This short methodological appendix serves to provide the reader with a more detailed overview of the methods used in gathering the empirical data found in this book, the samples of participants and the limitations of the data utilised. I also make a short statement on reflexivity, given my own positioning towards the data and the argument I have made.

Interviews

Twenty-three in-depth, semi-structured qualitative interviews lasting between 60 and 90 minutes were conducted with individuals working in senior positions in policy, research and communications at UK charities. All participants were provided with information about the study and were asked to provide their consent. Interviews were recorded on a digital recorder, before being transcribed by a professional transcription company. Interviews were first coded by a research assistant, and then by myself.

These practitioners were recruited through a snowball sample and were from a range of organisations and worked in various fields, such as voluntary sector infrastructure, housing, fundraising, volunteering and youth engagement. A breakdown of their organisation's focus, their role and their gender can be found in Table A1 below.

Interviewees were asked about issues such as their ability to influence policy, the impact they feel being a charity employee has on their ability to gain access and do their job, and issues of charity branding, marketing and persuasion. They were also asked specifically about the Lobbying Act, the politicisation of the charity sector, and discussed the remembrance poppy, all in all taking a 'state of the sector' approach. The names of interviewees and any organisations have been anonymised (apart from in the case of Andy Benson from the National Coalition for Independent Action, who wished not to be anonymised). At various points throughout the book, small and inconsequential details have been omitted in order to protect interviewees' identity. Interviewees were generally located in Sheffield and London, with the majority of London-based participants working for charities focused on delivery at a national level, and the majority of those situated in Sheffield working locally. Throughout the book the location of the interviewee is presented, apart from when this could impact on anonymisation.

Table A1: Interview participants

Organisation focus	Role	Gender
International development	Director of communications	M
Students' union	Community engagement officer	F
Community foundation	Fundraising manager	F
Homelessness A	Director of communications	M
Homelessness B	Chief executive	M
Homelessness B	Policy officer	M
Homelessness C	Chief executive	M
Homelessness C	Fundraiser	F
Children's health	Chief executive	M
Housing	Chief executive	M
National Coalition for Independent Action	Director	M
Advocacy	Policy and communications officer	F
Voluntary sector infrastructure A	Policy officer	F
Voluntary sector infrastructure B	Director of policy	M
Voluntary sector infrastructure C	Director of policy and research	M
Voluntary sector infrastructure D	Chief executive	M
Private fundraising consultancy	Chief fundraising consultant	M
Youth volunteering A	Chief executive	F
Youth volunteering A	Research director	F
Youth charity	Policy officer	M
Addiction support	Chief executive	F
Hospice	Chief executive	M
Disability	Chief executive	F

Nine of the 23 interviewees were female, and all of the interviewees were White British, which I recognise as a limitation of the study, emanating from the combination of purposive and snowball sampling processes which were employed, and which speaks to current concerns about the lack of diversity within the sector (Guo and Musso, 2007; Charity Commission, 2017). Respondents were not asked to self-report their social class, or about their age. This sample is not meant to be representative or to provide definitive proof of what all those working in leading positions in the charity sector think, but to provide some authentic insight into the 'doing' of charity, and the role symbolic resources play in that doing.

Focus groups

In order to explore how young people perceive and experience charity on social media, a series of eight semi-structured focus groups with young people aged 18–25 were conducted. These focus groups lasted up to 60 minutes, were digitally recorded, before being transcribed professionally, and were then coded and analysed, first by a research assistant and then by myself. All participants were provided with information about the study and asked to provide their consent. All participants were given a £10 voucher for taking part.

Focus groups started with a general discussion of charity on social media, prompted by questions such as, 'What sorts of charity activity do you see online?' 'How do you engage with such activities?' 'Have you asked others for support or been asked to support others' charitable activity through social media?' Following this semi-structured discussion, participants were each given a tablet computer with access to a manufactured Twitter feed. This was put together by myself and a colleague, and consisted of a series of Tweets of charity news stories, fundraising campaigns, videos of charitable activity such as the 'Ice Bucket Challenge', infographics from charities and other similar content (see https://twitter.com/digicharityshu). Participants were given five minutes to scroll through the feed, and were invited to click on links, read stories, look at videos and interact with the material as they would if it were their own social media feed. They were asked what particularly stood out to them, and what they felt worked and did not work. A Twitter feed was chosen both because it is a common medium for charities to use, and also because (after testing the approach with Facebook and Instagram pages) it was found to be the most suitable platform through which to curate a set of content independently. However, given the myriad social media platforms participants subscribed to and used, focusing just on one will always give a partial picture.

Participants were asked basic demographic, education and employment details (see Table A2), and also to list which social media sites they belonged to and used regularly. Demographically the sample consisted of 20 female and 17 male participants; in terms of ethnicity, 32 identified as White British, three were White Eastern European and two were British Asian. The mean age was 20.5.

The social media sites our participants used are listed in Table A3 below.

As Table A3 shows, Facebook was used by all of the focus group participants, with Instagram, Snapchat and YouTube used by over

Table A2: Focus group participants

Demographic	Category	Number (% of sample)
Gender	F	20 (54.1)
	M	17 (45.9)
Age	18	6 (16.2)
	19	6 (16.2)
	20	5 (13.5)
	21	11 (29.7)
	22	5 (13.5)
	23	2 (5.4)
	24	1 (2.7)
	25	1 (2.7)
Ethnic background	White British	32 (86.5)
	British Asian	2 (5.4)
	White Eastern European	3 (8.1)
Education status	Completed A-levels/GNVQs	2 (5.4)
	Current undergraduate student	30 (81.1)
	Completed undergraduate degree	4 (10.8)
	Current postgraduate student	1 (2.7)
Employment status	Not employed	15 (40.5)
	Employed part-time	16 (43.2)
	Employed full-time	6 (16.2)

Table A3: Social media sites regularly used by focus group participants

Social media site	Users (% of sample)
Facebook	37 (100)
Instagram	32 (86.5)
Snapchat	29 (78.4)
YouTube	29 (78.4)
Twitter	25 (67.6)
WhatsApp	25 (67.6)
Reddit	6 (16.2)
Pinterest	2 (5.4)
Tumblr	1 (2.7)

three-quarters of participants, Twitter and WhatsApp by two-thirds of participants, and some other sites used by only a few individuals.

In terms of representativeness, the limitations of the sample for making definitive claims about how all young people perceive and experience charity online are recognised – 35 participants (94.6 per cent) were either studying for or had completed an undergraduate degree at Sheffield Hallam University, whereas, for example, only a third of 18-year olds in England enter university. The other two participants had completed A-levels/GNVQs (post-16 education) and were now in full-time employment, meaning that none of the participants were currently unemployed; 16 participants worked part-time and 6 worked full-time.

Drawing only from a sample of student research participants and seeing them as emblematic of the wider pool of potential young donors and engagers with charity raises questions about class dynamics and the wider generalisability of findings. Undertaking this project with a wider range of participants would, in all likelihood, produce different responses, with, potentially, non-student participants having a different style of engagement with charity on social media or different social media usage habits. While specific class and background data was not collected from participants, Sheffield Hallam University, as a former polytechnic university, recruits students who would traditionally be thought of as upper-working-class/lower-middle-class, with internal university data showing 40 per cent of students are from NS-SEC social classes 4–7, and 97 per cent of students educated at state schools or colleges. In a further limitation, all of the participants were aged 18 or over, and younger people, such as those aged 14–18, may provide different insights, especially given that many indications show that this age group are moving away from sites like Facebook (a site used by 100 per cent of this sample) because it is associated with their parents (Sweney and De Liz, 2018).

Both these studies generate a tremendous amount of data. Further publications (for example, Dean, 2020) will be developed making use of this data.

Reflexivity

In previous work on methodology, I have examined the role of reflexivity, the task of assessing one's own positionality when conducting research (see Dean, 2017; Dean et al, 2018). In that work, a key recommendation was that all researchers need to do the work of reflexivity in order to offer the reader some insight as to the conditions in which the research was collected and whether the resultant interpretation of data may be affected as a result, as social science is not conducted in laboratory conditions, as illustrated by my occasional presence in the text. I am wary of reflexivity being the be-all and end-all, however – the data and the argument must come first – but it would be remiss of me not to offer a short reflexive comment here.

I like charities, and the people who work for them. Any researcher who starts to get a feel for the field they are engaged in, once they can say with more confidence that they know what they are talking about, will, by nature, get attached. Visiting charities and community centres, and meeting people trying to get homeless children a place for the night and a sense of security, or offering counselling to people addicted to alcohol, or encouraging the richest to invest in areas sorely in need of attention, is quite humbling. I remain hugely sympathetic to critical arguments about the right role for charity in society, and there is a reasonable view that governments should be doing all three of those activities. But frequently they are not, and seem to have little inclination to do so. While universities have real problems, they are still a relatively secure environment, and I'm certainly well paid with a good degree of autonomy. So yes, there's a tendency, just by dint of comparison, to want to give charities the benefit of the doubt. But checking your privilege at the door of charitable organisations is not the same as checking your critique. I can hear fundraisers, and charity chief executives, thinking that by focusing on how charity can be operationalised by people to make themselves look good, that's writing off a lot of true goodness. Writing a book that I hope will be of interest both to those working inside and studying the charity sector, and those doing sociology and allied disciplines more generally, I have felt at various points that the former will think I'm being too critical and the latter that the judgement isn't critical enough. We will see. But as I addressed in Chapter 6, speaking to people working for charities is an overwhelmingly rewarding experience because they tend to draw links between their own work and wider structures, policy changes and key events. The general public also have strong views about charity, something they care about deeply, but that brings its own retinue of pre-loaded narratives, assumptions and myths. So in terms of positioning, as someone who is employed and gets a livelihood from talking to students and others about charity, this data was collected with the idea, pre-emptively bringing theory to the analysis, that there are unsaid realities to charitable life that need to be analysed and understood, and that the theoretical framework of symbolic power enables us to see what makes charity work, and allows others to use it.

Index